BEHIND THE

A curated collection of knowledge, insight and experience from the UK property industry

Tej Singh
&
Friends

First paperback edition Q2 2021

ISBN: 9798503757903

tej-talks.com // tejinvests.com // tejsingh.me

This book is dedicated to Surjit Singh Kalra, my Nana Ji.

This book is about collaboration, sharing wisdom and encouraging thought. This is exactly what he stood for and instilled in me. A Master of language, communication and kindness. A loving man who had boundless strength, even in the hardest times.

His words, actions and thoughts taught me so much and he is a beacon of peace in my mind.

CONTENTS

"…grant me the serenity
to accept the things I cannot change;
courage to change the things I can;
and wisdom to know the difference."
- Reinhold Niebuhr

INTRODUCTION

Greetings,

I'm Tej, I'm a property investor, podcaster, author and public speaker.

I grew my portfolio from 0 to £1.3m in 9 months, raising £648,000 of Investor finance along the way, with a further £200,000 added since.

My podcast has had over 675,000 listens in 100+ countries now, it's got the most reviews of any UK property podcast and is ranked in the top 0.5% of podcasts in the world. I've interviewed a range of fantastic people, who have taught me a lot and educated and entertained my listeners. I'm very active on Instagram and have grown a strong following by documenting the reality of property and business, with no fluff.

This book is a compilation of people I know in property, who's experience I've followed and learned from. I was very selective when choosing people for this and I tried to get people I've known for a bit of time.

The idea is, I gave 42 property investors a selection of about 30 questions, some property related, some mindset and business, and a choice of more quirky ones. They provided their answers and insight to their chosen questions. I aimed to make the questions somewhat interesting, so the answers would be compelling and offer you something to learn from and implement.

The order is not random, nor is it an order of 'greatness' or the best answers first or anything like that, it's a strategic mixture, laid out in a way that you hopefully learn more from, whilst getting a variety of ideas and approaches.

I've broken it up with some quotes that I love, and some *'Tej's Tips'* to throw in some more sauce for you.

This is a book you can read as you like, all in one go, person by person, or dip in and out when you need some inspiration, motivation or a knowledge top-up. Make it yours.

There are people who unfortunately couldn't contribute to this book, but I'm very grateful to those who put aside the time and put effort into their answers and are a core part of this book.

The guests have been very humble I must say, many of them have purchased, built or controlled 10s if not 100s of assets and have been in property for a very long time, and have made a difference to their areas. Lots have raised £multi-millions from investors and created £millions of equity and profit, doing what they love.

If you enjoy their contributions, please take a picture, upload it to Social Media and tag us, let them know!

Thank you for purchasing this book, please do **leave an Amazon review** when you're done, it's really important to me as an author and it really helps more people like you find these resources!

Tej Singh

Tell me about your biggest failure in property so far?
Oh, where do I start? If you follow my Instagram, you will have seen all of these as I went through them. My failures are endless and were never-ending at the start. Every one of them taught me so much though, and I didn't make the same mistake again, so it's not a bad thing. Although, most of these cost me money, and not a couple of shillings either, but £100s or £1,000s, so they really stick with me.

I've been way too trusting with a builder, who I've since given two CCJs, and sent the bailiffs around to recover my funds. So, you can see how that fairy-tale ended! I had multiple refurbishments on, I was avoiding finding a new builder because I believed that no one else would be as skilled as him (big fat L O L at that) and I suppose I was busy with my brand, podcasting and other elements of my business that this slipped. Being 150 miles away made this hard too, because I couldn't regularly check in and verify work, as he would send pictures that looked way better than the result. He even dangerously rewired a house, forged an EICR certificate from his 'mate' who's an actual electrician and thought that was OK. Guess who's spent £2,500 on a new, safe rewire that has to be trunked, whilst there's tenants in? The house is gorgeous, but this has been a total headache. Horrible experience, in situations like this I think it's 'laugh or cry', I tend to laugh. Sometimes I cry though, I really do.

Although he's a scumbag, at the end of the day all of this is my fault, for being too trusting, for not checking in enough, for forgetting my basics because I was so desperate to finish these refurbishments, get them rented and repay investors. The pressure was real, but also created inside my head. I think as entrepreneurs we are responsible for 98% of what happens, in some shape or form, I accept that, and I've learnt so much from this.

Another is taking 2 months to decide on what to do with one of my BTLs turned flip, it needed new render and a new roof (significant jobs and cost) but I just sat on it. I didn't think, I didn't want to. I don't know. But it just was hard, I struggled. I didn't know what to do, and I didn't ask for help which is unusual for me. Yeah, it was a strange time, I think. Discovering that my first builder was also a compulsive liar, his team were unskilled, and he has no clue what he's doing. I was processing the emotions and basically being cheap trying to avoid these extra works… but they had to be done. I almost went into a 5% renewal fee on the bridging loan because of my delay. Ouch. *(It would have been less, I negotiated using our relationship).* I had to sell it slightly below value too, and the investor tried to mess around near completion, but I kicked off (surprise) and it was alright. Looking back, if I didn't have time pressure and I made better decisions, I could have still kept this house.

I've made plenty of other smaller mistakes that compounded to create bigger issues. One of the biggest lessons from those is to just spend the money. Some jobs, or aspects can't be cost-cut and are essential, just get it done. My life has been easier, and maintenance has decreased since I took this approach.

What areas of property need the biggest change?
Don't get me started.

Land Registry are absolute dinosaurs. Everything is in paper; everything is done on paper or by fax and they seem to primarily accept cheques or actual coins posted to them. Sorry, but are they based in 1987? It's shocking how easy tech is to build, use and maintain yet our centralised store of data on this is antiquated. Their website is pants too, looks like a primary school website project built on windows 98. They have so much to improve on, if they did, maybe applications wouldn't take 5 months to process, and the whole market and economy would benefit. I know people who work there, and it's as old school as it appears on the outside. We need a digital, centralised and secure platform for this data.

Conveyancing. One solicitor shuffling papers louder than the other, then the other blames one for not having documents, then the postman loses it, then it's the client's fault, then they send letters or faxes instead of emails, oh they can't witness IDs over video call and the clients are in Magaluf on a jolly for 3 weeks. I said don't get me started!! I love my legal teams, honestly, I think they are fantastic, and we have a great relationship, but the general principles are just so old school. The whole process isn't clear *(I do have a podcast with my conveyancer which helps clarify it)* so we as investors don't have clarity on the key steps or what's supposed to happen when. Most solicitors are not pro-active, they are reactive. Often sellers or buyers who are not savvy investors like us will go to the cheapest most dull solicitors on the high street, read 0 reviews and just get sucked in by the promises or not even care about the speed. Again, technology can really benefit us here, I believe there are things being done, but it's a frustrating process for all, I think.

Planning. I haven't experienced this first-hand yet, but from my learning and research this is a tricky one. The government want us to build as they consistently fail every single year to hit housing needs, and we try to help, but it appears most planning departments make life difficult. The government passes legislation then gives each council the power to use them as they see fit. That's helpful, not. Some planning portals are shocking and barely function, I'm not sure how technology would help here with the process, but we need clarity. We need people in the council to be helpful, proactive and to work with us. There are good planners of course, and plenty that are helpful, but I don't think that's the 'norm', from my limited experience and conversations.

I can only see one area that is ahead of the game, or innovative or doing something extra special to be honest. I would say that Prop-Tech is doing that, whether it's land finding software, property management or data sources, they seem to be doing well. Lots of opportunities here, lots of investors are old school so getting them to take these on will be a bigger challenge then actually creating something awesome, I feel.

Generally, do you buy to hold or sell, and why?
Of the fifteen I've purchased when writing this, I sold three and kept twelve. The aim from the start was to sell three, so I've done what I should. One made a loss (£-6,500), one was a healthy profit (£24,000), one was a very minor profit (£6,000). I did this because I wanted 'passive income', and the flips (buy to sell) paid down any money left in my BRR deals, to my Investors. Which means my ROI is even higher and I can pay them

back in full. I like holding assets which I think many guests in the book will also say, because of the capital appreciation over time and monthly cashflow. Tenants are not always easy to deal with, and it certainly carries a risk element as they are so overprotected by the law, but the first day of the month is fantastic when it all lands in the bank!

Although most of what I've done is held and rented out, I really love selling. Doing a flip is the most fun, because you can spend more on the design, do the extras you wouldn't normally do so someone falls in love with it. Interior design and the refurbishment are my favourite parts, so flips allow me to do both with extra sauce. Plus, big chunks of cash? Yes please. It's not 'passive' every month, but just spread it out over 12 months and it is! You don't have tenant issues too, it's much 'cleaner', in and out. If you compare single lets to flips, profit doesn't compare in the certain time frames. Especially if you can take the chunks from flips and reinvest in multiple asset classes and earn a better ROI % anyway.

Now I'm flipping closer to home, London, Hertfordshire and Bedfordshire *(got any deals for me?)* the profit is 5-10x what I'd make flipping in my BTL area, so it just makes even more sense. Especially when building-to-sell Holding here would give me a terrible ROI and I don't see any benefit in it for me. That's important by the way, 'me', what works for me may not for you – think about your own goals and timeframes.

Lots of people want to go straight into owning BTLs, but I always suggest you consider flipping first, especially if you have limited funds. Build up your cash pot, rinse and repeat. When you have increased it significantly, then look at investing into assets you will hold. I think it's underrated and not discussed enough, BTLs can be really slow, especially without momentum and investor funds.

What makes you a good Landlord/lady?
I think and know I am a good landlord or 'property manager'. I self-manage, at 150 miles away, they are all single lets (one SA – with a management company) so there isn't that much to do. People are scared to self-manage from far (or even close!), just think that's 10% a month extra that goes to you, for me that's £50 a month, £600 a year. That's a lot

of cheese. I find it straightforward, nothing I can't fix with my phone and the internet, plus my network. Also, if I was close by and there's a maintenance issue like a leak... am I going to be there in my wellies and a wrench at 11pm Friday night? No!

So, who cares how far I am?

I think the following are important when managing tenants, I implement them all:

- Communication and clarity are key, keeping things in writing and making sure there is no ambiguity, spell it out
- Firm, but fair. A contract is a contract, but you and tenants are human, so consider all things from that aspect too
- Speed of problem resolution is vital. You need a maintenance team, and multiple of the same skill/trade, so you can fix things quickly
- Tenants are overprotected by law, it's ridiculous. Bare that in mind when talking to them and resolving issues or conflicts, think twice before sending that text!
- Get it right from the start, make sure the house is fully functioning and clean
- Rent arrears are horrible but explore the reasons why and keep it open for the tenant to hopefully explain to you. Firm but fair again
- Pets – I don't mind, usually the deposit taken is bigger to protect against the smell etc. end of tenancy
- Join the NRLA, they have so much legal advice on the complexities of tenancies and so you know your rights

How diverse is the property industry?

This is an interesting question, one that only a few of my contributors have answered, with great answers. I think the corporate property industry is not very diverse, at least from what I see on LinkedIn, the news, brochures and social media. The non-corporate world is more diverse, but not as much as it could be across all aspects and elements of diversity.

I don't feel that I stand out as a Panjabi man when I'm at networking events, in fact I feel like there are quite a lot of South-East Asians in property. I do have friends from other backgrounds and genders who feel they do stand out, and the statistics and real world evidence support this. I would also say the industry is male dominated historically and currently.

What causes this lack of diversity in Property? Perhaps it's what has or hasn't been passed down by generations? The 'cultural' norm? Generational wealth or lack of? Discrimination and oppression across race, gender, sexuality? *(which very much exists in the UK. If someone doesn't see it and denies it then frankly, it speaks volumes of their privilege).*

To encourage people of different backgrounds and beliefs into an industry, I think it's important that role models exist. Someone who looks and sounds like you, who shows you that 'people like us' can be in powerful positions and achieve the same as anyone else. When the world doesn't provide equal opportunities, we must encourage people to push through the barriers and stereotypes and having someone to look up to who has got through, like you, is powerful.

If you could share one message to every single person on the planet, what would it be?
Be kind. Be understanding. Love more, laugh more, smile more. Live

Bridging Finance - expensive or very useful?
Both! Compared to a mortgage or sometimes a private investor, it is expensive, that's a fact. At the time of writing, bridges are at least double the % rate of a mortgage, likely three times more. But ask yourself - is it more expensive than *not doing a deal?* That's the real question. If you need finance, and you don't have your own cash you should realise this: If your deal can't take interest in the calculations because it makes it a bad deal… then in my view it's probably shit, and you shouldn't be doing it anyway! If the bridging cost eats into the margin, then a small error in the refurbishment cost, or duration or other factors can also eat into your margin so perhaps there isn't enough in the first place? Lower value properties are heavily affected by bridging costs vs. higher value, the rates and % are the same but the margins get tighter. The same rates and fees

will exist on £40,000 and £400,000, in fact at the smaller amount they could be higher.

Bridging is incredibly useful, and powerful especially when scaling quickly using your own or investor's finance in combination. Of course, it carries risks, some of which may be new to you (Debenture, First Charges, Personal Guarantees, ILA and Floating Charges) of which you should seek legal advice. Everything has a risk, especially borrowing money, which is just the way it is. Once you understand these, and you control the risks of your projects, it will be more palatable. Your deal analysis has to be very strong, if it isn't then you could be running into trouble here, I mean the kind of trouble you don't talk about on Facebook. I cover analysis in extreme detail in my eLearning, as it is central to your success. The Bridger won't necessarily do the sums for you on the deal, so just because you've been given money, doesn't mean the deal works that well! All the due diligence is up to you, and only you. So, make sure it's good.

I'd always rather use a private investor, as the terms are easier, the rates are usually lower and it's nicer to pay a human back some interest, than a bank/faceless company. I do like my bridgers though, and we have a great relationship. If you want an introduction, then DM or email me.

Don't be afraid of bridging. It's powerful, it costs, but it can be fast and 'easy to access' which can help you complete quickly. For auctions, most mortgages can't get near the 28-day completion, they are too slow. Bridgers can do it in days, I've done it in 7 days before (but they were ready earlier!). They also lend on 'unmortgageable' properties, what you and I would refer to technically as *'Shitholes'.*

Dorian Payne

An accountant by profession and property developer based in Wales, specialising in delivering high quality affordable, social and disabled homes. A Co-Founder at Castell Group.

Dorian has been active within the property sector since aged 16, being involved in over 80 acquisitions to date and is currently studying for an MSc Quantity Surveying.

Dorian has collaborated with a variety of private investors, having raised over £7,000,000 to date.

He has built a secured development pipeline of over 220 high quality, affordable, social and disabled homes with a GDV in excess of £35,000,000.

IG – @Dorianpayneproperty
FB – @Dorianpayneproperty
LI – @Dorianpayneproperty

What advice would you give a total beginner in property?

Starting out as a property investor, trader or developer can be quite daunting. Unless exposed from an earlier age or through experienced contacts, many people assume property is very capital intensive and only the wealthy can be successful in property. If you're reading this, you'll probably already know that is not entirely true; you can build a successful property business without being wealthy or experienced. Yes, having capital will allow you to accelerate faster in property, although it doesn't actually guarantee one will be successful. Money is a tool. Tools can facilitate in either construction <u>or</u> destruction, it's the operator that decides.

My advice to those starting out would be to spend significant time understanding the property industry and the different routes or strategies which can be implemented. I would start by reading highly rated property educational books, written by authors with a proven track record in the subject matter. Join social media property related groups and ask for suggestions that people have found useful. This is a low-cost route to having a foundational understanding. My personal advice is try to get a holistic understanding of how the strategies work.

Whilst you're doing this you also should be really thinking hard and deep about <u>what</u> you're expecting from this venture? What are you actually trying to achieve, is it a certain amount of income to cover bills, a pension plan, a lifestyle business or a large business? There's no right or wrong answer but you need to work out what your goals are.

In addition to this you must also be honest with what actual resources you have available. Where are you in terms of time, money, relatable knowledge (may be a QS/Builder for example).

With your initial knowledge and understanding of your personal circumstances, you may have a much clearer idea of the plan to achieve your goals, this is a perfect opportunity to find people who are doing what you are planning and ask them questions. You can find these people at property networking events or social media; you'll be surprised how many people are willing to give you information. It would be nice if you could offer to help them in some way in return.

Do I Build to Hold or Sell, and Why?

My business, Castell Group specialises in building high quality affordable, social and disabled housing for those truly in need. We do this by collaborating with private investors and registered social landlords. Currently all of our developments are 100% pre-sold and therefore we do not hold any completed properties.

At the moment our business model and funding lines are geared towards our goal of scaling to build over 500 homes per annum. To facilitate this growth, we are liquidating each site and reinvesting capital.

Any share of returns that are distributed to my holding company is currently used to invest in property assets to hold. These aren't new-builds but predominately single-family homes or multi-unit blocks (MUB) of apartments which are purchased in a state of disrepair. Equity is then added through the refurbishment process with the hope that the end value is higher than the total project costs. The property can then be refinanced at the higher valuation and majority of the cash inputted returned, ready to be used to acquire more. Also known as the Buy-Refurbish-Refinance model (BRR). Once the property is let to good tenants the returns come in and it is relatively passive. When there are issues though it can be a huge headache so having a good team around you will help. Doing a good refurbishment will also help reduce your maintenance worries.

Repeat this enough times and you'll eventually have a portfolio that generates significant cashflow every month. The asset value can also appreciate over time, which reduces gearing and finance risk.

3 Top Tips on Raising Investment

As of writing we have raised around £7,000,000 from private investors, some of them are small investors and some are very large. It has facilitated our growth and will continue to do so. If you wish to scale a property investment or development business, raising investment is a crucial skill. My 3 top tips are as follows:

1. **Be Likeable** – First and foremost, be a good, honest and kind person. That's a bit vague but what I mean is private investors are people. Underwriters are people (albeit with clearly defined lending criteria). One of the biggest personal traits you can work

on which will yield you significant results, is your pleasing personality. There's a saying that people like to work with those they "know, like and trust". The power of being likeable and having a pleasing personality is key. This is something I personally worked on extensively and some books on this are:

    a. How to Win Friends and Influence People – Dale Carnegie.

    b. Crucial Conversations – Kerry Patterson

    c. Never split the difference – Chris Voss (Negotiating book but it's about understanding the other side).

2. **Confidence** – Be confident, not arrogant. People are attracted to confidence but repelled by arrogance. The key points to remember is that when dealing with investors you can't predict exactly what they're going to say, think, feel or expect and you can't write a perfect script to deal with their responses. You will need to respond to their tonality, concerns, questions and feedback in a real-time instinctive manner. To do this with confidence you need to have a clear understanding of the subject. Get comfortable with your level of knowledge and don't rush to secure the first deal. Reach out to an experienced property investor / developer that will be happy to review any deal appraisal and potentially even do a role-play call with you. I've done these many times and they're very helpful.

3. **Be Consistent**
It can take a bit of time to find an investor who is willing to work with you. Many talks or agreements will also break down for a variety of reasons, it's important not to get discouraged and to remain consistent. There are a tremendous number of investors with all different lending and risk criteria. Remain active, keep networking and working on your people and sales skills. Remember not to just grab the first investor willing to work with you, don't forget to set <u>your</u> investor criteria out. What type of investor do <u>you</u> actually want?

The best non-property investment I made

I've always known I wanted to be a property investor and developer and I was working on various properties with my parents and helping them with their rental portfolio when I was in school. I was also involved in other businesses such as: buying and selling motorcycles, buying items from boot sales and selling online. One business I set up involved learning to source items from manufacturers in China and importing them to the UK to sell online and locally. I sourced an item called the expandable hose pipe and it was around the time It was making a big surge in the UK. My initial investment went well, I doubled my money! So, I did it again and doubled my money with easy sales. Just in luck, I was about to make a fortune. It doesn't take long with doubling rates to become a millionaire, surely? For some reason I thought I could squeeze more out of the situation and I contacted the manufacturer to try and reduce my product cost. I was offered an alternative material which was 20-30% cheaper, I thought great and put all my money into the order. I was set to make more than double my investment.

The hoses came and I started selling more and more, although after a few days I was getting phone calls from customers all requesting refunds. It turned out the cheaper material wasn't tested; I didn't get an agent to quality approve and they weren't fit for purpose. Once the hose filled with water the pressure would cause it to explode! The manufacturer didn't help, and I lost all my funds. The lesson for me at an early age was clear; I was chasing money at the detriment of the customer and I had no real knowledge of the business I was in. After that I stopped trying to become a millionaire overnight and thought more about building a quality scalable business that people would want to work with repeatedly. Money is now a by-product of delivering an excellent product at a fair price.

What is your deal analysis process?

There's a conflicting saying, depending on which business books you read. Some say you should start with the end in mind, and some say you shouldn't have an end in mind as that means you're not truly committed to the journey. Regardless, with property development I think it's really important to start with your end in mind. We have set large goals for our development company and one of the main ways we will achieve them is by acquiring and delivering good sites. One of the best ways to remain in control of this, is to have an excellent deal analysis process. We worked with experienced developer Richard Little to build our development process, then we further split the process into individual stages and are constantly reviewing it as we are delivering more sites. We also have a manual that helps our employees understand how each stage needs to be completed. Employees get delegated to the relevant stages and we monitor the priorities of the stages & tasks. As property development is quite slow, we end up with a lot of sites live in the pipeline at once and this type of reporting becomes very handy.

Our deal analysis process looks something like:
1. **Criteria** – Our first step is to have a clear criteria of what we're roughly looking for, if the opportunity falls outside this then we will pass it on to a land agent or disregard it. The key is to remain focused.
2. **Sourcing** – We focus on off-market sourcing methods using property tech such as Nimbus Maps or Land Insight. We identify sites using the mapping systems and planning portals, then acquire the vendors details through Land Registry and send a letter. When finding potential sites, we disregard those with clear material constraints which would render the site too difficult or unviable. We still look for deals advertised on the market if it matches our criteria.
3. **Appraisal P1** – Our initial appraisal is a 4-part process that can be done swiftly and covers the main points which normally renders sites unviable:
   a. Initial Assessment
   b. Planning Assessment
   c. High Level Numbers
   d. Demand
4. **Negotiation**
5. **Appraisal P2** – (still prior to acquisition)
   a. Design - Detailed
   b. Planning - Detailed
   c. Legals
   d. Funding - Detailed
   e. Construction - Detailed

f. Exit - Detailed

g. Sensitivity

6. **Renegotiate, Secure or Acquire**

What's really important to me in life?

I would consider myself a very ambitious and driven person with big goals and a (self-inflicted) busy life.

As of writing, my life currently consists of the following:

- I spend a significant time on self-development, reading or listening to approx. 2 books a week.
  - o Books are mainly on autobiographies of people I admire, mindset, property, construction, business growth, sales, marketing, negotiation and financial markets.
- I am currently studying MSc Quantity Surveying
- We are set to deliver close to 80 homes next year within Castell Group, with a target of securing an additional 100 and a growing staff count.
- I have a Wife and 2 children which I adore and try to spend time with.

In terms of what's really important to me, the good health of me and my loved ones and a certain level of wealth for comfort is important, as it would be for anyone reading. What I'm actually working towards though is to help further contribute towards society in a bigger way by investing in driven entrepreneurs with business concepts that could impact many people. I want to be surrounded by very experienced and highly motivated people who are willing to sacrifice and commit to growing. The goal for me is to eventually operate a form of venture capital/family office/ angel investment fund and spend my time helping entrepreneurs make a difference.

Dorian will be listening to Either Classical Piano or 60s Rockabilly, reading Principles – Ray Dalio and Shoe Dog – Phil Knight, whilst eating Barbequed Chinese Food in his office... with his thoughts.

Ayesha Ofori

Ayesha Ofori is a property investment specialist and one of Britain's leading female entrepreneurs. She is founder and CEO of three real estate businesses: Axion Property Partners, PropElle Network and Black Property Network. Through Axion, Ayesha works with investors who want to invest in property projects. PropElle Network is focused on female financial empowerment, by getting more women investing in property and Black Property Network seeks to increase financial literacy among the black community and help them to build wealth through property.

An experienced real estate investment specialist and wealth manager, Ayesha has previously held roles in Morgan Stanley's real estate investment team, and at Goldman Sachs, where she was a Private Wealth Advisor to ultra-high net worth individuals, managing over $500m of client assets. She has also won many awards and accolades. In 2020, Ayesha was named one of Imperial College London's Emerging Alumni Leaders and winner of the Black British Awards Entrepreneur Rising Star of the Year.

She is also one of Management Today's 35 Women Under 35, one of Business Leader's 30 most inspiring entrepreneurs, and winner of the Women of the Future Award for Real Estate, Infrastructure and Construction. Ayesha holds an MSci in Physics from Imperial College London and an MBA from London Business School.

IG – Ayesha.Ofori
LI – Ayesha Ofori

IG/LI – PropElleNetwork
IG/LI – BlackPropertyNetwork (UK)

Why are you in property?

I started investing in property because my husband (boyfriend at the time) and I had some cash between us just sitting in the bank. As bankers, we knew the last place to put cash is in the bank. We knew that we needed to invest our money and make it work for us, rather than us only working for money in our day jobs. Property investment ticked many boxes for me.

Property is a real, tangible asset, something I can see and touch (unlike equities for example), it should perform well in inflationary environments (like what I expect to happen as a result of all the money the government has "borrowed" to pump into the system during the Covid crisis), by personally managing my portfolio I have more control over how the investment behaves (versus equities or bonds) and I love the way you can use leverage to maximise your returns. Unlike when investing in equities and using leverage, where when the asset price falls you have any margin calls – with property you don't.

What do I mean by this? Well, let's say you get a mortgage from a bank (leverage) and buy a house. If the house price falls the bank doesn't call you and ask you to pay more money. With some leveraged equity investments if the price of the share falls you have to invest more money. So, by comparison, property has more upside that downside in my opinion. Also, when you use leverage, property returns are pretty much unbeatable over a long-time horizon and I'm a long term property investor.

Why am I still in property today? Because I found my life calling, my "why" - I focus on helping other people to use property investment to become financial stable.

What advice would you give a total beginner in property?

The fact you're considering getting into property is the first step – congrats! Now you have to keep going. I have a few tips: 1) Know your why. You have a reason for why you want to invest in property – it needs to be a good reason. Because when things get tough and you're not making as much progress as you'd hoped, you need to be able to remember your why and have it help to pull you through. 2) It's not a get quick rich scheme and it's not easy. If it was, literally everyone would do it and would make a ton of money and that's not the case. But, if you get it right, I think it is worth the hard work you have to put it. 3) Try not to get shiny penny syndrome. You'll hear about lots of new and different property strategies that work well for various people, but they may not work for you. Focus on trying to find the strategies (1 to 2 max) that work for you and not be distracted by what others are doing. 4) Don't listen to the haters. There are going to be people who try to dissuade you from investing in property. There will be those who try to bring you down when you become successful. You have to rise above all of that – stay true to yourself and your goals. 5) Have fun! You'll meet lots of people on the way, make new friends, make money (hopefully ;p), provide homes for people….it can be a lot of fun.

3 Top Tips on raising investor finance?

Investors will give you money if they like you, trust you and think you're going to make money for them and it's in that order. Be genuine – inevitably the people who give you money will be the ones who like you as a person. Also, don't be an ass, always put the interests of your investors first. If you don't they won't invest with you again and they won't recommend other people to invest with you.

The best investors are the ones who keep coming back and tell others to work with you. Lastly, make sure any investments you offer people are ones you'd be happy to put your money in yourself.

How do you decide who to JV with?

I have had good JV partnerships and bad JV partnerships. I like to think I did the "right things" when deciding who to work with. I asked around about the people I was thinking of partnering with (but not letting opinions sway me either way. It was more to get as much info as possible so I could make a decision myself. I've found sometimes people bad mouth others for personal reasons or repeat false rumours – the property world can be very gossipy and cliquey, - so I like to get as wide a perspective as possible). I speak to others who have worked with the JV partner, I speak to their investors and I do research on their background.

Look at their professional history and try to verify the things they say about themselves. Then I try to spend some time with them, lunch or dinner (when not in lockdown). But even after doing all of that I've still had JV partnerships that I've regretted. It's difficult to predict or find out how people will manage in various situations. You can only see some things when they happen.

When you're having a nice calm dinner with someone, they behave very differently to when you're in the middle of a million-pound development and the project is delayed because of them. I've learnt that you always have to do your homework as much as possible, but you can't pre-plan for everything. Try to make sure you have as many protections and agreements in place to account for the obvious things that can go wrong, but even then it's impossible to account for every possibility.

Is property a 'numbers' or a 'people' game?
It's both. You won't succeed in property consistently if you or someone in your team isn't good at numbers. You might be able to do a deal here and there and have it work out ok because you get lucky or because the market is rising, so any mistakes made are covered, but eventually the music will stop.

What's that saying..."when the tide goes out you see who's been swimming naked".

Equally you won't succeed long term if you're not good with people – whether it's needing people in your team (e.g., as architects, builders, brokers etc.) or renting to tenants or raising funds from investors you need to interact well with people and treat them decently.
I've worked with people on JV projects who, I unfortunately discovered a few months into the project, were awful at the "people person" bit. I never worked with them again.

How diverse is the property industry?
Not diverse at all, sadly. The property industry tends to be dominated by white men. I've seen a few publications coin the phrase "pale, male and stale" when talking about the industry. As a black woman I am somewhat

of a rarity – I know a handful of other black women in property, but we are few and far between. Also, from the wider female perspective there are significantly fewer women in property than men. But it's not all doom and gloom. Many in the industry are trying to change things, myself included.

I am the founder of PropElle Network, a property investment business for women. PropElle's aim is female financial empowerment, by getting more women investing in property. I also founded Black Property Network, which does what it says on the tin. It's a business focused on those of black ethnicity to increase financial literacy and help them invest in property as a means of creating wealth. I'm also working with the RICS and other corporates in the property sector to improve diversity and inclusion, particularly among black people and women. Change isn't going to come overnight and it's not going to be easy, but it's long overdue. A woman or a person of colour should be able to walk into a property event/ meeting etc. without feeling like the odd one out.

What differentiates you from your peers?
There are 2 very distinct property worlds from my perspective. A professional "corporate" property world where the people involved work at credible, established real estate firms, many have a track record in investing or development etc. Here I'm thinking of the CBRE's, JLL's, and Grosvenor Groups of the UK property world. Then there is what I call the SME property world which essentially includes everything and everyone else "in property" …and what you find here is a very mixed bag. It includes everyone from "mum and dad" landlords, to the postman who does rent to rent to those dabbling in development and those who have genuine experience but aren't big enough to be in the corporate property world. I straddle both worlds – I work on projects with large corporates/ large institutional property investors and I have businesses where I work with small developers who are looking for project funding and people who are just starting out and have never invested in property before.

This is one thing that differentiates me from my peers – most people I meet fall firmly into one of the categories or other, the "corporate" property or "SME property world, not both. I guess I'm able to do this and move fairly seamlessly between the two because I come from a corporate, professional world of investing. I worked at Morgan Stanley in their Real Estate Investing team and at Goldman Sachs as an Ultra High Net Wealth Adviser, but I also built a personal property portfolio with my husband, from the ground up, which falls within the SME property world.

The second thing that differentiates me from my peers is my professional investment background. I worked in Investment Banking and Investment management for almost a decade, where I was authorized by the FCA and managed half a billion dollars of client money, personally. So, I'd say I know a thing or two about working with investors and managing their money and investments. I meet very few people in the SME property world who have genuine investment/ financial backgrounds. Now there's no requirement for anyone in property to have any particular qualifications or track record for that matter, but I'm often surprised at the number of people who raise investor funds for property investment and don't really know what they're doing. What really amazes me is that many of them are working with investor funds in a way that's not FCA compliant and they don't have any idea they're breaking rules! It's nuts!

Ayesha is currently listening to Stefflon Don and Old Skool Drake, eating chocolate…at every opportunity! "Audible-ing" the latest books on entrepreneurship and business, at home with her family, embracing the lockdowns.

Jay Anthony Howard

With more than 18 years of experience dealing with all aspects of property sales and purchases, Jay is a trusted property expert. Jay is co-author of Amazon #1 seller Before the Hammer Falls: The Insider's Guide to Property Auction Success, which provides you with the tools and information you need to find success at auction. Jay also forms part of the judging panel for the Property Investors Awards, a testament of his respected opinion and authority within the industry.

Jay's interest in Blacksmithing combined with graduate degrees in Psychology, Classics and Law and extensive travel to archaeological sites around the world make him a singular entity within the auction space and the property market at large.

Jay is part of the team at HAMMERED –

Help to take the risk out of selling your property at auction. With 20 years combined auction specific experience, both from an investor/ trader perspective and from the perspective of someone who had worked in the industry.

HAMMERED know how best to market through the auction, which is the best auction for your asset and optimising the process and success of your sale. The service costs the same as going direct to the auctioneers (as we split the fee with the auctioneers). It makes sense to have two teams pushing for a good result.

FB – Jay Anthony Howard
W – hammeredauctions.com

How do you decide who to JV with?

There are some major considerations that I take into account before entering into a JV. A lot of people talk about the know, like and trust metric *(a little overused, not always by people with genuine intentions)*. It's a strong foundation to start, but certainly not to finish. Due diligence is the next step, just because you like someone, doesn't mean you should work with them.

What are the motivations and intentions of all concerned? Do they align? Can you communicate effectively? What roles and responsibilities will you share (have this written down, everything, and I mean everything needs to be enshrined in a JV agreement/ shareholder agreement and modus operandi to ensure success.

A JV is more than person X solves a problem or adds value to person Y and vice versa. It is a marriage. Don't let it be a marriage of convenience or a marriage out of duty. It must be love *(platonic is best for this purpose)*.

What's been your biggest success in property?

When I first read this question, my initial response was to talk about my Birmingham deal, which is impressive based on the level of uplift (purchase price of £500,000 and sold price of £5,000,000) over a 12-month period. This was in 2009 and is rather redundant 12 years later. Its good, but it's not quite Carling.

Planning gain is celebrated for being able to add significant value to an asset, permitted development and prior approval are the lowest risk routes to gaining planning. Here is our latest one and it was an absolute beauty. Four workshops at auction in late 2019 in Tooting! Purchased for £212,000 with £18,000 costs.

We solved some issues effecting the site, submitted an application for Prior Approval for conversion into four mews houses which was approved in January 2020. We then packaged the deal up and sold the site approximately 8 months later for £650,000 at auction.

The deal was funded by a private investor, with 10% funded by us as well as the £18,000 of costs, which created an IRR (internal rate of return of just over 3,000%, trebled the value of the site and produced a significant return for future reinvestment.

We worked the deal with several exits in mind and multiple ways to add value. We had the option to build out and submit for second stage planning but decided to leave some value add and meat on the bone for the incoming buyer/ developer to complete.

How diverse is the property industry?
The UK real estate industry is so beautifully diverse. There are so many different metrics to take into consideration when discussing diversity:

1. Asset Class/ Tenant type/ Leasehold - Freehold
2. Rural or Urban (London/ Home Counties/ North/ South/ East/ West)
3. Strategy (HMO/ BRRR/ Commercial Conversion/ Development/ SA etc....)
4. Sub-Markets (Off-Market/ Private Treaty/ Auction)
5. Landlords/ Developers/ Traders
6. Gender/Race/Religion/Creed
7. Age

I feel that the industry is well represented (or at least better represented) than it has been. With networking really coming to the fore in the last ten years, I think has made it possible or at least made property (investing/developing) far more approachable and inclusive investment vehicle, community, environment and industry.

Do you think most property investors are completely honest on social media?
I don't think anyone can truly be honest on social media. That is more a sign of the times rather than an issue that is specifically applicable to investor/developers. Everybody wears a mask, that's life, that's necessary. The advent of social media and social interactions in the technological age has had many different implications.

Some of these implications are good and some of them are less so. The ones you are most likely to see are (to the negative) the big, the loud and those with silver tongues and promises. We are social animals; however, I feel that social media isn't very social.

Social Media is an overly exaggerated mask, one that sits on top of the mask that we already wear (the mask that protects what's underneath).

I think if you are going to make your mind up about somebody just based purely on their social media, you are likely to come unstuck. Value like beauty is more than skin deep, so don't take people at their face value. You are either grossly overvaluing them or detrimentally undervaluing them.

If you could share one message to every single person on the planet, what would it be?
Good Words, Good Thoughts, Good Deeds.

Is there a quote that means a lot to you? Why?
"A room without books is like a body without a soul." - Marcus Tullius Cicero, Roman philosopher, and lawyer (circa. 107-43 BC).

You are more than flesh and bone. You are more than the sum of your parts (tangible, intangible and more).

Fiction or Non-fiction, it doesn't matter. You will grow, you will gain knowledge, perspective and understanding. You will escape to other worlds, you will feel joy, heartbreak and your depth and breadth as a human being will be greater for it.

I do not know what the worth of a soul is, I have not sold mine and I do not know the going rate. What I do know is that a life without books (learning) is a life lesser for its absence.

What differentiates you from your peers?

Apart from my sparkling and effervescent personality, not much really. I think I have positioned myself in such a way that I am perhaps a bit of an oddity in the small space I occupy in the market.

The first property I purchased at the age of 17, was purchased out of auction, it was a commercial property and during my term as owner, the property blew up. Approximately 4 years later, I started trading properties through auction. I haven't really stopped since.

I was the auction manager at a London real estate auction company and a business development director for a national auction brand. The experience, knowledge and understanding gained from working both sides of the fence is immeasurable.

I started my first degree at the age of 11 (psychology), my second degree at the age of 17 (classics) and my third degree at the age of 21 (Law). I think the inclusion of the areas of study independent of property and my property experience, make me an oddity and perhaps unique.

Which books do you find yourself going back to after the first read?

These are the books that I revisit the most and are in no particular order.

1. The Art of War – Sun Tzu
2. Never Split the Difference – Chris Voss
3. Mr Nice – Howard Marks
4. The Divine Comedy – Dante Alighieri
5. The First Fifteen Lives of Harry August – Claire North
6. The Complete Sherlock Holmes Collection – Sir Arthur Conan Doyle
7. 12 Rules for Life – Jordan B Peterson
8. Rise and Kill First – Ronen Bergman
9. The Alchemist – Paulo Coelho
10. Oversubscribed – Daniel Priestley

It's a bit of a mixed bag, but I hope that shows diversity.

What's the best non-property investment you've made?

In 2008 (late 2008) I was looking at alternative investments to help carry me through the property (and economic) crash. I had just finished working with a developer (family member) and we had just disposed of an optimised site in West London (nunnery with planning for 52 residential units – uplifted with an overage clause via Crest Nicholson and Notting Hill Housing Association to 64 residential units).

I had a decent pay-out with time on my hands and the desire to re-invest. At that time in my property career, I relied quite heavily on UHNWI (Ultra-High Net Worth Individuals) clients for funding and a family member to help run the investment delivery with me.

I was spending a lot of my time watching Bloomberg and CNBC as well as other news and markets channels. At around the time the government was releasing TARP funding to banks, I realised the bank that I banked with Barclays, didn't accept the government TARP funding, instead they were offered very attractive funding from the Middle East.

To keep a long story short, I put a good 80% of my not then so inconsiderable wealth into Barclays shares. I traded them (went short) quite a bit, but by the time I sold them off (end of Q3 2009) I had increased my personal wealth seven-fold. Shortly after this I had purchased the largest property deal, I had done to date.

Jay is listening to Harry Belafonte drinking a Moscow Mule whilst reading The Divine Comedy by Dante Alighieri in Port Douglas, Cairns with the 'Double Trouble' (Gorgeous Wife and Beautiful Baby)

Pippa Mitchell

Pippa Mitchell is a London-based property investor, developer & manager with 10+ years' experience.

Pippa has two key focuses in business:

RegentsView - With her family she is building RegentsView, an income-generating property portfolio that has created an establish buy-to-let portfolio and is now focused on investing in London HMOs

PippaBenoit - With her partner, Benoit Gallaga, they run PippaBenoit, a boutique property management portfolio specialising in managing residential investment property in Prime Central London using the serviced accommodation rental model to maximise rental yields and provide a hands-free management service for the property owners.

Pippa's past projects and experience range from her personal investments with a £1.3m GDV to super prime developments such as The Shard, London Bridge and No.20 Grosvenor Square, Mayfair. These projects had construction budgets of £50 - £100 million. Pippa is also to co-host of the No.1 PPN networking event in the UK alongside Tej, PPN Knightsbridge.

Pippa holds an MSc in Construction Project Management, obtained from Oxford Brooks University.

Pippa is passionate about enjoying the process of building strong businesses & investments. When she isn't working from their house-boat in London you'll find her and Benoit in the SW of France working remotely close to the beach.

IG – @pippamitchell
FB – @pippamproperty
LI – @pippamitchellproperty

What makes property such a powerful asset to you?

For me property is a powerful asset, because as the Covid-19 pandemic has proven, everyone needs a place to call home. It's a fundamental requirement for most people. For most of our tenants buying a property isn't an option, and for a number of reasons this is a reality set to increase. Therefore, for me, this makes property a long-term profitable & stable asset class to invest in.

I take great pride in providing good quality safe homes for tenants to enjoy with their families. Whilst they aren't always the easiest to manage, the tenant type I feel is the best for renting my buy-to-let properties to are single-parent families. This is because they are usually young mum's who haven't had an easy start in life. I sleep well knowing that I'm providing single parents with the peace of mind and pride of a high-quality home, and their children with a lovely safe place to call home.

What advice would you give a total beginner in property?

Never forget it is your life and copying someone else probably won't give you what you want.

So, before you choose a strategy:
1. Get clear on what you personally want to create and consider your strengths and weaknesses.
2. Then, get to work. Learn, work and connect with people who inspire you and who you can learn from. Step-by-step you will make progress.

Along the way, learn & take inspiration for people further ahead in the industry, but whatever you do, don't compare. Comparing your Day 1 to some else's Day 1000 is a losing game.

Whatever you do, along the way constantly keep your eyes and ears open for partners. Partnership in life & business allows you to play a much bigger game than you ever could solo. I have personally found that partnership has made success far more likely, and the process of creating a life that I love so much more fun!

How do you cope with the stress of Property?

For me stress comes in waves, but generally I stay positive & relaxed since I own the fact that:

No one is putting a gun to my head forcing me to buy property, build an investment portfolio or a property business. It is my choice.

For millions of people around the world property investment is impossible, and the kind of freedom we have is only a dream. Every day I appreciate and value that I get to choose the work I do, where and when I do it, and who I work with. For me this was always the goal, so everything else is a bonus. I have found keeping it this simple leaves a lot more space for good quality work and enjoying life!

Getting to this point has taken trial & error and has become much easier since I started doing 2 things:

    1.   Saying no more often.
    This has been a game changer because over-committing myself relentlessly always tends to lead to exhaustion, and no one can do their best work or really enjoy life when they are exhausted.

    2.   Living according to my values.
    The more I stop valuing other peoples' opinions and living according to my own priorities the better life has become. For me this is a game changer improving fulfilment & happiness in my business & life in general.

Generally, do you buy to hold or sell & why?

I buy to hold. I do this because property income & capital appreciation are the two key features of my long-term investment strategy.

Having spent 10 years as a construction project manager on Prime Central London residential developments, and the past 6 years on my own property investment and renovation projects I know too well how much work goes into buying, renovating and refinancing a property. I am not interested in repeating this work any more times than necessary.

Therefore, I prioritise holding property assets wherever possible on my projects.

For example:
369a Limpsfield Road.
Purchased for: £120,000 in 2014
Re-financed for: £220,000 in 2017

This project benefited from the magic trio of
1. Below Market Value purchase price
2. Added value through £20,000 Refurb
3. Capital growth over time

Investing around London we expect at least 2-3% capital appreciation per year on average over a 15-year period. We are definitely looking forward to collecting more capital appreciation over the next 10-15 years.

How do you decide who to JV with?

During my career I have a learnt a lot about people and how to choose who to work with, and even more importantly who you want to become financially involved with.

For me there are two key features of a great JV partnership:

1. Different resources, skills & experience
2. Aligned values

I'm a firm believer of not forcing a partnership and never following the money. Having prioritised the money before - I am speaking from experience that it isn't worth it. If an individual or a company isn't a good fit day one, this won't change over time, so focus on finding partners who are a great fit for you & your business, and you will find great business partners and hopefully life-long friends who you can enjoy doing working with.

What areas of property need the biggest change?
Big-Picture Change for the Industry – for me it would be the credit rating system on which so much of high-street mortgage lending is based.

For me, it is an archaic legacy of the classist British financial system that is fundamentally flawed and needs replacing. I have learnt that this system is not used as a means to accept or refuse lending in other European countries and I would welcome fundamental changes to this system in the UK. Changes to this system would help a lot of people obtain mortgages more easily and at more affordable rates, not just property investors.

When you feel overwhelmed, what do you do?
When I feel overwhelmed, I stop what I'm doing, take a step back & get practical:

> Q: What outcomes do I want?
> Q: What is the correct order of priority? (not the order I find easiest)
> Q: Who can help me & how?

Getting to this point hasn't been an easy road, and sometimes it still requires my partner or business partners to stop me in my tracks and insist that I delegate and share my workload to stop overwhelm creeping in. I've spent far too many nights plugging away doing work in the wrong order, not asking for help & waking up exhausted. In my experience this isn't a sustainable way to live & work, and frankly it's is how burn out shows up, which is never the goal.

I do consider that I've experienced burn out several times to varying degrees. Usually, my body breaks one way or another and I find myself being beaten up on the massage table by a very strong osteopath or as I did in one case booked a 2-month solo trip through Europe to get away from my work phone (summer 2015).

What I learnt from these experiences are that none of these coping mechanisms actually bring down stress levels long-term. The pattern just runs on repeat. In my 20s, each time I would say never again and then it would happen. I can thank Covid-19 for breaking this negative cycle and changing my day-to-day habits for good.

As a partner & business partner, having been in a state of overwhelm enough times to recognise it in someone else, I try to offer my help and take more tasks on if someone else is on the road to overwhelm, whether they realise it themselves or not.

Who do you look up to/ who inspires you?

So, I don't have a particular person or icon I look up to.

I am inspired by brave people. I admire people who are willing to search, try and probably fail along the way to create the life they want. I have a lot of respect for people who are clear on what they want from their life experience, it doesn't have to change the world, it just has to be true to them. For me, this clarity is interesting because it's unique to each of us. I love to spend time with people who are prepared to do life differently, on their terms, because often they have some of the best stories, which makes for a lot of fun!

The people who have given me the most inspiration in my career to date are the *'tribe of mentors'* I've been lucky enough to collect. These people mostly work in the property industry, but have had very different careers, with very different stories to tell.

I don't want to emulate any one of their successes specifically but learning through them has helped me choose my own path. I find it interesting that they are all men, although this is in part due to the fact that the construction industry is majority-male. My mentors continue to cheer me on, give me honest advice and help where they can. They are generous with both their time and thoughtful advice, both of which I'm always grateful for.

What do you do in your free time?

I feel like I need to preface this question with the statement: I'm a recovering workaholic.

In my early 20s the reality for me was – I didn't really have 'free time'. There was always something to do, and it was often work related.

My life had become faster and faster from my teens and through my 20s. I knew how to be busy & I knew how to do nothing, but I didn't know how to slow down & enjoy the view.

Thankfully things have changed.

Over the past few years, I have learnt through my French partner the pleasure of long, delicious meals, in a beautiful setting, with family & friends. It feeds my soul & makes me very, very happy. I have also learnt that there is no time of day that it's unacceptable to drink champagne (in France at least).

The French cultural influence I've experienced through my partner & his family has been a game-changer for me. Thanks to my property business & investments I've been able to spend 3-4 months a year in France more the past 2 years & this has been incredible.

There is no going back now!

What's an unusual or weird thing you love?

So as much as I love travel & adventure, which is a lot, I equally love the peace of home, because at home I get to make things with my hands, and for me for many years that has been cross-stitch. I know, I know… it's not 1880, but there we go. It keeps my hands and my brain busy, which must be a form of meditation, and I always create something beautiful & useful that I keep or gift.

In the UK's lockdown 1.0 I created 12 traditional German miniature Christmas Tree decorations. I'm so proud of them I wish I could include a photograph. So proud in fact I brought them with me to my French family for Christmas. We used them on the tree & I love knowing that they are something I'll use for many years to come!

Since Covid-19 has given me more time on my hands and sewing is more of winter (OAP) hobby, I've decided to learn something new and that happens to be gardening. I realise like sewing, it keeps my hands & brain busy, but even better it's physical too, saving a trip the gym.

Most recently I've created an herb garden in old wine boxes & have taught myself how to prune very large old lemon trees. I'm excited to see everything in full bloom come summer and enjoy spending long lunches & dinners on the terrace surrounded by beautiful colours & sweet-smelling flowers!

During the first 8 years of my career, I spent a lot of time designing and building stunning homes filled with marble & other luxurious finishes in central London. Whilst I do love marble, I fell out of love with luxury finishes & the design ethos driving super-prime property developments. I realised that a home to me was somewhere I had created, that's personal to me. So far, I've prioritised building my property portfolio over owning my own home, but I look forward to creating my own home further down the line and using everything I've learnt & created to make it special for me, my partner & our family.

Pippa will be listening to Fleetwood Mac on repeat with a glass of Champagne & everything her French mother-in-law cooks! She enjoys reading Unshakeable by Tony Robbins, between her London houseboat, and the SW of France working remotely by the beach, with her partner & his French family.

Dan Hulbert

Dan is the co-owner of Hulsford Property Group. He is a property investor and developer who started on the tools to then project managing his own developments.

Hulsford Property Group own and control a £35 million portfolio, they have raised over £5 million in private finance and also host their weekly 'Building on Solid Foundations' podcast where they share real life situations and solutions with warts and all.

Their goals are to 10X their controlled and owned portfolio and to help as many property investors as they can grow and scale their business or portfolio.

Their mission is to help property investors build on solid foundations with a mixture of theory and practical based Earn and Learn investments, Joint ventures and Project Mentoring.

IG – @dan_hulbert / @building_on_solid_foundations
FB – danielrichardhulbert
LI – Daniel Hulbert

Why am I in property?

I got into property when my Dad was investing back in the early 2000's where he was flipping properties part-time while working full-time as a teacher. I have always learnt from doing and being very practical, so for me being involved in this and getting my hands dirty was hard work but it was fun as there was no pressure. I enjoyed watching the TV shows where people would take old, battered houses and turn them into something cool, I still watch Grand designs to this day. One of my personal goals is to buy an old Edwardian house and turn it into an amazing home for me and my wife as our forever home.

So, after several years on the tools and running my own contracts, I decided I wanted to do my own projects and to be honest I had a push and pull relationship with a cash flow or capital appreciation strategy and I did exactly what I now tell people not to do, and that was I didn't have clarity or a plan, I just winged it. I chased the shiny penny and ended up working with an investor where we did 14 HMO's in about 14 months and I earnt my builder's wage and a small profit for the business but no assets, cash flow or capital gains because I just jumped on the opportunity with no focus and made that person 'rich'.

I realised with the help of a mentor that cash flow was king and for me to do the things I wanted to do I needed to replace my income, which I did by doing single let BRR's using none of my own money. Buying below market value, adding value and refinancing pulling out all of the initial seed capital and interest for the investor giving me and my business partner at the time an infinite return of investment and 25% equity. I then went on to do HMO's for myself, but these were different. I would leave investors' money in after refinance and give them an annual return for a fixed long-term investment, at the same time I was packaging HMO investments in Kent and working with UK based investors and through third-party international investors.

The reason I am still in property and growing the business is because I am now in business with a partner where we have completely opposite skills and really complement each other. We can both do the things we enjoy doing and can really get into our flow. Funnily enough most of what I do now is business development, marketing and building strong relationships with investors who get involved with us at different levels through our Earn and Learn opportunities, Joint ventures and project mentoring and I don't have much to do with the day-to-day property, refurbishing side at all. I set out to be my own client and along the way realised through personal development that what I wanted was a successful business I can be proud of and within that business do the things I really like doing and to find a team that can do the rest. We are building towards that on an even larger scale now.

How do you manage refurbishments?

Now this is an interesting question to me, because I have spent nearly 20 years on projects by working, coordinating or fully managing them. I have come to realise that I actually really do not like this part of property investing. It just so happens that I have done it for a long time and got good at it by learning from mistakes and putting better practice in place.

The refurb makes or breaks the deal! Yet so many people do not give it the attention it deserves, and this is where most of the problems and stress come from.

There are four ways to manage a refurbishment:

1. You manage the individual subcontractors and all the professionals.
2. You oversee the individual subcontractors and manage the professionals, but you pay someone on that team a bit extra to help you run the project.
3. You manage a main contractor and professionals, and they manage all the subcontractors.
4. You manage the project manager, and they manage all the contractors and Professionals.

Each way has an upside and downside! Now when I say professionals, I mean Architects, Surveyors, planning consultants, structural engineers, building control Damp surveyors, R&D Surveyors, contractors are professional too though hehe!

Managing individuals is potentially a great way to save money but if you are inexperienced and manage them incorrectly it could end up costing you more and the time input to your project is almost full-time.

Overseeing the subbies and having someone help you by paying them a bit extra will help you save money and maybe time, but the bigger the project the less likely this will work without a management structure in place.

Managing a main contractor has the benefit of saving you time on site and only having one point of contact but the downside is it will be slightly more expensive as the main contractor has overheads and profit to add onto the quote.

Managing the project manager is where you get into bigger projects and this will help you organise your time, money and reduce stress, the downside is the additional expense of a PM, but this should outweigh the cost if they are good.

I now do not run this side of things as much my business partner does as it is more his flow and I oversee the project and help out when needed. The smaller refurbs are run with subbies and we have a main guy that is paid extra to run the project day to day and Gary oversees him, on the large developments we will go to another level and have a full-time contractor's manager.

What advice would you give a total beginner in property?
One of the biggest misconceptions in property is that things happen quickly. Property is a marathon not a sprint and the challenge is that we live in a quick buck, instant gratification world. The access to information through the media is just that 'Instant' and that is what people expect from everything else. If we look at the way things have changed with businesses like Amazon where you can have items posted to you the next day or Netflix where you can watch an entire series in an afternoon, don't get me wrong I love these businesses and I am an avid user, but property

really doesn't work like this. You need a good 3 to 5 years to build a solid foundation and this still depends on your current position.

Now, as this question is for beginners, my advice would be to get clear, by having clarity on what type of investor you want to be, you can choose a path that suits your needs best and then you can specify your plan and get ready to take action. I would say do not focus on anyone else's journey, as comparison is the thief of all joy; however, if you are following, listening or watching for inspiration or learning that is a different matter, although I have one caveat to this and that is you don't become a mere follower but a student to soak up the knowledge and then whatever you decide to action is a product of your own conclusion.

Tell me your biggest failure in property so far?

At the time I had 3 partners, my Building business partner, my property business partner and my lovely wife. I was building in Kent (South), investing in the Midlands and the North West, whilst my wife and I were going through fertility treatment. All I can say is I was stretched, physically and mentally. I had a period of 5 years that was one of the toughest times in my life, my building partner decided he wanted to leave and go out on his own, the timing was brilliant 'right before Christmas' he then took most of the skilled labour with him. This meant I had to find other labour and this came through 3rd and 4th tier connections.

I didn't really know them or vet them, but I had 8 projects to get done and keep clients happy. I also had 4 of my own investment projects happening in the midlands and up North. Wallop… and shit hit the fan. One of the projects I was running the builders hadn't fitted a steel properly and the building moved, this caused structural issues and led to an 18-month litigation battle with a high 6 figure deficit for me. The anxiety I experienced at this time was unbelievable. I had to sell out my portfolio and amicably split with my property business partner who was very good about it all, but I still had debt to pay.

Then to top it off my wife and I found out that we couldn't have children.

My life felt like it was turned upside down.

I quickly fell into depression and struggled to see the point in things.

I came through this because of a book I discovered called 'The Breakthrough Experience' by Dr DeMartini and part of his teaching is that everything in your life happens for a reason. I did struggle with this concept to start with, but I got through it and now look at life with balance, that things happen *for me, not to me.* There really are hidden blessings in everything whether it is perceived as a good or bad experience it will give you either Love or Wisdom.

I came along way mentally with this collection of experiences and now I imagine adversity as a 'seed'.

Let me explain, I take this seed, I sow it, cultivate it and harvest it, meaning I accept it for what it is, I learn from it and then I take the lesson to build for future growth.

What are your thoughts on property education/mentorship?
Property education and mentorship is a good thing; however, I do believe there are too many people selling education and mentorship that just see it as another stream of income and offer no real value. I have been through education courses and they have been great but also, they have been lacking because they are for the masses. There are a high number of people that attend these events and do not do anything with it, this is partly human nature, but I truly believe that the deeper issue is because they don't believe in themselves enough to step out of their comfort zone into the fear and then growth zone.

It is also that they don't know what they want in life and when you don't have a plan, there are hooks with very good marketing and sales pitches to lead you down a path you think you need. Clarity is key and personally they should work on themselves with a coach to truly look at what they want in life before making 'quick' expensive decisions that could affect their life moving forward.

Theory is needed but what I feel people really crave is practical wisdom. I think it is funny that a lot of people teaching property education say the traditional teaching system is broken but yet they teach the same way with an academic approach filling people's heads with content and theory, but without action knowledge is useless! I.e., knowing how to read and not reading, means you are no better off than someone who can't read. The challenge is we all go through the academic teaching process 'school' and if you learn well in this academic learning style, it teaches the student to gain knowledge, which makes them think they know more. Whereas practical based learning and in my opinion are more entrepreneurial, these students learn by doing and the more knowledge they gain the more they realise how much they don't know.

We are all individuals and for someone to really get on they must concentrate on their individual needs. This is a personal mission to that individual and if they don't focus, they see a lot of shiny pennies and never commit to anything but end up paying loads of money out for courses you don't need (and I have done this) wasting time and money just because you want to feel part of something. I personally would have rather paid £25,000 into an 'earn and learn' mentorship with £20,000 being invested and £5,000 on mentorship, that way you can get the theory that you need and the practical experience you crave. The problem is this model isn't scalable in academic property education scenarios, it is about having bums on seats to scale and make money.

'A numbers game'. I hear the educators say "If you don't succeed, we don't succeed" but because we are very British, we don't say anything because we want to save face. I believe property education will start to change because of COVID and the situations we find or found ourselves in. Theory can be learned for free or low cost online; it is then a matter of gaining practical experience and having support on your journey when you start building your property business or portfolio.

Personally, I would rather scale my property business with education as part of that but have a 90% success rate with 10 individuals a year, than have a 5% success rate with 100 individuals.

Dan is currently listening to Fleetwood Mac eating a toad in the hole with a cold bottle of Heineken whilst reading Arsene Wenger's autobiography in his home office with his wife Emma, 2 Frenchies Delilah and Arthur and their Cat George.

Sanjay & Malkit

Malkit Purewal and Sanjay Kumar are childhood friends who embarked on their property journey over 20 years ago by purchasing a property in auction while both in fulltime employment. The guys continued building their property portfolio while working until 2008 when they embarked on adding value to property by developing or extending properties.

In 2010 the guys purchased a HMO in auction which was used for LHA tenants. They used this HMO as a template to learn how to provide modern contemporary Co-Living HMOs for working professionals. By learning from each project Malkit & Sanjay have gone on to manage over 300 tenants in HMOs for themselves and Landlords in South East England.

In 2013 Malkit & Sanjay took advantage of Prior Approval planning rules to repurpose commercial properties to residential use. From 2013 until now Malkit & Sanjay have repurposed numerous commercial properties to residential use. This was recognised in 2020 by the Property Investor Awards where Malkit & Sanjay won Commercial Property Developer of the Year Award.

Malkit & Sanjay have featured in Property Investor News Magazine, Your Property Network Magazine and are regular writers for HMO Magazine.

IG – @savoysproperties
FB – Savoys Properties
TW – @savoys_prop
LI – Savoys Properties
W – savoysproperties.co.uk

What makes property such a powerful asset to you?

We chose to invest and develop properties to make a difference to the property market and then make a difference to the tenants that we house.

However, property is a powerful asset for us for the following reasons:

Property is an understandable & controllable asset. When purchasing a property, you are purchasing a physical asset, something you can see and touch rather than something conceptual like shares, futures or bonds. With property you do not require specialist knowledge, making the knowledge barrier to entry lower than complex investments such as currency trading or cryptocurrency. Investment properties are more stable than stocks, funds and cryptocurrency during economic instability. As the population continues to increase, demand for housing will remain ensuring the stability of house prices.

A big advantage is that you have control over your asset, unlike other investments. Property investment has the option to add value to your asset growing the income and value of the property. In addition, you control when and where you buy, sell and if you want to adjust rent as the market changes.

Regular Income. With investment property you are able to predict cash flow and have a reliable constant income. Income is more certain because you receive constant rental payment from the tenants. If the rental income is higher than the mortgage repayment of an asset, the loan will slowly pay itself and you may also have surplus funds to cover any property costs incurred. The best way to ensure that your return on investment remains consistent is to minimize the time between tenants (voids). This minimizes the time when the rental income is less than the repayments on your mortgage.

Capital Growth. Property markets in the United Kingdom have historically enjoyed stable long-term growth. Should this continue, any property investment should grow in value. Commonly, property investors will purchase run down properties and renovate them to increase the value. When the time is right to sell, buyers see a greater return on their investment.

Portfolio Diversification. Property is one of the largest asset classes and we believe it is fundamental to a well-diversified portfolio. Property investing can be split broadly into the residential, commercial, industrial and retail sectors. An advantage is that property can be both directly owned, such as most residential property, or indirectly owned. Indirectly property can be managed through a fund, syndicate structure or a real estate investment trust (REIT).

Wealth preservation. We see property as a strategy that ensures our assets grow while providing a legacy for our families. Historically property has outperformed inflation and over the past 20 years we've witnessed that property is a key for preserving wealth for the future generations of our families.

Why have you chosen your strategy?
Our main strategy for over 10 years has been HMO and when we started, we adopted the saying that "*The only way to go is HMO*".

The reason we chose HMOs for a number of exciting reasons:

- HMOs offer better yields & cash flow: HMOs offer up to 3 to 4 times higher rental yields dependent on the area than standard properties, this makes them a great investment choice. It's important to bear in mind that location, condition, and interior design will determine your overall rent & tenant type.
- HMOs have fewer void periods: When you rent out a property to one tenant or family, you have to consider void periods. When the single tenant or family moves out and then you have to wait for another tenant to move in. With HMOs it's likely that at least some of your tenants will remain, even if another one is vacating, so you won't lose all of your rental income overnight.
- Arrears less likely: By letting out a house to multiple tenants, you balance the risk of late payments. If one tenant falls into arrears, the rest will still be contributing.

- Tax benefits: HMOs benefit from Capital Allowances. Capital Allowances allow HMO owners to claim qualifying items of capital expenditure as a tax deduction and are a valuable tax relief. The aim of Property Capital Allowances claims is to recover tax paid and reduce tax liabilities for companies and individuals that have spent capital buying and/or improving HMO properties. Please revert to your accountant for specialist advice.
- High demand: We find whether you're letting to students or multiple households, demand for HMOs has never been higher, particularly in cosmopolitan cities. Always identify the demand and competition before you invest in a property to maximise your returns.

What advice would you give a total beginner in property?

Historically property prices have doubled every 10 years and rents have doubled every 20 years. With this in mind I would strongly advise a total beginner to be starting their property journey ASAP.

However, it isn't as straight forward as opening the Rightmove portal, looking at a property, calling an agent and making an offer.

We think a total beginner should take the following steps:

- Identify Your Financial Position. This will allow you to establish how much money you have to put towards a property and what you need to raise.
- Educate yourself on investment strategies and choose one. There are many strategies out there and many individuals share this information online for free.
- Pick a Target Area for Investment. This area should be within your budget and have an active rental market.
- Decide Your Property Criteria. What are you looking at buying? Freehold or Leasehold? Studio, 1, 2 or 3 Bedrooms? It's important to get this criteria right as it will form the basis of your investment strategy.

- Build Your Power Team. To be successful in property you need a power team and for us the below people / companies have been essential to us for our success:
  - Independent Mortgage Broker
  - Property Specialist Accountant
  - Property Specialist Solicitors
  - Estate Agents / Property Finder
  - Wealth Manager
  - Letting Agents
  - Builders
  - Maintenance Team
  - HMO Insurance Specialist Broker
  - Mentor
- Create a Plan to Find Deals. Great deals don't fall on your lap, it's more like a treasure hunt and you need a plan to find them.
- Have Your finance lined up? We would suggest you speak to you broker early in your property journey. Their initial advice can crucial once you find your first deal.

Generally, do you buy to hold or sell, and why?
We generally never sell. Over the course of 20 years, we have only ever sold 5 properties and we only sold those to purchase other properties which had greater potential.

The reasons we like to hold are:

- Wealth Creation
- Property is a top-performing asset-class
- You can leverage one property to buy another or raise funds for other purposes
- Your tenant can pay your mortgage indefinitely
- Property offers both capital and income growth
- You don't have to sell your home when you move

Should people invest in the North or the South?
There is no right or wrong answer here, it all depends on the investor and what they wish to achieve.

We think it really depends on whether you are looking for:

- Higher Yields. With experience over the past 20 years, we have witnessed the North outperform the South with higher yields. However, the capital growth has been lower than inflation. Therefore, if you wish to achieve great yields then the North is the place to invest.
- Capital Growth. For the past 20 years we have actively invested in the South. What we have experienced is lower yields compared to the North however the capital growth has been exceptional. With the housing shortage in the South we see capital growth in the South not slowing down anytime soon.

Bridging Finance - expensive or very useful?
When we were both at college our business lecturer explained the pros and cons of having a credit card. The pros being if you use the credit card in the right & sensible way it gives you 56 days interest free credit. However, if you miss use it, then it can be very costly, and this is where Bridging Finance is very similar.

We typically use bridging loans for 6-9 months on properties which are unable to obtain a mortgage or our works would not meet mortgage terms.

We find the key advantages of Bridging Finance are:

- Fast to arrange
- Flexible lending criteria
- All types of property can be used as security
- Property that is in a poor state of repair
- Lend against non-standard property construction
- Multiple properties can be used as security

However, there are cons which you need to bear in mind with Bridging:

- High interest rates

- Increased fees
- Currently unregulated for investment purchases
- Widely varying lending rates and terms

On the whole we like bridging finance; we have used it in the right way, and it has been pivotal for us in expanding our portfolio.

Is there a quote that means a lot to you? Why?
"Men lie, women lie, numbers don't." *(Jay Z, "Reminder")*

Within the property industry people tell many lies regarding numbers to get a deal completed with the loser being the buyer. These numbers relate to current values, developed values, rents, commissions, build costs, etc. What we found during our years within property is the only thing that speaks the truth is the numbers.

People can promise you a certain rent or return however the true number is what the market offers or returns to you. Once we understood this we stopped taking 'experts' advice as gospel and started trusting ourselves and our numbers when it came to property deals. We have not looked back since.

Malkit and Sanjay will be listening to U Don't Know by Jay-Z, drinking cappuccinos whilst reading Empire State Of Mind: How Jay Z Went from Street Corner to Corner Office by Zack O'malley Greenburg, in their office.

Jess Leader

Jessica is the founder of Next Level Living, a property development company in the Midlands led by the vision that everyone deserves to live in a home in which they can flourish. She focuses on co-living and residential developments – all with human impact at the heart.

Before her property career, Jessica was an internationally award-winning marketer, working for both start-ups and some of the biggest marketing agencies in the world over 14 years.

She has always been driven by what excites her and this has led her to work with charities, female empowerment initiatives and now, with the values that together, we can achieve more.

IG – @jess_leader
LI – Jessica Leader
FB – Next Level Living

What makes property such a powerful asset to you?

Property is a vehicle through which you can determine your own life. Want a simple life? Choose a strategy and scale that keeps things easy. Want a lavish life? Dial it up, work harder, for longer, and you can fulfil your heart's wildest desires. Although not immediate and often not easy, it's totally in our hands. Which means if we don't have what we want, that's the perfect feedback to change something about what we're doing.

Property also is a perfect feedback mechanism to what we need to improve in our businesses, teaching us excellent business lessons. If you're a sourcer not shifting deals quickly enough, the feedback is to focus on your buyer contact list and CRM systems. If you're a developer not generating enough private finance, the feedback is to spend time focussing on your investor pipeline and relations. If you listen for the feedback, which often presents through our frustrations, it's incredibly powerful.

Then looking wider than ourselves, working in property gives me the ability to create homes where people flourish: the very ethos behind my approach to property investing and the end products I create.

Why have you chosen your strategy?

A property friend of mine maintains of himself that "[my] strategy is making money. How I do that simply comes down to different tools in my toolkit and which tool suits each 'box' [building] best." So, he simply feels that the more 'strategies' he knows, the more money he can make. Others choose to pick one strategy and strictly F.O.C.U.S. (Follow One Course Until Successful) until they've mastered it, choosing to diversify only then. This itself is proof that you have to decide what YOU want to achieve and then work out what will get you there. It's personal. No comparing.

I focus on HMOs and flips.

HMOs were an obvious choice for me: from my own perspective, I wanted to create maximum cashflow and return on my efforts. I also wanted to own in order to be able to control the assets and benefit from the capital gain as well as the monthly cash flow. My initial property goal was to create a monthly cashflow to equal and therefore replace my monthly salary, which would give me choices around my work in marketing. It took me about 3.5 years to get to this point. Yes, the effort is higher, but so is the reward. From my investors' perspective, I wanted to be able to create high returning assets that would offer solid performance and high returns. Which I do.

Flips for me create balance in my portfolio: whilst HMOs require large amounts of capital, flips balance that out to 'fill the pot' back up. Whilst I invest using investor, bank and also my own funds (I think it's important to show I have capital equity in the game, as well as sweat equity), capital generated from flips gives me a cash reserve, or a safety net, if you like. Reassuring for both me and my investors.

How do you decide who to JV with?
How do you decide who to date, or who to marry?

JVs are very powerful tools in upscaling your business and I have a couple of JV relationships. BUT you have to choose carefully and conduct thorough due diligence before you go into a JV arrangement. I didn't with my first and, although this has led to no disasters, it's meant my approach is different now. Here are some of my top tips on choosing your JV partners:

- Do you know this person? This might sound ridiculous, but the number of approaches I've had to JV with people I've met that day on a course, or from a social media connection shows that JVs are created between practical strangers.
- Do you have the same values? Regardless of any opportunity, do you like this person; are you aligned in your missions; what niggles do you have about things they say or do; do you have similar, or at least complementary, codes of conduct, do you see property in the same way, etc. etc. For example, a person who sees property purely as a money-making vehicle above all else will clash when assessing priorities in a project with a person who sees their purpose as creating efficient, welcoming or eco-friendly homes, as examples.

- Will you enjoy working with this person? In a job, we work with who we are teamed with. In our property businesses, we choose. Make it fun and a joy to come to – after all, we do it Every. Single. Day.
- Have you worked with this person before? My latest JV partner was an investor for 2 years prior to us deciding to take our professional relationship to the next level. I know how he thinks about risk. He knows how I behave when things don't go to plan. We trust and understand each other.
- What's the benefit? I personally advocate JVs which are fair exchange of funds, effort, skills, knowledge, time or position. A JV should benefit both parties and bring something to each they could not otherwise achieve, or perhaps not as quickly.
- Talk about EVERYTHING. Go through every scenario before you start working together – if the sh*t hits the fan, you're going to have to talk about it anyway, so best to do this in a state of clarity and calm upfront. If someone isn't willing to have open conversations with me, that's a red flag for me.
- Make it legal. Go to an expert and get the paperwork done. Your relationship might not just affect you and them, but your and their families.

I could go on. For excellent guidance on choosing JV partners, and how investor partners choose their developer partners, follow @helenchorleyinvestor to name but one of many valuable resources.

What is your deal analysis process?
In a word: anal! I value my word too much to make careless mistakes.

My process includes both manual and automatic steps and is now based on a set of tried and tested criteria that allow me to quickly assess whether a deal is feasible.

The initial automatic or process-led steps include assessing location, floorplan, saturation, competition and GDV comps, as the basics. Much of this is done by my VA.

Then I use my deal analysis spreadsheet to stress test each variable, including interest rates, voids, costs, etc. I do this for each potential exit, making sure each property has 3 exits that stack financially.

I also sense check things with my broker and lettings manager, particularly in these pandemic-driven changing times. Asking questions like 'What are banks cautious about at the moment?', 'Are you seeing patterns in what's holding its value or getting down-valued at the moment', 'What are tenants asking for most at the moment' allow me to keep current and to get a realistic short-term perspective of what will / won't achieve the funding or GDVs I want, even when I believe that, long term, they will hold.

How important is interior design? Any tips?
Absolutely key.

Financially, the positive impacts of strong interior design can include higher rents, quicker uptake, longer tenures (so lower new tenant costs) and higher GDVs.

Strategically, interior design can be used as a tool to attract at retain your preferred tenant type.

Health-wise, interior design in its fullest sense, including spatial planning, functionality planning, design of flow and visual design has everything to do with wellbeing of tenants.

A couple of tips:

- As with any marketing, identify your target audience, understand what they want and create that solution
- It's helpful to understand what your competition is offering and decide where you want to sit against that: if you want a typical price point, offer a typical product. If you want a higher-than-average price point, figure out how to offer a higher-than-average product.
- Decide if you want to create a unique brand look. If you do, spend time developing this in a way that is unique to you and your values

and that creates the tenant experience you want to evoke as part of your 'user experience'.

My ethos is to design spaces where people flourish. Interior design plays a critical role in bringing this to life. To talk to me more on this, come take a look at my website, nlliving.co.uk/nldesign

Bridging Finance – expensive or very useful?
It is both. Bridging enables funds to stretch much further and I have used it multiple times.

Taking this very simplistic example applying two scenarios to the same situation:

Property purchase price:	£150,000
Development costs:	£60,000
Purchase costs and fees:	£10,000
Project subtotal:	£220,000
Total investor funds available:	£250,000

Scenario 1: property fully funded by private angel loan/s

Example angel interest @7% of £220,000	£15,400
Project total:	£235,400
No. of properties purchased with angel funds:	1

Scenario 2: property funded by private angel loan/s and bridging

Bridging 75% of purchase costs:	£112,500

Funds required for project
Cost of bridge @10% (approx.):	£11,250
Deposit:	£37,500
Development costs:	£60,000
Purchase costs and fees:	£10,000
Project subtotal (angel fund requirement):	£118,750
Example angel interest @7%:	£8,313
Project total:	£239,563

No. of properties angel funds will stretch across: 2

So, you decide if you think the extra few thousand pounds is worth it.

My personal preference would be to fund deals fully with angel loans: firstly, I would prefer to give that finance cost to my angels as opposed to Bridgers and secondly, working with people is far better than working with institutions. But they are very helpful leverage tools.

What has property allowed you to do? What has it given you?
Apart from a few more grey hairs? For myself, I have been able to derive my income from property and therefore entirely change my day-to-day life. That's hugely satisfying and as someone who always wants to make themselves proud, it's also highly fulfilling.

For my investors, I have been able to send families on holiday, grow retirement funds and grow nest eggs for deposits for children's first homes.

What differentiates me from my peers?
First, my product: I create homes where people flourish. Once a deal stacks, creating these is the highest priority.

In how I work, the priority for me is relationships. With my team, my investors and my tenants.

I treat my tenants as customers and that they feel important and heard in their homes is a key priority for me and therefore how I operate with my letting's teams.

I aim to act with integrity, transparency, fairness and respect. I work hard to live true to my word and hold that most highly. It's always a bit awkward writing about yourself, but feedback tells me that my differentiators include fantastic clarity and communication, strong relationships and high emotional intelligence.

Is there a quote that means a lot to you? Why?
"There are people less qualified than you doing the things you want to do purely because they decided to believe in themselves and take action."

Property throws many challenges your way. This quote reminds me that I have all the resources available within me to deal with any situation and constantly level up.

Jess is listening to the '*calming music to work to*' playlist on Spotify. It's not cool, it doesn't scream any vibe, but she finds words in songs too distracting when working, so sound with no lyrics work best for Jess. She'll likely be eating healthy food, reading The 12 Week Year by Brian P. Moran and Michael Lennington in her home office. One day it will have an uninterrupted countryside views.

James Sahota

James Sahota has a vast array of experience when it comes to property development.

He is highly skilled in a range of areas such as new build developments, land planning, co-living (HMO) houses, flat conversions and significant back to brick house renovations.

A Masters graduate in Industrial and Product Design, James spent the early part of his professional career in the education sector but, he soon realised his lifelong love of business and entrepreneurship could not be kept at bay. In 2009 James set up a Signage and Print business that focused mainly on the events and exhibition sector.

James scaled this business to a several million-pound turnover company with major accounts such as Google, Facebook and Microsoft.
James has always invested in the property market, and it was in early 2018 that he realised his true passion was in property development and he made a move to focus on this solely as a full-time career.

His current focus is on providing high-quality new build homes in London and next level co-living HMO's (Houses of multiple occupancies) in university towns and sought-after locations, a high cash flowing model which he has perfected over the last few years.
Having spent the early part of his career in lecturing and teaching, James naturally has a love of education, learning, mentoring and growth.
His online Liquidaction Academy, and one to one Titanium Property Mentoring are always in very high demand.

FB – James Sahota
LI – James Sahota
IG – @jameshsahota
YT – James Sahota

Tell me about your biggest failure in property so far?

It's pretty horrific to be fair, I lost £100,000 to a building firm, worse still this was a so-called friend from the local gym and actually came highly recommended. My biggest failure here was the lack of due diligence done on my part and the lack of education on how to correctly pay for works and stage payments.

I was naive and thought handing over a chunk of money would mean the job would get done. To further add insult to injury, the builder didn't actually know what he was doing, it took the local neighbor who just happened to be a commercial architect (and his office window looked out onto the site), he actually called me very concerned and said "James, I think you better get to site, it looks as if your building has been built at the wrong height"

To my shock horror, the neighbor was absolutely correct, instead of starting to build the house 1.2m below ground level, these idiots decided to start from ground level.

The whole building needed to be ripped down and started again, I look back now and I'm glad it was ripped down as God only knows what other horror lay beneath what I could see.

Lessons:

- Don't hand over large chunks of cash over to builders
- Make sure you vet your contractors no matter how close they might be
- Make sure you check the previous jobs your builder has carried out and ask to speak to previous clients
- Make sure you are on-site regularly and understand every aspect of your build
- Hire a project manager if this isn't your full-time crack and you need to help
- DON'T GIVE UP ON YOUR FIRST MAJOR FAILURE.... KEEP GOING!

What are your thoughts on property education/mentoring?
I'm a massive fan of Education and mentoring, I know the topic has some very mixed opinions but my whole outlook on the topic is this, "Why not get someone to show you the blueprint so you can get to the end goal quicker". There are lots of free resources out there and I'm sure by consuming this free content you could probably figure out what to do but how certain would you really be. Free advice will only take you so far in my opinion.

I often get asked the question "James why do you have a mentor?". My simple answer to this is why do professional athletes have coaches for all aspect of their training? If it's good enough for the world-class athletes it's good enough for me, obviously in the property sense.

Having been mentored by some of the world's best and in fact, right now I'm being mentored by the world-class "Darren Hardy" (Author of The Compound Effect book) I decided it's about time I put out some world-class training of my own. As you are probably already aware the yellow tee man (Tej) has already released an excellent book that educates you on everything property-related and also his even better eLearning programme which provides a new way of interacting and learning online. I feel the whole space of education and mentoring is changing, out with the old bullshit trainers and in with the new real-life investors and developers living, breathing, eating property day in day out and teaching others how to do it properly.

Watch this space for some mega exciting things dropping in 2021.

3 Top Tips on raising investor finance?
Tell everyone what you do, is the single biggest bit of advice I can give. Make sure the whole world and his dog know you're a property developer and you actively look to work with investors and offer healthy returns.

Make sure you document your journey, show people and followers how you do property, share all the positives and negatives, be a realist, show them how you mess up and then show them how you overcome these issues. This shows you're a real problem solver and knows how to deal with challenges, you will be surprised how many investors like this trait. Our very own Tej does this extremely well you only have to take a glance at his Instagram and you within a few swipes you know exactly what he does.

Remember to make sure your personality shines through on everything you do. An investor will invest in you first before they actually look at the deal. If the investor likes you than chances, are you will get an investment.

Treat everyone with respect and don't be a dick, you never know who is watching!

What's been your biggest success in property?
I've had a number of big successes in property but the one that sticks out the most was the planning uplift a good friend and I got on a property we purchased.

So, here's how it goes, a lady in my friend's office inherits a shop which has a two bed flat upstairs, the property was located in Croydon just around the corner from the new Westfield shopping centre. The lady wanted a quick sale and my friend, and I just happen to have the £300,000 she wanted for it, she had no idea other shop owners in the parade had successfully got planning to convert the shops into flats.

Fast forward 3 months from purchase we managed to secure planning to turn the commercial into a 2-bed flat. We did think about building this out but when someone offers you £425k for the building it seems silly not to sell it. These kinds of deal don't happen all the time but when they do it's like Christmas has come early.

It goes without saying we used this money to buy ourselves a nice car each...How stupid we were back then, nevertheless this really was making money for very little work.

When you feel overwhelmed what do you do?

Feeling overwhelmed is part and parcel of property investing and knowing when you are feeling overwhelmed and how to identity it's happening to you is very important.

I recently felt massively overwhelmed only 2 weeks into the new year and although part of me felt like I was failing I knew I needed to address this quickly and deal with it before it got out of hand. I decided it was important to stop and work out what was happening, I spent a couple of hours brain dumping everything going through my head and decided it was important to put all of this down on paper, so I knew exactly what was going on.

It turned out I had 193 open tasks that needed to be completely before I could take on anything new. No wonder why I was feeling overwhelmed I had so much to do and was trying to add more to my plate.

Think of it this way if your stomach is full of food, you're not going to add more food to your system until the first lot is digested and the waste has been removed from your system, adding more will only result in you feeling sick and that's exactly how I describe overwhelm as.

I now run my whole life through apps such as Trello and Asana which help me to see exactly what needs to be done and allows me to remain calm and collected at all times. If you have a clear plan that's broken into chunks and it's all out of your head than it's all a lot easier to address and handle.

My advice if your overwhelmed – don't add to the baggage, take a minute to take a step back and work out what's on your plate before you move forward.

Who is really important to you in life?

My mother is hugely important to me in my life. She's been very influential in the decisions I have made, and she gave me the best start she could with her limited resources. If it wasn't for my mother making me buy a house at the age of 23 whilst all my friends were buying cars, I would never have got this far down my property journey.

If you follow me on Instagram *(shameless plug @jameshsahota...LOL)* you will know I have often posted site tours with my Mum in them and made her a real integral part of my journey. It's been great having her smash things up; help cut trees and generally just get involved.

Sadly, in November 2020 she was diagnosed with a very aggressive form of brain cancer and although she has had an operation and treatment to try and cure this, it is sadly terminal cancer and I've had to face facts that one of the most important people in my life won't be around much longer. One of my biggest fears was always losing my mother and now sadly I have to face it head on, the only consolation being I can prepare for it and it's not a shock to the system.

Never take life for granted. Be nice and love everyone around you as you don't know what's going to happen tomorrow. One minute my mother's working with me racing at 200mph and now she's laid up functioning at 5% of her former self.

You would never have guessed I was going through this looking at my social feeds, right?

Be kind - you never know what someone else is going through.

You will find Uncle James listening to Lo-fi beats with a hint of Nigerian Pop, whilst eating hot chili grilled chicken with roasted vegetables, reading the compound effect for the 5th time. In his home attic office with his 4-year-old JV running around asking to explain CAD drawing and structural drawings to him

Susannah Cole

Susannah is one of UK's most successful self-made property investors. Starting her first business at the age of 22 she knew she had and entrepreneurial spirit which could not be constrained by J. O. B (Just over broke). Breaking out of the corporate lifestyle she followed her dreams and took the risk to set up the Good Property Company which she has now been running for over ten years.

With determination and the right knowledge, Susannah believes anyone can make millions from property. It is possible to succeed even with very little money starting out. It only took Susannah 3 ½ years to becomes a property millionaire, and in her first 3 months as a deal packager, she made £12k as a kitchen table start up with a phone, a kettle and computer. Susannah went on to source, buy or let out more than 200 properties with a value of £45million and an agreed purchase price of £30million (before refurb). She then invested her capital to develop her multi-million-pound property portfolio consisting of HMO's, single lets and serviced accommodation.

Susannah's passion for property is infectious and she loves to give back and share her knowledge. Her top priority is to help people reach their potential as a property investor and achieve (and hopefully surpass) her own successes! Whilst she is currently taking a sabbatical from her mentoring programme, she has created a large range of educational materials which fit all budgets and are available to download on her website.

FB – Susannah Cole TGPC
LI – Susannah Cole
TW/IG – @SusannahcoleUK
YT – goodpropertycompany
W – thegoodpropertycompany.co.uk

Why are you in property?

Security, stubbornness and family protection started it and later the community, the entrepreneurial drive and energy I enjoy in my peers and myself and the fun we are having! I think it evolves, but in the early days it was all about protecting my beautiful children as I was a young head of household who wanted a strong financial future for my family.

What makes property a powerful asset for you?

The fact we can buy houses wholesale. The only difference is that you can't go to the wholesalers, there is no special shop for them, you need to spot the wholesale deals nestling amongst the retail details. But the beauty of property is that it is so a numbers game. To get a wholesale property, they are 1 – 2% of all properties sold, so you know that in every 100 properties on the market, you will be able to find (if you put the work in) between 1 and 2 wholesale deals.

I like the dependability of the numbers when you are looking for them: I built my first property business on those reliable numbers, as we sourced over 200 deals, £45 million of property at an agreed purchase price of £30 million in less than 5 years.

The flexibility also excites me – you can get into property with very little money, like I did, and package on discounted (wholesale) deals to happy investors, who pay you a high sourcing fee, within weeks. So quite quickly you can build up your own funds as well as getting great experience finding property and working with dynamic cash rich investors.

How do you decide who to JV with?

Well early on, like most inexperienced investors, we looked for people with money, who qualified for PS 13/3. But quickly we realised there is a heck of a lot more to a JV relationship. A JV relationship takes time, both to develop and then to maintain while you are doing a project. As a result, spending time with the right JV partner becomes super important to your long-term success as a property investor.

The right JV partner will rinse and repeat deals with you, happily and you with them. The wrong JV partner will be a weight dragging you down in a flurry of blame, recrimination and anxiety.

This is due to a number of things, but ultimately when it comes down to it, property development and flipping (I only JV on flips) is inherently risky. So, whilst I do EVERYTHING in my power to mitigate the risk – such as seeking up to 45 pieces of research to establish the end value of a property, get fixed price quotes from builders, check their insurances, always having a Plan A, Plan B, Plan C for the property, at times speedbumps occur. These could be my mistakes, the builder's mistakes or simply the market not responding as we would like, despite all our research.

At that character defining moment you want to be shoulder to shoulder with your JV partner. Working as a team. You identify the problem, come up with the solution and your JV partner reflecting then either agreeing or adding value by bringing an even better solution to the table.

What you don't need is someone screeching down the phone at your team (had that) driven by fear, anxiety and the inability to navigate the risks and speedbumps that property does at times bring.

This does not mean to say you ever do a project half hearted – absolutely not – you always put everything you got into working on a JV to the best of your ability. But sometimes things don't go to plan.

This is where screening your JV partners is critical.

As we did more JVs, (at one point we had about 30 on the go at the same time) we saw repeating patterns.

First, there are a ton of people out there with money. So, don't grasp the first person, check them out. Second behaviour counts.

We ended up with a 5-point JV partner screening check list:

1. Are they nice to the team? This is important as pretty much everyone was nice to me, but who they are to people they might not directly get rich working with counts for more. Subtle behaviour is important.
2. Are they fast and accurate on paperwork; an easy JV partner to work with, who won't lose a deal through delaying the purchase or sale?
3. Will they be an ambassador for us – would they naturally think and say good things about us to others. Do they believe in what we are doing over and above the personal gain they will be making?
4. Do they behave selfishly in a group, or are they considerate to others? We used group Investor Days yes to attract JV partners, but later when we were inundated with applications, to mainly assess the behaviour of potential JV partners. People can usually be nice one on one but show their true colours when in a group.
5. Will they add value? Meaning, apart from the money they bring, will the relationship bring: fun, joy, expertise, knowledge, good energy, business acumen, enjoyment.

Isn't it fascinating that none of the screening questions – and we scored every applicant JV partner – had anything to do with money?

I'd strongly recommend you assess your JV partners for behaviour first, and only accept the fabulous ones! Life is too short to be hampered in a poorly performing business partnership, even if it is only for the lifetime of one flip.

What's your secret sauce for Finding Deals/Sourcing?

This is something we know a thing or two about – we sourced over 200 deals in less than 5 years – 217 to be exact.

There are 4 routes to stock:
*   Estate agents
*   Auctions?
*   Direct to vendor

- Direct to house

But after the first year which saw us spending £4,000 per month on leaflets, we primarily focussed on the 'free' ones, which are estate agents and auctions.

Estate agents: set yourself up to succeed with a population density search area of 250,000 and 100 estate agent offices – branches of the same brand do count. Then get busy, this is a numbers game.

100 calls, 25 viewings, 21 offers will statistically get you a deal.

The key here is to ensure you offer on 85% of properties that you view. If your conversion rate of viewings to offers is lower than that you are wasting time on viewings that you do not offer on, so get better at the calls.

Second secret: I have never EVER looked for a deal online. EVER.

Why? That is where everyone else goes – I call it property porn!

With estate agents the sweet spot is to get a call in early when a property has come onto their books but is not yet advertised and if the agent can get it sold to you, it keeps their life simple. Finally, be good to estate agents, they are the route to around 90% of the deals you will find!

What is your morning routine?
I generally bounce out of bed as I love what I do. I have a gratitude diary and daily (or almost daily) write 3 things I am grateful for.

This is a technique I read about in a well-researched book called 'Authentic Happiness' by Martin Seligman. It enables you to focus on the good in your life, rather than problems, and increases your happiness levels, which I am all for.

I then set out my key tasks: I aim for 3 a day, made up of 2 important tasks, which will move the business forward. Important tasks don't yell, they whisper. Yet if you neglect to do them, they become firefighting issues within about 6 months. I much prefer to be front footed in my business, rather than firefighting. I'll endure the cacophony of a few of these tasks at times, and only focus on one daily, with the remainder of my time driving my business forward. This technique really works as you move from being on the back foot to the front foot, but it takes a couple of months to tilt forward.

Exercise is important: CrossFit, yoga, weightlifting, walking, and meditation as well as good food and strong connections with friends and family.

Now I live in both Bristol and Barcelona, I am often working remotely, which means a walk or run on the beach is pretty much a daily trip when I am in Barcelona.

What has property allowed you to do? What has it given you?
Property has been a fun journey and allowed me to express my creativity, my drive and my stubbornness to run my life the way I want to live, rather than being cooped up in an office. Now as I have a property portfolio that more than pays for my living, I live in both Bristol city centre - a funky city I love, and Barcelona where I have a 1920s Art Deco apartment close to the beach. I have a grown child in each city so get to enjoy family, travel and sun with the people I love. I now work part time (because I enjoy my property work) and spend a lot of time travelling and with the people I care about.

I have also had the fun of setting up a key UK property YouTube channel with over a million views, an online busines with great education and ran a very high-quality mentoring programme for over a decade – I'm enjoying seeing others succeed.

Susannah will probably be listening to Nina Simone and Aretha Franklin eating Vietnamese street food, reading non-stop! Every night without fail, a combo of business books, food books, health research and a good old story or two. You'll find her partly in the centre of Bristol, in a hidden cobbled Georgian Street, working at her window desk overlooking the city and part in Barcelona in her 1920s Art Deco apartment near the sea, with a roof terrace and hammock, with the people she loves!

Dee Ludlow

Dee Ludlow is the founder of Interlinnx Group LLC, a US based company focused on building a group of Gas & Electrical Businesses and he is also founder of The 5am Club, a community of likeminded individuals that want to explore the world of wealth generation.

Before devoting his time to building an educational community and coaching program, Dee has been investing across assets and building businesses since he left school.

In addition, Dee is a business consultant and has worked with 8 figure turnover companies to restructure their processes and systems to maximise profitability.

Dee now spends his time travelling and networking and continues to work on his vision of generational wealth for his children.

IG – @deeludlow
FB – Dee Ludlow
LI – Dee Ludlow
YT – Dee Ludlow
W – www.jointhe5amclub.co.uk

How do you handle the stress of Property?

Mentally I cope very well with property, I brainwash myself with positivity on a daily basis and even if something goes wrong, I have a story my Dad told me once that plays in the back of my mind. My dad has stage 4 cancer and has gone through multiple chemotherapy treatments, and he told me that he went to see his Oncologist to see where his tumor markers were at, and the oncologist said,

"Martyn, this is the 3rd time we have gone through this, and you're the only one from the previous 3 groups that has survived, aren't you scared?"

My Dad replied,

"Would it help?"

That to me was so powerful and it made me realise we take on so much stress over things that sometimes are out of our control, from that day anything that comes up whether in property or my personal life I ask myself *'would it help if I worried'*, this helps me cope with any stress that arises in property. I also apply first principal thinking when I run into a problem, I very quickly work on the solution and what could make a core impact instead of dwelling on the fact something may have gone wrong or something hasn't gone to plan.

Property is a people's game, as much as we factor in the numbers of 'the deal' or 'volume of viewings and offers', without the people, I.e., the agents, the build team, the broker, accountant and your overall network, stress then becomes an even bigger obstacle. I read a great book called Who Not How and it's all about finding the 'Who' as in the person that can get the job done, not trying to find out 'How' I do it, so systemising and creating Standard Operating Procedures relieves stress - don't become a busy fool! We all have been one at some point.

What are your thoughts on Property Education/Mentoring?

I think education is imperative in anything that requires a specific skillset, property is one of those things that without the correct knowledge, you will experience some very costly mistakes. I will caveat this though, even with the correct knowledge you still can experience some very costly mistakes.

ETHICS ETHICS ETHICS… this is what REAL education & mentorship comes down to in my opinion. There are many mentors & educators out there, and the stigma around unethical selling is a double-edged sword, if someone is providing knowledge that they have acquired through experience over a period of time and someone else is willing to pay them for that knowledge, I don't see what the problem is?

The only thing I think can be a little misleading is the claimed stacks of value that an educator provides on a low-cost seminar that leads into a high ticket upsell that doesn't provide a great deal of follow through.

Paid education as a whole is a great way to fast track your knowledge on a specific topic. People often ask me *'Dee, there's so much free content out there these days why do people pay for education?'.* Yes, there is tons of free content that is amazing, but time is the most important commodity in life, so I believe that finding the right mentor or education platform that is passionate about helping people and giving them REAL value means you're then paying for TIME. I also believe if someone is providing education that can create a road map to success and wealth *(whatever you define that as),* then why shouldn't they get paid? If someone is giving up their time and knowledge, then I believe there needs to be cost attached to value.

On another note, if you have time to research, with YouTube being the best education platform in the world in my opinion, you can find out a lot of the information you need on there, and, also on podcasts and not to forget networking with active investors, but this requires TIME.

Food for thought: 'You pay for your education one way or another'.

What is one thing people misunderstand about property investing?
When an investor first starts out after either attending a property webinar
or after doing some research on property, I think quite quickly they forget
about what makes the property market a business in the first place.

People forget about the 'money', the outstanding value of all residential
mortgages was £1.5 trillion at the end of 2020 Q1
(source: finder.com/uk/mortgage-statistics - 12/08/20).

The key component to the housing market is the availability of credit.

People get so obsessed with fast tracking a portfolio to 'Financial
Freedom' as quick as possible and they lose track on the key metrics that
make the market move. The reason for my view on this, is when people
are taught 'how to buy property', most of the time the implications of
costly mistakes or not doing the correct due diligence are left out. Now
due diligence is something that gets emphasised in the property
education sector. But, as the educator teaching is usually not an
accountant or a finance broker, naturally things will get left out, and often
some of the costliest things.

This goes back to my thoughts on delegation and allowing the
professionals do their job. People also get taught a short-term mindset
from my point of view. When the BRR model gets taught, generally
people focus on getting an investors money to get 'in' and 'out' of a
property deal in a specific time frame and then, the investor gets paid
back and the deal is done, add it to the portfolio. I have spoken to many
investors that do not think past this point, the show is not over here - at
this stage most people have taken out a financial product that they are
tied into for usually 20+ years. The real estate model is a business, it's not
just finding properties, doing them up, refinancing or flipping and so on.
The business model of property when creating a rental portfolio is to
leverage debt to create a business that cash flows, now debt is a good way
to scale if it can be serviced correctly. When building a portfolio, people
need to constantly monitor their overall exposure on their portfolio, does
the next project make sense or fit in to your current holdings, have you
stressed tested a fall in property values, have you accounted for non-

payment of rents, have you factored in 6 months mortgage payments in reserves? If you take on this next deal, have you calculated the downside and prepared proper risk management?

Being an investor in property, the financial markets or even a venture capitalist, the play book of weighing up a whether a deal has greater probability to succeeding than failing is very similar, it's the same metrics and risk management across the board, this is more important when being an 'investor' than anything in my opinion.

What's the best non-property investment you've made?
If we are talking about within my current portfolio it would be buying BTC (Bitcoin) and ETH (Ethereum) very early on.

The real best non property investment I have ever made would be travel. I have met some of the greatest people in my life whilst travelling the world, I have been fortunate to experience some amazing people from different cultures and try food that tastes like its dancing in my mouth!

When I started travelling, it changed my whole perspective on life, seeing a lady in Thailand selling handmade souvenirs 11pm at night with her baby laying in a blanket on the floor while she is trying to make a living, or on the other hand meeting a billionaire on his Yacht in Dubai who has forgotten about the value of money as he has reached that milestone, or experiencing the thriving expat community in Hong Kong and Singapore where it feels like everyone wants to help you grow. Those are just a few things that have really inspired me to progress towards 'Freedom', and by freedom, I mean freedom of movement, freedom of choice - to decide if I want to wake up and work or, spend time with my family. Investing in travel means you are investing in understanding people and how the world turns. I think that alone puts you steps ahead in life and gives you a broader outlook on business also.

What is your morning Routine?
- Wake up between 5am-6am
- Drink a pint of lemon water
- Go for a 30 min walk whilst listening to an audio book/podcast

- During my walk I find grass/sand (take my shoes and socks off and just feel the earth) and just focus on gratitude & vision
- Once home after my walk I have a healthy breakfast with a coffee
- last but not least… shower, then get to work!

Which books do you find yourself going back to after the first read?
- Who not how by Dan Sullivan
- Principles by Ray Dalio
- 48 laws of power by Rob Greene

Tell me about your biggest failure in property so far?

I have not really failed in anything to date *touch wood*, my biggest mistake would be, not understanding how trades work before I worked with them. I looked at them all as 'builders' instead of individual trades, this led to hefty costs which could have been avoided if I didn't overlook the importance of this before taking action. I trusted the wrong person as a project manager or builder as I referred to him as at the time, he was the person doing the plumbing, electrics, carpentry etc. Once I realised, I needed to plan my project better and employ individual trades that specialised in what they do, the project was completed quickly and efficiently and more importantly stress-free (I overspent by £8,000 on this project!).

My overall thoughts on property are as follows; I like property as an asset class, but I would not rely on it solely to provide me with my only income stream, the reason for this is things are changing with Tech in exponential growth and I believe the typical property cycle isn't one that we can only follow anymore. Property is a great asset to hold on to and if it provides an income stream or has potential for capital appreciation that's a bonus. I will continue to invest in property in the UK across different strategies but also looking at global diversification within the asset class as there are emerging and frontier markets that have some great opportunities.

So, if you are worried to take that step and you are a total beginner, I would tell you to be very resilient and prepare for more bad days than good. There's a lot of things in property that you have to figure out yourself whilst doing it to really feel the impacts and reality of it. I would also say no matter how hard you plan things will go wrong, but once you overcome all those obstacles it's a very rewarding feeling and also builds a strong character and who knows where you could take it.

Is there a quote that means a lot to you? Why?
"A journey of a thousand miles starts with a single step". Buddha

You can find Dee listening to Jay Z, eating Wagyu Sliders, reading Ray Dalio Principles in his home office in Dubai whilst his 3 daughters are making a lot of noise in the background acting out a Destiny's Child music video! (Yes, it's manic!)

5 THOUGHTFUL QUOTES

"We are more often frightened than hurt; and we suffer more in imagination than in reality."
- *Seneca*

"There is no try, only do"
- *Master Yoda*

"Silent in our suffering, loud in our laughter"
- *Dave*

"Not everything that is faced can be changed, but nothing can be changed until it is faced"
- *James Baldwin*

"The person who says they can and the person who says they can't, are both right"
- *Confucius*

Dr Lafina Diamandis

Dr Lafina Diamandis is a GP, Lifestyle Medicine Physician and Property Investor with over 10 years' experience of investing in residential property in London. She is an NHS Clinical Entrepreneur and co-founded social enterprise Eurekadoc with the aim of helping doctors to diversify their skills and enhance their careers. She is the author of Amazon #1 Bestseller Property Investing for Doctors and has delivered education and training to thousands of doctors all over the UK.

She is also the founder of DEIA Health and works part-time as an NHS GP alongside her private practice. Lafina is interested in housing as a social determinant of health and explores this fascinating relationship on her podcast: Health Meets Home. She is regularly asked to speak at health & housing events such as Grand Designs Live.

At DEIA Health, Lafina has developed a unique consult style blending influences from cognitive neuroscience, Western medicine, evidence-based lifestyle interventions and health coaching. She works with highly motivated professionals and entrepreneurs who are ready to reset and rebalance their health using a holistic, whole-person approach.

Lafina has offered a generous 15% discount to all readers who purchase a health screening or coaching package at DEIA Health before 31/12/21. Quote 'TEJ TALKS' at booking.

IG – @drldiamandis
TW – @drldiamandis
LI – Dr Lafina Diamandis
W – deiahealth.co.uk

Why are you in property?

In the beginning, property was simply a vehicle for me to be able to invest and create an alternative income stream from, it was great fun and I enjoyed working with people in the property sector, but I didn't think about it much more than that. However, over the years, thanks to my medical background, the relationship between health, housing and the places we live has become of great interest to me and I see the impact that housing has on the health and behaviour of my patients every day. I'm currently in a position where I have enough experience to combine my medical expertise with my experience in property which presents a very exciting opportunity to work with investors and developers on projects with a health or wellbeing flavour.

How important is interior design? Any tips?

Very important! Paying careful attention to interior design benefits everyone whether that be tenants, landlords, investors or developers. It has certainly helped me break records when it comes to £/sqft when selling as well as renting out properties and everyone knows that well priced, attractive properties go fast. If you are doing the interior design yourself and feel overwhelmed by the number of decisions you have to make, my top tips would be to:

1. Research your market - your interior design may vary significantly depending on whether you are selling or renting and who your target market is. For example, properties with a strong or edgy interior design can work well whereas more neutral colour schemes tend to work better when selling a property to end users who often want to personalise it themselves
2. Ask estate agents, letting agents and other investors what sort of interiors work well for your particular strategy and area
3. Put together a mood board on Pinterest for inspiration and to help you put together colour schemes and soft furnishings
4. Small details make a big difference when staging properties, don't forget to use small accessories, plants and soft furnishings like cushions, throws and rugs to bring a room together

5. Finally consider whether your time is better spent elsewhere, employing an interior designer can save time and reduce 'decision fatigue'!

Is property a number or a people game?
Both!

Whether to invest in a property or not should be all about the numbers and whether it fulfils your specific investment criteria. But property is also a people business - investments don't run themselves. You soon learn that strong working relationships are essential and can make or break deals at any stage whether that be when sourcing, financing, refurbishing, renting or selling your property.

When you feel overwhelmed what do you do?
Take a break, meditate, exercise, say 'no' more than 'yes' to opportunities, eliminate all non-essential tasks from the 'to-do' list, focus on self-care, that means eating, sleeping, resting and exercising regularly, share the problem with someone - this always helps, particularly if you feel isolated or aren't sure what next step to take.

Small business owners and entrepreneurs are particularly susceptible to stress, overwhelm and burnout as they are usually juggling several different roles within their business and when you work for yourself you tend to work longer and harder than you ever have before. We all get anxious and overwhelmed from time to time but I can't stress the importance of self-care routines, boundaries and dedicated relaxation time enough. Chronic stress and burnout can really damage your physical and mental health and can be challenging to overcome, so it's essential to pace yourself and enjoy the journey of building a business rather than burnout.

What is your morning routine, why is it so?
I wake up around 6.30/7am, read for half an hour or so in bed then I get up, do a 10-minute morning stretch routine and a 10-minute meditation before having my breakfast. I love to do this as it makes me feel like I've given some time to myself before the day starts; the stretch routine wakes

up my body and I've found the meditation very grounding, it brings me peace and clarity before the day starts to unfold. I then check my diary and focus on the top 3 things I want to achieve that day - I love using a Passion Planner or Clever Fox desk diary for this because of their brilliant layouts.

What's the best non-property investment you've made?

I never think twice when it comes to investing in my health whether that be getting a massage, a health MOT, going on a retreat, or cooking nutritious food. It isn't until our health is taken from us that we realise just how precious it is. Our body and mind work so hard for us every single day and it's easy to take this for granted. All the money in the world can't buy you good health once it's gone so for me, it has to be the best investment you'll ever make.

What has property allowed you to do? What has it given you?

Investing in property has allowed me to develop business and investment skills, broaden my network, create alternative streams of income and develop an entrepreneurial mindset which has been immensely beneficial to my medical career as well as property investments.

Do you think most property investors are completely honest on social media?

Err no. While there certainly are some property investors who are pretty transparent and do post honest insights or experience on social media, the vast majority don't. We have to remember that what we see on social media (whether it is someone's personal account or business account) is the highly curated version of their life or business that they want you to see. We have no idea what is really going on 'behind the scenes' and I take everything I see with a pinch of salt!

What do you do in your free time?

I'm lucky to have a career that really fascinates and fulfils me and I spend quite a bit of my free reading books, listening to podcasts or researching new developments in health. I'm particularly interested in lifestyle medicine, the mind-body connection and the capacity that the body has to heal itself which is not currently well understood. I also love to do anything that involves a connection with nature and throughout the pandemic have really benefited from having more time to take long walks through parks and woodlands observing all the wonderful changes that come with each season. There is so much we can learn from nature and it's a great way to relax too! Trying out new watersports is also something I like doing, particularly in the summertime! Last year I went sailing with some friends in Greece which was brilliant and they convinced me to do the competent crew course on the Solent this summer! Sailing is a sport that can be a bit hair-raising at times but it really stimulates mind, body and soul - I'd recommend it to everyone!

Currently listening to Give Me One Reason by Tracy Chapman, eating one of my fave foods used to be Sushi but since going plant based and watching Seaspiracy, I don't think I'll be eating fish again unless I catch it myself! Reading How To Do The Work by Dr Nicole LaPera in London.

Jack Jiggens

"When Jack was only three years old his mother caught him up on the scaffolding with a cigarette butt in his mouth helping the builders. It was meant to be".

Jack is a third-generation property enthusiast.

Every property Jack lived in as a child was built by his father. With 16 years exposure and 6 years full time experience in property running his own projects and own businesses. Jack combines traditional methods with a modern twist to capitalise developments, flips and rental portfolios.

As Jack started his career on site, he understands the end-to-end working on developments, new builds, conversions and more. His previous roles include project/site management of a £7m office fit out, multiple-million-pound flips, management, new build land and planning enhancement. Jack's forte is acquisitions, he can also be found on site every 6 weeks in recent years.

With a business and marketing degree behind him, Jack brings a solid outlook on finance and strategy, and has been successful with creative structures that provide a win-win scenario for both buyer and seller.

Jack leads the acquisitions team, ensuring the XP project pipeline is full of high-returning opportunities. His expertise has been achieved after many years of relationship building with local agents and by using technology to help identify potential investments.

FB – Jack Jiggens
LI – Jack Jiggens

EXP Property LI/IG/YT – EXP Property Investments

What advice would you give a total beginner in property?
Hard work beats natural ability every day of the week.

Property is not so different from anything else you may want to make a go of. Hard work, learning (textbooks and from others), practice, consistency are good foundations to success. What a lot of beginners get bogged down with is selecting their strategy, then implementing it effectively to not get bored before breaking inertia.

Firstly, it takes time. Setbacks will be plentiful. Everyone starts somewhere and many people have already made mistakes before. Build relationships, both to deliver projects but more importantly for people to learn and seek advice from. Take realistic steps that are in line with your goals and ability. You'll hear all of this 'work hard not smart'. My rule is to stick to both, then you're always on a game.

What is your deal analysis process?
Our deal analysis is forever changing, and I think it always will. The most important fundamentals we ensure across the board are:

- The first scenario to analyse is de-risking the project and seeing what that looks like. What does de-risking mean? What happens to the model if you do not achieve planning, or that extra bedroom or the low-cost investment? It means what could you deliver without any 'luck' or bonuses.
- The second scenario is the project overrunning by 6 months, gross development value going down 10% and build costs going up 10%. Pretty much every scheme we do still turns a profit given all three of these factors happening.

Moving on from the desktop side of things, what does the process look like?

1. High level stack before viewing to ensure you are not wasting time. Basically, to sense check you are not wasting your time.
2. Actually, view the place, measure up, take loads of photos, drive the surrounding areas.

3. Final review before offer and make sure you bring in a second opinion from the team if you need to stress test.

We always structure our stacks in the same way. With three outcomes; 1. Worst case 2. Most likely 3. Largest value enhancement possible, which we aim to achieve. This is mentioned above as de-risking.

For example:
TAB 1: What is the worst case, if planning fails, build overruns, sales overrun etc.
TAB 2: Likely case of planning, variables, which are yet to be confirmed etc.
TAB 3: More optimistic value enhancement, well more so than Tab 2.

All stacking tabs have realistic purchase price, conservative build costs, conservative finance costs and professional fees, 10% contingency and always conservative end values. We also have a section which shows the profit if the scheme were to suffer 6 months overrun, 10% build cost overspend and 10% drop in GDV. If the deal does not make a profit subject to all these factors, we will not pursue.

What's your secret sauce for Finding Deals/Sourcing?
An average developer/ investor will find deals. The best *creates* the deals. You don't find deals; you create the deal.

Over the last three years across my businesses, I've averaged a purchase every six weeks.

When you get in a simple effective routine you realise just sticking to the fundamentals is key:

- Understand where you bring value, you might be the cheapest builder, you might have a good eye for design, you might have contacts in estate agencies. Whatever it is, use it
- Rate the deals you review, size, location, competition of other buyers, before you spend time on them

- Don't just look in one place. We use agents, direct to vendor, our own network and also previous pipeline or offers. We revisit these regularly.
- The right deal will come with the right amount of hard work, KPI, process improvement and so on, be patient

If anyone is reading this and not sure about where to find their next project, feel free to reach out. I have spent far too long before looking in the wrong places and I am finally starting to find it simpler with processes in place.

Should people invest in the North or the South?

This question is actually my pet peeve. You do not need to look up north for a good yield. Yes, it is easier to find a good return as rental pulls heavier on property values. Oxfordshire (where I live) is the second most expensive real estate outside of London and has been for decades. Our HMO portfolio is in Oxfordshire, where we achieve AVERAGES, yes averages across the portfolio of 10-12% Gross Yield, 30% return on capital invested. I agree it's easier to find double digit yields up North, but

I would rather work harder to ensure I don't have to spend hours on the motorways to maintain a portfolio.

Do you think most property investors are completely honest on social media?

In short, No.

I warm to those who are honest.

I listen and follow people that are honest. I struggle to grow in a community where people exaggerate and sometimes lie. In property, it is a small industry where I feel some people feel an urgency to deviate from the truth to sell courses, processes and the worst part, dreams. Property is like any other business, you do not get there from a secret formula, it's hard work, commitment and goals.

Tej Talks

3 Top Tips for raising investor finance?
- Be genuine and open, things do go wrong, it's how you deal with them
- The first is always the hardest so prove the concept
- Investment isn't about the first option, goals and values need to be aligned. Be patient.

With all of the above you should have no problems. I would like to stress being patient though, it will come, and no one wants to invest in anything short term or desperate.

Who do you look up to?
My Father. Why?

I listen to podcasts, YouTube videos and entrepreneurs daily who tell you to read a book a day, meditate and exercise to become successful. This guy (my Dad) has not read a book in his life, spends as much time in the pub as possible but has always worked his ass off. He is a self-made millionaire who succeeded the 'old school' way, which is often overlooked with modern day entrepreneurs using buzzword bullshit.

I could highlight a list of other inspirational people, the above does not include the powerful partnership my father has had both in business and marital. Both of which are just as inspirational.

Being ambitious and consistent you tend to naturally gravitate to amazing people, I don't have the space today to go into too much detail and reel off all my inspirations, I wish I could. That said I am forever grateful for the people I have met over the years and can call my friends.

What has been your biggest success in property?
Firstly, finding my business partner Ben Richards, Founder of Aura Architecture. Investment, projects and business is interchangeable. But the right business partner is invaluable. I am forever grateful to find someone who brings the best out in me, challenges me, outperforms me in other areas and most importantly someone I can call a good friend.

Property is an industry which promotes partnerships and joint ventures. Often the process of finding the right partner or joint venture partner gets overlooked. Start with morals and work ethic, you shouldn't go too far wrong.

Secondly, finding my flow. Being an entrepreneur can be a slow start or sometimes difficult to see the light at the end of the tunnel. For a long time, I was wondering if I was just being a busy fool. Plenty of long nights, early starts and stressful days. It took a long time to finally click. I finally understood what I was good at and when you start to build momentum it all starts to pay off. Roger Hamilton writes about finding your flow in his book *'Your life, your legacy'*, 100% worth a read.

Who is really important to you in life?

It has to be my wife, family, our team and the right partners. Business and being an entrepreneur is tough, sometimes lonely and often requires a change of pace. I am fortunate everyone around me supports and understands what I am doing. That helps a lot. I can't remember the last time I worked an average week. It's the loved ones around you who humble you and can take you away from the hustle.

Favourite quotes?

"I thought I had everything in my and our family life under control, I realise now that I have no control, nothing in life is under control. Life is for living, I have a choice, live my life dwelling in the past dramas or dogma, or deal with it and move forward, it is an amazing place, moving forward… I wish I hadn't left it so long." *(Simon Gale - Very close family friend, 2016)*

"The only person truly watching you is yourself. 5 years from now." Cringy as it sounds, this quote is self-made. It's to always challenge myself and keep myself on track no matter the potential external changes or circumstances.

Tej Talks

You can find Jack with his wife Kelly and dog Moose. Listening to Kygo, either drinking coffee or beer, depending on what side of the day you fall. Reading Wealth Dynamics, either in Henley or out in San Diego, soaking up the sun surrounded by loud Americans talking.

Ben Richards

Ben is a business owner, property investor, property developer and an architectural engineer – depending on what time of the day it is! He started AURA Architecture in 2017 and they've grown 100% year on year in revenue over the past three years by creating fantastic homes for homeowners and adding maximum value to SME property developers which he's very proud of. This year's target is £500,000 revenue and 25% net margin.

Since meeting his business partner Jack Jiggens *(also in this book)* in 2018 they've also grown a property development business now employing seven staff members (at the time this is written) and have built a development pipeline with a £7,000,000 Gross Development Value (GDV) and a projected profit of £800,000 deliverable in 2021.

Follow them on Social Media to see how this plays out!

FB – Ben Richards
LI – Ben Richards
IG – @benrichards_property

EXP Property IG/YT – @expproperty
Aura Architecture – @aurahomes

Why are you in Property?

I used to love puzzles as a kid. But not just normal puzzles - Puzz 3D *(You know if you're an 80's kid!)*. Lego, Meccano, building blocks, you name it I wanted to build it.

The property industry affords me that sense of creation daily. Every property is different, each day is varied, and there are challenges at every stage. That's why I love it!

I guess like a lot of people reading this you're probably wanting 'passive income' which most of the property education platforms tout as being the dream. In reality though it's never passive, but it can be close if you put in the work upfront and systemise as much as possible. It's not the main reason I'm in property, but ultimately it is one of the perks.

What advice would you give a total beginner in property?

Both in property and in business - It's hard! You will probably struggle in year 1, but perseverance will pay dividends after years 2 & 3. You need to build solid foundations first so don't get disheartened and do stick it out. Absorb as much information as possible via books, podcasts, networking, YouTube but like with everything there is no comparison to actually getting out there and doing it. Just make sure to start small.

There really is a lot to be said for learning to walk before you can run. It's easy to get distracted by bigger and better things, but with bigger things, comes bigger risk and you need to be prepared for that.

If you haven't got the basics right, then mistakes and failures can be exaggerated in larger schemes and cost you a lot of money.

Is property a 'numbers' or a 'people' game?

Okay, so I deviated from property after graduating from Uni. I gained a master's degree in architectural engineering so was well placed to work in property, but I found a passion for poker in 2010, and I was good at it!

"So, you gambled for a living" I hear you say, and I get it. If you don't understand the game, then from an outsider's perspective that's what it looks like. But it's much more than that.

It's a game of strategy, mathematics, risk analysis, understanding people and ultimately a game that needs a bit of nerve to pull the trigger and go all-in.

Now read the last paragraph again. Sounds like property investment/development, right?

My year-out playing poker for a living gave me many things:

- The realisation that I'm a people person and good at understanding what people need
- A greater understanding of risk, and what my thresholds are
- The ability to look at the numbers, think logically, and not get swept up in the emotion
- A nice chunk of deposit money to buy my first Buy-To-Let property!

If you're a numbers person then find a partner who understands people, and vice versa. Both skills are imperative in property.

Tell me about your biggest failure in property so far?
Not necessarily a failure, but a key learning especially in development. Cashflow is key - Development is typically lumpy cash. Make sure you have funds in reserve or build an asset base that cashflows well before stepping up to developments where profit payout is delayed and can take 18-24 month to crystalize.

The only other failure *(and this is for everyone!)* is that I didn't start soon enough. I bought my first BTL when I was 26 but even that is too late. I wish the traditional education system catered for young entrepreneurs more and gave people a solid foundation on financial education before heading out into the big wide world. Property is a fundamental for wealth building, so the sooner you can start compounding returns and building assets the better.

How do you cope with the stress of Property?
Talk. Share ideas. Share problems. Having an understanding partner in your personal life, and a business partner that is calm and methodical when problems occur is important. Property is stressful, so expect it. In all honesty, it's not for everyone - you need to have the right mentality to see obstacles as a positive challenge and not a barrier.

I started AURA on my own so I'm talking from experience. Having Jack as my business partner in XP Property opened my eyes to sharing the journey with someone with the same goals. Having someone to bounce ideas off, share the wins, and share the lows will help you through it.

Don't do it alone.

3 Top Tips on raising investor finance?
- Start networking more. It can feel like a slog, but people won't invest in you unless you've built a relationship with them, the classic 'Know, Like, and Trust' is very true
- Share your journey on social media *(warts and all)* because in today's world it's much easier for people to build relationships and connect with you vicariously through these platforms. We've had many investment partners say *"I've been watching you on social media and have £X to invest. Do you have any projects coming up that we can discuss?"*
- Never say 'Other People's Money'. It makes me cringe seeing this type of marketing talk. At XP, every investor we work with is a partner, that's how it should be.

How important is interior design? Any tips?
Incredibly important. With marketing and media today, there is so much noise. To sell/rent fast you will need to cut through the noise with a product that stands out from the rest.

My top tips for interior design:
- Keep the main shell basic and bring colour to the rooms with furnishings and fittings when styling. This way, the style of the room can be changed cheaply and quickly, and the potential buyer can put their own stamp on it if they wish
- Interior Design isn't just colour and fluffy cushions *(albeit my Technical Director at the Berkeley Group called Interior Designers 'Cushion chucker's')*. Yes, colour and texture is important but it's also about how the space flows. Does everything have a place?
- Try and appeal to all the senses. Too often people think interior design is about how something looks. What about how the textures feel? Smells of a staged property can help sell/let any good marketing suite. Have you thought about how a large open room will echo and could feel cold? These may feel like marginal gains, but a cumulative effect of all of these considerations will make a huge difference to the consumer
- TOP TIP: for heaven's sake put the shower valves on a wall away from the shower head – I don't want to get a wet arm when turning on my shower!

Is there a quote that means a lot to you? Why?
"Whether you think you can, or think you can't, you're right" – Henry Ford

Self-belief has always been instilled in me by my family and I think it's incredibly important in any venture you undertake. Be confident.

You will always run out of cash in property, so getting external investment should be a top priority. If you don't fully commit and believe in yourself/your project, why would an investment partner?

What differentiates you from your peers?
I worked as a Technical Manager for the Berkeley Group which gave me insight in to one of the most profitable property development businesses there is. Hopefully some good stuff has rubbed off!

Tej Talks

In addition to my technical abilities, I believe there are two other key things which set me apart.

Vision:
I see things others don't. For a long time, I just took for granted that everyone saw things the way I did. They could see the solutions quickly and process how best to get there. It turns out they can't, and this skill has added a tremendous amount of value to my own developments, and also helped my architecture clients to increase the value of their sites significantly too. For example, my first property development was a new-build two-bedroom end terrace house in a large garden plot. I bought the existing end terrace house with planning permission already granted for a two-storey side extension creating a larger 3-bed property. This was great as it established the massing, but a new-build 2-bed house and a sub-divided plot to create two houses was far more valuable. And that's what I achieved. That one idea, and tenacity to execute the plan added circa. £150,000 of additional value to the property.

EQ – Emotional intelligence:
I don't see this talked about often but it's so fundamental to property development. I touch on it above from my poker days but essentially this is the ability to understand, use, and manage your own emotions in positive ways to relieve stress, communicate effectively, empathize with others, overcome challenges and defuse conflict. I'm often asked how I cope with spinning many plates and stay so calm when shit hits the fan. I think it's because of my EQ.

Have Podcasts been important on your journey?
I've never been good at finding quiet time for reading books, so podcasts have been extremely important in my property journey. It's the main place I go for business/property knowledge, and a great place to find tips and tricks for new strategies from people out there doing it.

The beauty of podcasts (and other audible platforms) is that you can multi-task whilst listening. It's something you can tune in to on your commute, at the gym, whilst doing the washing up etc. so I feel like I'm learning at times when historically the time may be wasted.

The added benefit is that you can control the listening speed to 1.2x, 1.5x or even 2x so can cram more content in a shorter timeframe!

Ben is probably eating Chewy sweets instead of chocolate *(controversial?)*, listening to Saxaphone House Mix on Spotify listening to anything business/property-related in St Albans with his better half – Laura, and little boy Lucas.

John Howard

John Howard is one of the most accomplished property developers, traders and investors in the UK today, with four decades of experience in the industry. John's proficiency stems from the purchase and sale of over 3,500 houses, apartments and developments within the UK.

With a rental portfolio similar to many investors through his numerous property companies, John's experience is vast; including traditional houses, hotels and large scheme developments. Having worked in residential and commercial property for many years, John has formed many valuable partnerships with leading industry contacts, adding breadth and depth to his expertise and knowledge.

The latest acquisition in John's portfolio is a £26 million development funded by Homes England.

John and his business partners purchased Auction House UK in 2009. The company was developed significantly before the partners sold their shared in 2018. John is also director and shareholder of various property management companies, financial service providers and numerous estate agencies, including Fine and Country Norfolk and Exquisite Home. All of which provide an all-encompassing understanding of the property world.

LI – John Howard
IG – @johnhowardpropertyexpert
WS – johnhowardpropertyexpert.co.uk

Why are you in Property?

Well, I've been a property developer and investor for over 40 years, and I was very fortunate in that my father had been a greengrocer in Felixstowe a small town in Suffolk and when he was in his early 60s, he decided he wanted to become an estate agent.

So, he purchased an existing small business and ran it for a number of years with modest success. I used to help him by holding the measuring tape and do the odd viewing on my bicycle while I was still at school.

When I left school at 17, I joined him, he had been seriously ill in hospital and there was virtually no business left to run. This is a great way of learning fast as you learn far more when things are tough than you do when it's easy.

To cut a long story short I purchased my first property on my 18th birthday with the help of my mother and the bank manager. I purchased the business when I was 19 and changed the name and had moderate success until I sold it when I was 24 years old when I met Robert Boyce who became my Backer for a number of of years.

The great thing about property is leverage. Which means if you have £30,000 to invest you can actually invest £100,000 with the help of the bank.

These days especially if you've got a great deal but no funds someone like me will put the funds up for you and share the profit 50-50, that was very hard to do 40 years ago!

What advice would I give a total beginner?

The first thing I would say is go and read and absorb as much property education as you can which doesn't cost you a penny. Please don't jump in and spend fortunes on all these property courses and weekend retreats and the like, there's so much information you can glean free initially. Then, when you've got some idea of the business, I would look to spend a small amount of money on further education making sure that the person you are investing your money and has a long successful track record and not just started selling education courses because they've done one successful deal!

Before you start investing any money in your first deal you must know and understand what sort of investor or property developer you wish to be. For instance, I have a friend of mine who buys lock-up garages, he has over 2000 and makes a fantastic business out of it. There are lots and lots of ways of making money out of property you have to decide which you want to do.

And please, please do not give up your job just because you think you have a property deal to do! The great thing about Property is that you can use it as a second income, in other words your main income can pay all your costs, your second property income can then be reinvested back into property after the tax has been paid.

Please remember it is a business whether you are full-time at it or part-time at it, it must be treated in a professional way and respected, it's very easy to lose money if you're not completely committed to the business.

How do you decide on a JV partner?
This is a very pertinent question for me at the moment because I've just launched the John Howard joint-venture fund where I will invest in other people's deals and share the profit 50-50

The first thing to remember with any joint-venture partner is it is a business arrangement, you don't need to be going out for dinner with them every night and going on holiday, but you do need to respect them.

There is also absolutely no point you both doing the same job, in other words if you are the one that goes and finds the deals then you need a partner who will come up with the money and deal with the financial side of things. During my 40-year career I've always been the one to find of the deals so it's quite ironic that I'm now being sent many deals to do as joint-ventures where I'm the one putting up the money!

Remember always check the person out financially who you're thinking of joint venturing with. It's similar to a marriage and just as hard to get out of if it goes wrong!

How do you cope with stress?
That's a great question, remember I started in business when I was 17 years old so I learnt to cope with the stress very early.

Interestingly in my seminars I have pulled people to one side at the end and said "I don't really think this business is for you" If you worry a lot and find it difficult to sleep at night then property is really not the thing to be in.

I have a method of coping with stress and that is by doing other things apart from property whenever I can. I jokingly say that my dog Ivy is on the payroll to destress me as is my tennis coach who I hit with once a week and my cycling pals who I cycle with regularly. Exercise for me is by far the best way of getting rid of stress. I also come up with some good ideas normally when I'm riding my bike or on occasions a horse, I forgot to mention that!

Should people invest in the North or the South?
One of the reasons I started getting involved in giving advice and writing books was the type of education that people are unfortunately receiving from certain so-called experts.

The answer to that question is actually very easy. There is absolutely nothing wrong with investing in the north or the south so please don't listen to all these so-called property experts who will tell you, you can only do one or the other you can quite comfortably do both.

There are a few things to remember such as there is a massive housing shortage in the south of the country but no housing shortage in the north.

On the whole property prices in the north are cheaper in certain areas but of course there is a reason for that you need to find out what that reason is. Make sure it's a reason you can deal with for instance, it could well be that there has been very little capital growth over the years in certain parts of the north of the country compared to the south.

Remember property is a micro market, it differs hugely from area to area - even in the property recession certain towns and cities won't go down whilst others will go down a lot depending on employment and other issues.

So potentially if you're looking for a high rental return it may well be just be better to look North. If you're looking for capital growth it might be best to look south. Of course, if you can get a property that does both that's even better!

One quick tip though, always check whether the area you are investing in has got perhaps just one large employer, because if the employer goes into liquidation you may be vulnerable to a downturn in rent and property value.

The other thing is to check whether the population in the area is declining or increasing you'll be amazed in certain areas it is decreasing even though the population in the UK is going up all the time.

You can find John listening to Motown and anything soulful, eating Chinese food*, reading Donald Trump "Part of the Deal" and working in his country house office in Suffolk, where he has been for 35 years.

*I'm very fortunate that I've just let one of my new commercial units to a very successful Chinese chef so hope to get a free meal soon!

Jemal Mazlum

Jemal is a full-time property investor, he left school with just 5 grade A-Cs (5 Cs to be precise) the rest were Ds and Es. He dropped out of college at 17 and went to work at a chemical processing factory supplying chemicals to brewers. He took this job just so he could save and get a mortgage as all Jemal wanted to do was get into property. He says he thinks he spent more time hiding in toilets and taking extended breaks reading as many property books as he could get hold of then he did actual work though!

Jemal's goals are to retire at 40 if he chooses with a large portfolio to sustain a nice lifestyle which includes a few holiday homes for the whole family and friends to enjoy whenever they like. Also, to make sure his parents are always okay financially

He is from a very humble background. He was raised on a council estate in Nottingham but never went without. Always had food and clothes on his back.

Jemal has one older sister who is totally opposite to him in every way.

He comes from a large extended family, Jemal has over 15 uncles and aunties and over 50 first cousins but none have followed him in property.

FB – Jemal Mazlum
IG – ALS_properties
LI – Jemal Mazlum

What is your deal analysis?

I start with a few things when analysing a deal. Firstly, checking the basic things such as the recently sold prices in the area. What's for sale around that area and are they selling quick? Is the location good? Will it work as an HMO or single let? Are the Fundamentals strong? (Good schools, local amenities etc.)

Then comes the most important question I ask myself "how much money will I leave in this deal" so ROI is a big one for me. This allows me to recycle my cash and go again. So, I will look at how I can add value? I try to do this is several ways…. first am I buying at the right price? *"You make money when you buy not when you sell"* so buying at the right price is important to me. Secondly, can I add value through an uplift? Add a bedroom? Open up the kitchen etc. If all these are ticking boxes, then I will then start running numbers through a spreadsheet I have which is just like a calculator and spits out everything from ROI, to renovation cost, stamp duty, solicitors cost and more.

I don't buy just for yields I try and factor potential growth as well so again these things are important. One thing to add is, if am looking for an HMO then a specific item I look for straightaway is a floorplan. I can rule out an HMO in seconds just by looking at a floorplan.

Here is a real-life example of my latest project

Market listed price £140,000
I secured it for £110,000 direct to vendor
(Already I've made my money on the purchase not the sale)
I've then turned it into a 5 bed HMO which will revalue at £200,000 through my renovation. So, I've achieved an uplift in two ways here. This will pull all my money out on the refinance allowing me to go again.

How do you find an area to invest in?

I think local knowledge comes into play here - I invest locally so know most areas quite well which makes it easier, I know where to avoid and where to buy. If I was to invest outside of my area then I would get out there and do some leg work; go speak to local agents, both letting and estate agents, attend property meetings in that area and get networking, and piggyback off someone else's local knowledge. Have a drive around in the day and night, an area can look very different at night and I find driving around a few times will quicky highlight if it not as nice as first seemed

Should people invest in the North or the South?
I really think it depends on you. You tend to get higher yield up north, but growth normally lags, where down south it's the opposite. So, the question comes down to you - do you need that monthly income? Are you looking for property to be a way of supporting you financially straight away? Then I would probably look for higher yielding properties up north. You don't have to go too far though; I'm based in Nottingham and we have some areas which still have great yielding properties. If you jump in your car and drive for 1-2 hours, I think within that area you may be able to find something which works for you. Now if your buying for a pension pot for example, then you may want to factor in growth, so the further south you go, normally the better growth long term.

What are the Pros/Cons of your strategy?
Pros:
- We are going really high-end with our properties, so we seem to attract a good tenant type and they tend to stay longer than usual
- HMO's Can Provide unparalleled financial benefits. They give us great monthly   returns. For an HMO, rental yields can be as much as **three times higher** than a single let
- HMOS help spread the risk, ensuring that the income generated is spread across multiple occupants. So, even if one tenant falls behind, you still have multiple other occupants providing revenue
- Tim, we don't spend more than a few hours a week managing our portfolio. I believe this is due to the high standard of our portfolio. We rarely have maintenance issues

CONS:
- Upfront cost. An HMO has higher start-up costs than a typical buy-to-let property in order to meet health and safety regulations and you have to furnish the property

- Keeping up with the trend. Your properties don't stay high-end for long, so you have to constantly keep reinvesting making sure is stays relevant
- You as the landlord in most cases have to pay and manage all the bills
- HMOs demand more legislation and planning requirements compared to a more straightforward buy-to-let property
- It can be harder to obtain finance/mortgages as a first-time HMO investor and a larger deposit is often required
- Article 4, this has been implemented in most cities due do oversaturation, which now makes finding suitable properties a lot harder

How important is interior design? Any tips?
I class it as very important.

Interior Design should always be centered around what the target market expects from premium living quarters. Your choice of furniture should reflect what a room is going to be used for. I feel it's important to work backwards, so visualise the room finished and then go backwards.

A little tip is that there are people out there for a small fee who will do you layouts from socket positions, lighting and layout. This gives you something to work off and if like me your memory is that of a goldfish you can keep referring back to it. It's also super handy for your tradesman as from the very start they have clearly illustrated instructions on where everything is going, so there should be no confusion.

Communal areas, such as the living room and kitchen, are places where you can instill more character. Just be careful to not go overboard. I still like my properties to feel like a home and not a bar or restaurant.

Add art statements. Having large-scale artwork can provide a focal point to each room. Alternatively, mix up smaller pieces of artwork in frames to create a collage effect.

Lighting is a powerful tool that can dictate the atmosphere and tone of a room. It can be just as much an accessory as soft furnishings and ornaments. If you look at any of my projects you can see how I incorporate lighting.

Lastly there are great websites and apps to go and get inspiration from such as Pinterest, Instagram, google images and more.

Bridging Finance – expensive or useful?
Bridging can be very useful if used correctly which is for "short term funding" it does what it says on the tin…. a fast, temporary and interest-only funding solution.

The key to a bridge I feel is having very high levels of flexibility to pay the loan back at any time, as well as features like rolling interest into the loan so that cash outflows can be managed. It is also a lot more flexible in terms of the types of property that can be borrowed against.
For instance, a property with no kitchen or bathroom would be deemed 'unmortgageable' by a mainstream mortgage lender, whereas a bridging lender would consider taking on the higher risk if the borrower has a credible exit strategy, such as refurbishing the property to a mortgageable standard, before refinancing. Also, it can give you advantages over certain properties if someone is using a mortgage as effectively you are a 'cash' buyer, and this can reflect in your offer
I've used a bridge successfully several times, mostly in situations when speed has been the dominant factor with the seller. I've used a bridge to purchase at a discounted value, done a light renovation and then mortgaged it onto a buy to let mortgage at the new higher value, paying off the bridge loan and putting money in my pocket and bear in mind crucially, there are typically no Early Repayment Charges on a bridge, compared to a mortgage.
My final point is this, Bridging can be SUPER expensive though if not done correctly. Anything over 12 months (or your agreed term) can become expensive and run into fees and you must factor this in, but this is where a good power team comes into play as a strong commercial broker should advise you on the best course of action

Tej Talks

What is one thing people misunderstand about property investing?
Property prices always go up…This is incorrect. Long term trends do show an upwards trend but along the way you will have many ups and downs, so don't buy always assuming your property will go up in value. I know some investors who purchased property in 2007 and the price they paid then is still more then todays value.

There are plenty of factors that could make your property drop in value, locally and internationally but the point is that your property is not immune from decreases in value that have little to do with your or your approach to homeownership. These considerations do not include things like mold, curb appeal and structure maintenance, which are within your control and could boost or decrease your property value.

Jemal is currently listening to anything RnB or Motown *(In the past year he's slowly started to like house, mostly the recent stuff as it reminds him a little of the old school garage which he loved),* you'll find him eating Turkish Cypriot food or a medium/rare steak, whilst enjoying a glass of red and the odd whisky. He'll likely be reading Arnold Schwarzenegger's or Richard Branson's book in his home office.

TEJ'S TOP 10 PROPERTY MISTAKES

1. Not firing my first cowboy builder quick enough

2. Taking on too many refurbishments without the knowledge or help

3. Overspending on refurbishments in the wrong areas, which actually made it harder to sell, or took longer to rent

4. Not thinking from a buyers/tenant's perspective, they are your customers, so you should be aiming to meet their needs

5. Taking too long to make key decisions on properties, this cost me money, time and really wasn't good for my mental health

6. Underestimating how hard a simple refinance on a BTL can be

7. Not buying more property whilst the market was good for Investors!

8. Not going to enough physical networking events, social media is amazing, and the reach is huge, but these events are fun, and you always learn something, and meet great people in Property

9. Thinking I could learn it all for free and being a tight arse *(which cost me more anyway in losses, time and relationships)*

10. Refusing to find a mentor, which would have saved and made me £10,000s early on

Tej Talks

Paul Nicholson

Paul is an award-winning landlord and property developer. He is a prominent leading North West property personality, with one of the largest private property portfolios across the Liverpool City Region. Paul's property portfolio which was established in 2008 is valued in excess of £32,500,000 in 2021 and is set to reach £52,000,000.

He is a highly experienced and trained property professional with 10 years' experience. Paul has received various accolades throughout his career canvasing much media attention for his visionary schemes and approach to business along with a raft of awards from local to national recognition.

Paul started his portfolio acquiring terraced houses and building a performing buy-to-let portfolio. As his knowledge and understanding grew so did the size of his projects. Paul is now leading the regeneration of a northern town called St Helens. He has successfully completed 5 projects to date taking advantage of permitted development rights. His group of companies has secured further sites which will see further projected developments of 200 apartments taking his portfolio size in excess of 500 rental units.

IG – @teamnico_uk
TW – @teamnico_uk

What advice would you give to a total beginner in property?

I would take your time and consider if it is for you. Have you got the time to dedicate to it and can you cope with the stresses (both emotional and financial) that come with property investment? If the answer is yes, then don't plunge in at the deep end. Take your time and learn all aspect of the particular property sector you wish to be involved in.

Speak to people who have achieved what you want to achieve, read books and there is a wealth of knowledge online. It is eye opening how what can be viewed as a simple idea – buy a house, rent it, collect money – can have so many different and complex moving parts to it. Start small, mitigate your risks and get a thorough understanding before scaling as costs can soon spiral.

Generally, do you buy to hold or sell, and why?

My strategy is to buy to hold. I like the concept of having passive income *(if you can call it passive)* each month, whilst paying down the debt and increasing my equity. I believe this concept allows for monthly income and a second windfall which is on potential sale, although I have no plans to do so and I am to create a legacy. With holding the asset, providing you have a good relationship with lenders you almost have a guaranteed exit where on sale you could be waiting some time to fund a buyer slowing any expansion plans.

If like my strategy you buy value-add opportunities, there is an opportunity to release equity from the initial refinance adding to your cash base and holding on to monthly income. It can be difficult to find such opportunities that allow enough room to achieve that strategy, though.

How important is interior design? Any tips?

This is one of the most important elements in any property project – would you buy a hideous looking pair of trainers that hurt when you walk? No, so - the property design needs to be both functional and attractive. This can be extremely difficult when converting older properties such as Permitted Development Right projects where often you are stuck with a supporting beam in a living area. You need to be inventive and here we integrate innovative lighting design to create to separate lit areas in the room making it 1. More appealing on the eye and 2. Functional as the end user could say have a dining element and lounge area split by the beam. I am forever taking pictures of hotels I visit or interesting buildings and have a folder I take inspiration on when undertaking a project with interesting features.

Is property a numbers or a people game?

Put simply, both. If the numbers don't stack why even bother? and if you can't get the right people, you won't achieve your vision. I often finding the numbers the easy part, if it doesn't stack it doesn't proceed. The ones that do - I have a vision of what I want to achieve and its imperative that you share this vision with your team and convey it clearly, which can often be extremely difficult with competing interests.

The developer wants the best-looking product for the cheapest price and the contractor wants the least work at the highest price. Be prepared for some battles which makes it even more important to convey what you want and expect at the outset, with clear targets on the deadline and finish to try and negate such issues.

What is your morning routine? Why is it so?

I generally wake early (5:30am - 6:15am) and as any landlord will no doubt do log straight on to my online banking to see if the rents have cleared the account. If not, a list is sent to my property manager to prepare him for what rents he may have to chase (once reviewed again at 9am as they are all payable via standing order). I then check over my emails and respond to the "easy" ones to reduce my workload. I review my to do list for the day, so I am conscious of what I need to do and achieve that day. I then exercise for 90 minutes, which is a mixture of weights and cardio. This gives me some "me time" and I often find when I run on the treadmill, I run through my long-term vision.

I have to do something to get me through the dreaded cardio! I then get ready for work and off I go safe in the knowledge that no contractor I face that day or tenant complaint will be harder than that run!

Tej Talks

Why are you in property?

I was a solicitor specialising in property and finance, which gave me a great insight and head start for the business I ended up pursuing. It opened up my eyes to the financial success my clients were experiencing and the possibility of creating a legacy and generational wealth for my family. I always wanted to be in control of my own destiny and be my own boss, I hated being told what to do and having to report to someone else, so being employed certainly wasn't for me.

I had set up other ventures and the idea of creating my own brand and company with a team around me really appealed to me, little did I know quite how hard it would be!

What are your thoughts on property education/mentorship?

I think 99.9% of the courses are a waste of time and aren't conducted by people who have created any real wealth/success on their property journey. If you are minded to attend a course, ask them what is their financial position and current portfolio. A mentor I believe is essential and I have had a few during my career, especially in the early days. I have forever spent hours on the phone to my father about the issues I have in my business, him being a sounding board for me has often given me clarity, I had the answer just needed to get it out of my head! My poor fiancée gets this relentlessly!

I had a client when I was in the legal profession (who was also a former solicitor) who helped me understand the strategies that could be deployed when refinancing. A mentor is a very wise move especially for a novice, spending thousands on a course when the material is on Podcasts and YouTube, I think you would be better placed using that money to actually buy a property!

What is one thing people misunderstand about property investing?

It's easy.

I'll be a millionaire in a year.

I can quit my job. Buy a house, rent it, collect money and sit on a beach. If that's your understanding, then don't quit your day job. So much money pours out the door each month and it gets worse the more you scale. Although large portfolio holdings are impressive it doesn't reflect financial wealth. The other misunderstanding, I see is "I'll just get to 10 properties that'll give me a nice lifestyle", if you are anything like me there's always another deal you want…. here I am still going since my first purchase in 2008 and I've never sold a single property.

Valter Pontes

Valter Pontes is a multi-award-winning property investor and entrepreneur. His vision is to create luxury boutique co-living spaces where people are proud to live in. He was in university when he decided to go on a gap year and make his vision a reality.

Valter went onto winning Simon Zutshi's Property Mastermind and was nominated as The New Property Investor of the Year by the Property Investors Awards. Since then, he has won several awards, and Forbes magazine wrote an article on how he changed his life and on his mission in the property industry.

His company Your Best Place is focused on making luxury the new norm for rentals and it won the Real Estate Company of the Year award in the North by the Corporate LiveWire Prestige Awards for setting an example of a company that's number one focus is the client, the tenant, and creating luxury co-living spaces that take the inspiration from luxury boutique hotels around the world.

This year Valter was nominated as the Entrepreneur of the Year by the Growing Business Awards and he got recognised in America for what he is doing in Europe and won the CEO of the Year Rising Star Award in the prestigious CEO World Awards and one of his HMO's won the HMO of the Year by the Property Investors Awards which is one of the most competitive categories in the industry.

Alongside his mission on creating luxury accommodation, Valter is a consultant, and it has become a mission of his to share his knowledge so that people who are looking to start on their property investment journey can replicate what he has done.

FB/LI/YT – Valter Pontes
IG – @valter_pontes_
W – valterpontes.com

Why are you in Property?

I think everyone knows that property can be a powerful investment vehicle for long term wealth creation. I always wanted to invest in property, but I thought you would need a lot of money to start with. Therefore, I thought I would be an actor first and then later in life start investing in property. I remember after reading the autobiography of Arnold Schwarzenegger, he mentioned that he started as a property investor before starting his career as an actor. So, I decided to do the same. Also, I like the idea of an investment that outlives me, and I can leave a legacy to the future generation.

What advice would you give a total beginner in property?

I would say to everyone who wants to start out to invest in themselves first. If you would like to be a doctor you go to university and study for almost 10 years to be a doctor. There are a lot of things you need to learn in property. It does not take 10 years, but it does take knowledge and time. You can make a lot of money, but you can lose a lot of money as well. So, definitely, investing in yourself would be my advice. Warren Buffett *(who is considered one of the greatest investors who ever lived said: "The best investment you can do is in yourself.")*

Tell me about your biggest failure in property so far?

Most people see me now as a very successful investor. I cannot say that I have done badly but I did make a lot of mistakes and failed quite a lot. I think my biggest failure has been in construction. I trusted people too much and I went into bigger developments too fast. You should learn how to crawl before you can walk. So, you should start with a small development, and master your craft and then move on to the bigger ones. Patience is the name of the game.

Generally, do you buy to hold or sell, and why?

I only buy to hold. I know a lot of people who are very successful in buying and selling properties. But my belief has always been, why do all of this work and then sell the property? Also, you will have to pay capital gains tax when you sell the property *(Tej - If it's in your personal name)*, and you will only make money once. If I keep the property, I can remortgage the property as many times as I want if the property goes up in value. (Which tends to be the case over time in some parts of the country). I might not get 100% of the value of the property but some banks could lend me up to 85% of the property free of tax because it is a loan and you do not pay tax on the loan. So, I love keeping property for as long as I can. The only time I would sell a property is if it was losing me money or giving me a lot of heachache. If I decided to sell it, I know I would take that money and reinvest in another property. So, for me it's about buying and keeping the properties forever. Imagine if we had a member of our family who had purchased a property in Oxford Street or in South Kensington in London and left it for us. I am sure we would be very happy now!

Should people invest in the North or the South?
I think you should do both. In the beginning you should focus on cash flow. I think most people have heard that cash is king. So, focusing on cashflow first is essential. However, over time, after you have a solid cashflowing portfolio: meaning properties that produce you profit after you pay all the bills, you should think of investing some of that money in the South where properties tend to double every 10 years. So, you can get the capital appreciation which can make you very wealthy over the years.

How important is interior design? Any tips?
I think it's very important. Particularly, now that the market has changed. Now customers have a lot of choices, so having good skills in interior design can help you to have your rooms filled. I need to confess, I am not very good at it myself, so I have an inhouse interior designer to help me with the design of our houses. Remember, you don't need to be good at everything.

What's your secret sauce for Finding Deals/Sourcing?
I started as a sourcer because I did not have any money when I started out. In fact, I had to use my student loan to start educating myself. *(I do not recommend using your student loan to do that but that's what I did)*. Starting as a sourcer gave me the edge. Because now, I am using these skills to find great deals for myself. So, having the skills to find properties is a good skill set to acquire. It's like buying and selling businesses. You need to know what a good business is to buy and what is not. I know

more than 15 ways of finding deals, so I can find the great ones in the bunch.

There are many methods to find deals. I tend to divide marketing in two separate parts, Offline and Online. Here I will share two uncommon ways:

A good method to find offline deals that does not cost you any money is Gumtree. There are many properties advertised on Gumtree every day. Normally, the vendor who advertises in Gumtree does not want to be working with an Estate agent or he or she wants to try to sell the property before thinking of going to the Estate agent. So, you can contact them directly and see if you can help them and get a deal directly from the vendor.

An online method which is very hot at the moment is Facebook ads. Facebook ads are very cheap at the moment and you can get a lot of leads from them. In the property industry very, few people are utilizing Facebook ads. That is a great way to find off market deals direct to vendors. Of course, you should do the free methods first before thinking of paying.

How do you find an area to invest in?
When the biggest brands that we know about decide to expand to a different area. They tend to do huge due diligence to check if there is demand for their products or services in that particular area. As an investor I think it is important for us to have the same approach. So, when I look for an area to invest in. I like to think of it the same way as the biggest well-known brands would think. There are quite a few key factors I like to look at before deciding where to invest. Here are some criteria I take in consideration when I invest and the reason why I take these into consideration. Also, I will give you the websites where you can go and check this data for yourself. All of this data is available for free. The government tends to spend a huge amount of money to collect these types of data. Here are some of my criteria:

1. I would like to know the population of the area. The reason why I like to see the population in the area is because I like to invest in a place where there is enough people living in that city or postcode that I want to invest in. I like to invest in postcodes with more that 80,000 people in total living in that particular area. You can find this information by visiting a website streetcheck.co.uk. You need to type in the postcode and select the tab "people". It will show you how many people are living in that postcode area.

2. Next, I want to know the demographics of an area. I want to know how many of these people are potential customers. Now that I know how many people are living in that particular area. I want to know how many of these people might be interested in the products that I want to create. For example, let's say my strategy is to convert a 4 bed in a 6 bed HMO to rent for students. To put it simply, I want to convert a normal house into a house that I can rent room by room for students to live in when they are in University. So, I know my demographic has to be people from 19 to 24 because these are the people who are most likely to be in university. Therefore, I want to know how many of these people are living in the area. Whatever the strategy is you want to pursue you want to make sure the demographic is right for that particular area. You can find this information also on Streetcheck under "people" tab and scroll down to see the age group. It will show how many people from a certain particular age group are living in that area.

3. The next step in my due diligence, I want to focus on the houses itself. So, the first thing I want to know is the average price in the area. The reason why I want to know that is because I want to know how much the entry point is to buy a property in that particular area. Also, I like to choose areas that are higher than the national average. By the time I am writing this the average price in the UK is £256,000.00. (This data can be found in the government website Office for National Statistics). The reason I like to invest in areas that are higher than the average price is

because it will be harder to buy a property in these areas. Therefore, you might find less competition.

4. The next step is that I want to know if there are people trying to do what I want to do. I do not like to be the only one doing that strategy in that area. Seeing that there are people doing the same thing gives me more confidence that this particular strategy works in that area or that there is demand for what we want to create. The only thing we can do is to make sure we differentiate ourselves from the competition by finding our Unique Selling Proposition (USP). You can find this information by visiting a website called SpareRoom and by putting the postcode of the area you are thinking of investing in. You will be able to see what type of rooms are being advertised in that area. That will give you a good idea about what your competition is doing.

These are some of the things I tend to look at before picking an area to invest.

Normally I'd say you can find Valter listening to something... he knows it will sound weird, but he doesn't listen to music at all. Normally, when he is working out, he listens to podcasts or audiobooks. He loves eating but doesn't know how to cook, he has a chef who cooks for him. Valter tends to read 200 to 250 books a year. You'll find him in London or Leeds.

Matt Baker

As a serial entrepreneur, Matt wears many hats:

- Property developer
- Property educator and mentor
- Coliving management operator
- Podcaster
- Professional pianist

Through his many hats runs a connecting thread which is woven into his coliving and Next Level HMO projects. Matt's passion for teaching and sharing knowledge began with his love of music, as it inspired him to set up a music school in his late twenties, which he later sold when he found myself drawn to the property world. He started investing in property in 2015.

Despite his inexperience, he had chosen a path that would carry him successfully forward, one he realised, anyone with the right mindset could make a go of, if they just had someone to show them how. In only his first four years, Matt built a portfolio worth nearly £5 million, and had done so primarily by way of investor financing instead of having to use all of his own money.

His success, specialising in HMO and coliving, and his desire to teach others to achieve similar success and security, drove Matt to write a book, *Next Level Landlord.* In it, he reveals my five principles of how to become a Next Level Landlord through investment and development in this niche market. And he's so intent on sharing this knowledge so that others who share my passion to be a quality landlord that I included a quiz in my book to help them decide if this is the right path for them. You can find it on his website.

IG – @clearlymattbaker
FB – @clearlymattbaker
LI – @clearlymattbaker

Why have you chosen your strategy?

Having been a musician from an early age, primarily a pianist, I knew the hours and hours of practise, with very few opportunities to perform, made it a lonely endeavour. That is, until my rising disinterest came to a jarring halt in my early teens when I discovered jazz. I joined my school's swing band and found myself abruptly immersed in something social, collaborative, where the output was greater than the sum of its parts. This experience led to me finding and creating more opportunities to play with other like-minded musicians striving for a great output.

As I grew older, I naturally wanted to make money playing. I began doing gigs and club nights, and selling second-hand furniture when I discovered that my gigs weren't lucrative enough to support me. With an eye towards a career, I opened a music school that soon developed a long waiting list of applicants. And then I came upon property investing. How, I wondered, could I combine that with my desire to add value to my community? It wouldn't take long for me to find the answer: coliving. I promptly sold my school to a buyer, who was delighted to run with the baton, and turned my attention to property.

Specialising in HMOs combined my passion for building communities and connecting people with building a successful business I could be proud of. But more lay ahead. I found my strategy transitioning from creating high-quality HMOs into desirable, well-functioning coliving in the late 2010s. It was a market whose demand was growing, but with tenants who were becoming more discerning. Yet, as the market became busier, I saw that despite tenant standards rising, the quality was primarily still poor. That, I realised, was where opportunity lay.

Our strategy is for every one of our properties to be in the top 5% of all shared living premises by way of quality space, quality design and quality service. We did it by listening to tenants. We provide that by developing the spaces to suit our target audience, and follow through by managing them under our co-living management business, co:home.

What areas of property need the biggest change?

I'm admittedly passionate about effecting change in the coliving sector, and, in my opinion, the biggest gap between supply and demand – what's out there vs. what tenants want – is the quality of the tenant's experience. We need properties that feature quality space, quality design, *and* quality service. We accomplish the first two by using an inhouse team that understands the coliving market inside out. That enables us to maximise our projects to deliver optimal space, layout and design, something we also offer to support other landlords' portfolios, landlords who participate in our mastermind programmes at The HMO Platform.

For the third, quality service, we are spreading the word about the need to raise service standards in property to encourage other landlords to do so – we also want them to connect the dots: providing better service to tenants boosts their bottom line. Happy tenants are habitual tenants.

We believe in leading from the front, and so we're actively changing this sector through our management company, co:home (thecohome.life). It's the antithesis of most standard letting's agents, who see tenants in residence as a liability, rather than an asset. Property is no different to any other business: to succeed, it must be driven by what the customer wants and needs.

What's been your biggest success in property?

My biggest success to date is linked to the first 2020 pandemic lockdown. It forced me into networking more than before, and to be open even more to ideas and collaborations. I met a group of amazing investors, operators and technologists as a result, and we created what's now a successful UK-wide coliving management agency, called co:home.

Co:home resulted from our and many others' experience. HMO management was, on the whole, quite poor around the country. We wanted quality *and* consistency. We wanted a tenant in the midlands to enjoy the same experience as a tenant in the north west. Having more control over the overall product and service means we have a positive impact on the business. Nobody cares more about a property than the owner/manager.

Why do I see this as my biggest success? Because it has a far wider reach and impact on the shared housing market than is possible with only our own developments. Our own developments are great, but by having that direct touchpoint with our end user, we can have more of a positive impact on their lives now and in the future.

3 Top Tips on raising investor finance?

At Scott Baker Properties, raising finance is one of three integral parts to our business – finance, deals, delivery. In fact, we operate almost exclusively with investors, whether they be sophisticated or high-net-worth angel investors or joint venture partners. Based on years of raising finance, here are my top three tips:

Be honest – People invest with people they like, know and trust. When having initial conversations, don't over-promise and get someone overly excited if you know you're just going to let them down later. This follows through into the project – if something is going right, shout about it; if something is going wrong, also mention it. Investors will generally work with you to solve issues as they arise, but they can only do that if they know what those issues are. If you wait until repayment day to tell them 'The project is delayed and I don't have your money', they are going to be understandably unhappy. Remember, they're giving you their hard-earned money. Give them open communication in return.

Be yourself – This follows in tandem with my previous point. Your goal when raising financing is to build rapport with the right person and the right time. Don't be who you think an investor wants you to be; just be yourself. My partner Niall and I have this rule when dealing with investors: Be smart-casual, not suited and booted, because that's who we are. If some people fail to take us seriously, that's their loss. We work with investors who would rather meet down the pub or over a meal vs. sit around a formal conference table. But, while we're casual, we aren't casual about what we do and how we do it. We take our business just as seriously as anyone else, and our investors know it.

Be resilient – Get used to rejection. You will face so many more no's than you will yeses. But remember, you are only one more conversation away from that potential yes. And you only need one yes most of the time.

What property tools/apps/software can't you live without?

We swear by our property management software, COHO. Before it came out in 2020, property management tools were clunky and cumbersome – not user-friendly. Managing HMOs is a complex thing to get right, and COHO takes the guesswork out of it, enabling us to manage our portfolio pretty effortlessly.

Nimbus Maps makes sourcing and appraising potential deals much quicker and easier. Ever since they released the HMO overlays and HMO-specific strategies, it has become a staple of our tech stack.

Trello is our go-to for tracking and managing projects. This board and list-style app means that the whole team can chip in and know what's happening with a project at any time.

Who's most important to you in your life?

My first thought is always family, when somebody asks me that, particularly my children who are still quite young. But that's a bit of a kneejerk response. I make a point to regularly assess my values – in true Dr John Demartini fashion – to see where my focus, energy and time go. Family is always up there, but alongside two other important things: business and music. Nothing else comes close.

They're also intertwined. Running multiple successful businesses affords me and my business partner the freedom and choice to spend our time with family, and frees sufficient time for me to focus on the creation, recording and performing of music with the amazing members of the bands and ensembles I play with.

So, the three groups who are most important to me are my family, my business team members, and the highly talented fellow musicians with whom I am privileged to play.

What makes property such a powerful asset to you?

Property, to me, is a hugely powerful asset. It has longevity as an asset. It is not about getting rich quick; it's about getting rich right, and the compound cumulative effect as you keep going, and keep investing, is massive. Demand for property is so high in the UK and it has a very long track record of increasing, year on year, over the long run, making it a very safe investment. Rental properties are increasingly more in demand as well, given that home ownership has grown out of reach for many these days. As people wait longer to buy their first houses, with some giving up altogether, the demand for long-term rentals has increased for all demographics and age groups.

I'm in it for the long haul. I intend to build a secure future for my children, to leave my share of our properties and companies to my children and their children. I'm playing the long game – building a legacy. And property is the cornerstone of this legacy.

Matt will be listening to his band Lo-Ke-Ba, enjoying a glass of cabernet sauvignon, whilst reading Think and Grow Rich on Worthing seafront, watching his wife and daughter splash in the rock pools.

Liz Baitson

Liz is a Director of Preneur Capital, which provides bridging and development finance, and is the founder of 'The High Net Network' – a high level business network connecting game changers in all sectors relating to wealth.

She holds a 1st Class degree in Maths and her background is Investment Banking – so numbers are her comfort zone. She started working in the world of Property in 2015, when she started as an Angel Investor. Since then she has dabbled in most of the property strategies before settling on property finance as her specialism. It means she understands property finance from the point of view of the developer, which gives her a greater insight and empathy.

FB – The High Net Network
LI – Elizabeth Baitson
WS – preneurcapital.co.uk

What areas of property need the biggest change?

I feel like our conveyancing process here in the UK is painfully slow. So often fabulous deals are left to fester, and all parties involved endure unnecessary stress. There seems to be an accepted level of "slowness" and complexity – even in the most straightforward of transactions. If we look to other parts of the world for inspiration, we can see with better communication, systems and expectations – this process could be quicker, smoother and less arduous.

Top Tips to speed up the conveyancing process:
Ask for recommended valuers/solicitors that are well versed in commercial transactions. Most lenders will have a preferred panel of professionals. Ensure your solicitor understands property as not all high street law firms will be familiar with the nuances of the process and could slow things down hugely. Finally, communication is key. Don't assume things are being done behind the scenes, keep on top of it with regular phone and email communication.

Do you think most property investors are completely honest on social media?

I would say the majority of property investors are honest on social media. There are always the few that spoil the reputation for the rest of us! I personally tend to think – the more ego and 'wealth' that is being used as content - the less likely they are to be truly authentic.

I work closely with High-Net-Worth Individuals – many of them are property investors on social media, and not a single one talks about their wealth. They are more interested in engaging in meaningful conversations with others or doing due diligence on those posing opportunities. I used to believe the hype on social media – until I was stung personally through a bad investment. Nowadays I would urge everyone to dig a little deeper before taking what you see on social media on face value. There is a lot of egotistical noise on social media and as a newbie it can be difficult to discern what is authentic – so now I suggest always getting a number of personal testimonials from people who have worked with the person or company in question before making any kind of emotional, mental or financial commitment. There are many truly

Tej Talks

humble, experienced and wonderful property investors on social media that ARE authentic, and in time you can spot these from the crowd. This is one of the reasons I created The High Net Network – to bring people of high integrity, professionalism and shared values together and effectively upgrade their network above the noise that the Social Media 'circus' around wealth creation can often produce.

How diverse is the property industry?

I am very fortunate that my personal property circle is very diverse. My mother immigrated from Egypt 43 years ago and I have friends and business associates from all corners of the planet. I am also aware that this isn't the case everywhere.

I celebrate diversity in every area of life – and I would love to encourage this more in the Property Industry. In actual fact – my dear friend Petra Foster and myself started a social media group in Clubhouse recently which is called Kings & Queens of property: Diversity! We have a diverse panel of property experts from every culture & background – so that when people join us – they feel represented and safe. Petra now runs this and is doing such a wonderful job at creating that togetherness and helping to break down those barriers.

Who do you look up to, who inspires you?

I am someone who is constantly looking for the best in the people around me. I have never really felt connected to business gurus or wealth creation experts. They have their place and inspire so many others – but I just see so much inspiration in my daily life from members of my family, my colleagues and friends.

My partner is someone I look up to and has made the greatest impact in my personal and business life. He reminds me constantly that I am ENOUGH and with his unconditional acceptance and love – I am empowered to go out there and be the best I can be. My dad also inspires me to set strong boundaries – his favourite word is NO *(said in a much less delicate way!)*. I used to hate this as a rebellious teenager – but now I understand the power of the word NO – and how essential it is to protect your own energy as without strong boundaries – you will be depleted and weakened, not only in business – but in every area of life.

If you could share one message, what would it be?
We are in this together.

Until we realise this – we will always be working from a place of separation. US and THEM mentality is the root of all evil in this world. My businesses are an extension of who I am. I love to share, I love community – to be a part of something bigger than me. Every successful organisation is based on people – the power of a single vision and a connection to a larger goal. This is the way I run my finance business – I wish for everyone we lend money to - to succeed – and come back to us over and over again. I wish for everyone in my mastermind groups to connect with each other and create the very best relationships and businesses – as their success is my success. I don't mean that financially – I mean that emotionally as I truly don't think you can have too many friends in this world – and the only real security is the power of your community.

Finances come and go – they are never truly secure – people, relationships, community and love can last a lifetime. This is what I ground myself into.

What do you do in your free time?
My 'love language' is food!

I love to visit open air markets and explore artisan produce and support local businesses. I would travel 100 miles for the right restaurant! Finding, cooking, eating with family and friends is the most glorious way to celebrate life and everyone knows if they spend any time with me it will involve some sort of amazing meal! I build communities for my 'work' and create events and occasions for great people to mingle - so you would imagine I would want some peace in my free time! That couldn't be further from the truth – I AM my work – it's an extension of me so free time is the same as not free time – it's all wonderful.

What's been your best investment outside of property?
My best investment outside property is in my personal development. I have spent thousands on courses in my early 20s that helped me go within and figure out who I am. It's something I feel everyone should create space for. You don't need to go on expensive courses – but you do need to create space to build the relationship with yourself at as young an age as possible – as it's the most important relationship you will ever have. It pays dividends to invest in yourself, in whatever form that investment takes.

Top Tips for choosing a property training course or mentor:

1. Always get testimonials from previous mentees. You can ask openly on social media for recommendations and testimonials – what you really need to find out is what results the delegates have had that they can directly correlate with the training/mentorship. Ensure you don't just get "groupie" testimonials – get several of them for a fair dataset.
2. If they put a lot of pressure on you - RUN! An ethical trainer/mentor will not 'pressure sell' – they will find out if you are suitable for the training and will give you time to consider it. Any scarcity tactics, harassment or anything that makes you feel out of control of the buying process – is a sign telling you they are not looking out for your best interests. Trust your gut instincts.
3. Find a training provider or mentor you get along with. A lot of training involves accountability which can be an intimate business relationship. You must feel aligned with the values and vision of your trainer/mentor. Take your time and do your research thoroughly.

3 Top Tips on raising investor finance?

1. Build relationships with potential investors BEFORE you need the money. Scrabbling around for investors when you have a deal that you need to close urgently can be stressful and force unwise decision making. Do not process financial transactions in a rush. No investors want to feel hurried while making a decision about handing over their hard-earned cash.

2. Do ensure you find out what the investor desires before you pitch what YOU need. Too often, people will start a conversation with an "ask" rather than a genuine enquiry into what the potential investor is looking for. Make it about them not you.
3. Upgrade your network. Diversify who you are networking with – if you think going to the same property networking event every month, seeing the same faces is enough - I would argue you are missing out on massive opportunity. Try other types of networking events, charity events, special interest and luxury car/boat/art events. You will meet a huge array of people and most will have an interest in property.

Currently listening to Kisstory, eating prawn cocktail, reading the latest quantum physics theories by Nassim Harramein in an English Countryside pub with her 5 kids, partner and Rhodesian ridgeback.

Romero Howe

A developer who paints a picture of how to progress steadily in property over a period of time & remain relevant in a market that is forever changing in order to grow. Born in 1990 Romero is a developer that truly goes beyond the norm and typically follows his own trend on what to invest in and how things will work.

Based in Nottingham but investing across the country, after his first few BTL projects he decided it's a great game but slow. Although BTL was successful for him and continues to be, he knew he wanted to quickly increase his cash reserves and so decided to branch into Bungalows and structural problem properties that require significant work to bring back to standard. With a few successful flips and BRRs he realised this strategy was working well and enabled him to rapidly grow into high cash incentive projects such as new build developments and conversions.

Now with experience since 2013 where he invested in his first simple £60,000 BTL when finishing university. This property has more than doubled in value. He has covered most of property from commercial to residential, new builds, extensions, simple buy to lets.

As a university graduated in Business Management and Marketing, his eye is always looking for new opportunities to take advantage of whether it be in planning or potential new build dwellings on vacant land. Romero has aspirations to be as big as possible and always says he's having fun. This was also a key driver in him leaving his full-time job in marketing in 2017 to enter property full time. He knew real focus was needed in order to further grow his portfolio. The dream of watching homes under the hammer with property seeming impossible, quickly became possible with drive and determination.

IG – @brighter_investments
FB – @brighter_investments01
W – brighterinvestments.com

Bridging Finance - expensive or very useful?

Expensive, if you're unsure how to use it on the correct deal or in the right manner. If the deal has a small margin that just doesn't work, then how can we expect Bridging to work? Alternatively, it's a very useful product if you have a great deal that has a good profit margin incorporated. Although still be mindful that any margin can be eaten into if the house remains vacant or takes a significant amount of time to be refurbished. A great profit deal that isn't refinanced or sold in 15 months at a high interest rate can soon eradicate a large chunk of profit from the bottom line.

Imagine a deal that, when purely funded with cash has a £15,000 margin? Add a Bridging loan to the scenario and the deal turns into a £5,000 profit deal assuming the property sells at market value. If it doesn't, then you either break even or potentially have a loss on your hands. In contrast, imagine a £60,000 profit deal with a bridge cost of £10,000 - the final profit on sale if sold at market value is £50k. Therefore, meaning for less money to get the deal done there was a substantial return on capital employed (ROCE).

Bridging is not for every deal and a rule of thumb is the bigger the deal the more effective a bridge can be, if the margin is bigger too. A potential cash purchase of £200,000 to buy and renovate a property could result in as little as £60,000 needed upfront with a bridge therefore, also enabling you to scale up to larger developments/projects much quicker without necessarily having the cash available outright to buy a bigger deal.

What is one thing people misunderstand about property investing?

Many people that I speak with seem to think it's as easy as going to the estate agent/auction and buying a property listed for £100,000 at £80,000. Therefore, meaning they can do some refurbishment work of £20,000 which then results in a £20,000 profit. Simple?

It is far from this as many properties listed with online platforms typically have a small margin or at auction, they are sold over the guide price. It's a numbers game and hard work, i.e., you have to be persistent across all offers to find out when a sale for example has fallen through and the vendor is now willing to sell the property for £10,000 cheaper for a quick completion. We have to be ready to take advantage of scenarios like this. I have known property investors searching for 6 months or more for a deal and struggling to find one. At this point they realise property is a difficult sector to be involved with.

What is your deal analysis process?
I always start from the GDV (Gross Development Value also known as the 'End Value') and work backwards. If the GDV is £320,000 and the refurb is £100,000, I then ask myself how much would I be willing to pay and what would give me my profit margin? Which for me, depending on the type of project typically is 20% plus for developments, which is aligned with the industry standards. However, there are certain derelict developments where I may look to push the boundary beyond 30/40% ROI (100% Plus ROCE if using financing methods).

The real deal and reward is made in the purchase - as if purchased for the correct price it means the refurbishment budget can be anything you want as it will not hamper the return. I often say if the deal has £100,000 profit and I decide to get a kitchen more expensive than originally, I scoped out. It's not a big issue - as the profit may then drop to £95,000 for example.

Why have you chosen your strategy?
BTL as it's the most stable and simple strategy, you also get to provide a loving home for a tenant that generally stays for a long time. I have some BTL's that have had the same tenant for more than 6 years, they also take great ownership of the property as they want a family and comfortable space long term. HMO's are great for the income generated but typically if within an Article 4 area the barrier to enter such marketplace could be quite high.

Generally, do you buy to hold or sell, and why?
Buy & hold. The greatest reward in property is in the long-term gain. It is purely an investment that will continue to grow over the years therefore enhancing the return on the original investment made. I have still engaged with flips over the years and still continue to where a factor, such

as the money 'left in the deal' may not work. Or even if it's a joint decision with a business partner we may have opted to sell.

What are the Pros/Cons of your strategy?

I take a risk buying the worst properties that have been derelict for many decades and have excessive structural issues. However, profits can soar way beyond the norm you typically see on most simple refurbishment projects. I typically buy a lot of properties that are sold as seen or have no entry for viewings due to their current condition. In my strategy I typically buy derelict buildings that need a full refurbishment back to brick or need a total demolish & rebuild. It is not guaranteed at the early stages to the extent of the damages, which can be a costly risk. Also, sometimes I need further planning permission to alter the buildings footprint or council authority to demolish which in itself is a risk of not being approved.

I prefer this strategy as when holding for the long term the property specification and quality of fixtures are at a high standard ensuring they stand the test of time to last way beyond 30 years before another refurbishment is needed. This is because we are starting totally from scratch or back to brick.

What makes you a good Landlord/lady?

Ensuring that you treat the tenant/s as if they constantly use your service therefore any amends/fixtures that are needed to the property by way of maintenance are carried out in a quick and efficient manner. You ensure they have the best experience all the way through their tenure of being in occupancy of a particular property.

How do you manage your refurbishments?

Typically, my contractor will provide aspects of project management. However, on any refurbishment under £30,000 I do have a designated project manager within my team. I always recommend for anyone starting out that one way you learn a lot is by managing individual trades as you learn each individual element of a project in its entirety.

This is something that when I started taught me a lot, so that now I'm more experienced I can challenge the builder's way of thinking should I not agree or be happy with it.

How do you find an area to invest in?

This depends on your goals and current focus. Right now, I concentrate on development & new builds, so I have found an area where less investors seem to be operating which is away from the typical big cities. The reason for the shift from large cities is that I'm competing with less investors to find some great deals that have a good level of margin. I'm based in Nottingham (which I class as an Investor-hotspot), I find a lot of the developments and land deals go substantially beyond what I'm prepared to pay for, here, due to increased competition. However, from a rental perspective if the focus was purely Yield based and looking to achieve 6% plus then Nottingham would still fulfil that objective. This was a focus of mine when beginning back in 2013 and therefore I have a strong BTL portfolio in my hometown.

However, when currently looking at larger developments and where I'm profit driven for ROI, I've found myself operating in Yorkshire, Lincolnshire and smaller rural towns.

What's the best non-property investment you've made?

Memory cards! Way before phones came with 8GB+ of storage. I brought around 50 memory cards on amazon at £6 and sold them at £25. I remember making £1000 within 2 weeks - it was exciting and that £1,000 went towards buying a Fiat Punto which I then sold but saved the money from the sale. So, in essence that £1,000 4 years later still went towards my first house purchase. I often talk about the percentage of income you can save, so doesn't matter if you make £1,000 or £10,000 in a month but the main thing is the percentage you can save. If you can save 50% of £1,000 as opposed to 3% of £10,000 then it's the principle of saving which matters and the lower income person will save more in the long run and therefore purchase a property sooner or be able to invest sooner.

What has property allowed you to do? What has it given you?
It has given me the time to not work Monday – Friday 9am-6pm. Therefore, giving me time to spend with family and more importantly with my children, with them being at a young age, this time is priceless. In the corporate world you work all day to then get paid at the end of the month. Whereas in property once you own a house, I don't class it as you then work to get paid. As its residual income and will come in whether you work or decide to not work.

Have Podcasts been important on your journey?
I started before Podcast became a thing in property so typically, I was from a time where going to networking events was a big thing and the only way of gathering information *(way before Instagram 2011 to be exact!)*. For me, I still think it's important to connect with the people on the podcast by this I mean going to see them or visit them actually onsite and actually talking.

Romero will be listening to Toast by Koffee, as it reminds him to be grateful of his life and how he can help others. Probably with a cookie as a snack after video calls to keep him going for the next few hours with a cheeky Ribena. He'll be reading Whitepapers on Property, at home with his Mrs and kids.

TEJ'S TOP 10 TIPS FOR BEGINNERS IN PROPERTY

1. Invest in yourself. Have a budget, whether it's books, courses, mentors, taking people to dinner or giving your time in exchange for knowledge etc., you need to spend something to learn

2. Take your time with your strategy and geography, you may get it 'wrong' at first, it requires some deep thinking, planning and an understanding. Ignore what others do, do what works for you

3. Learn about construction and refurbishments, I love it, I find it so interesting. You don't need passion, but you need knowledge

4. Don't jump into a JV with matey that you just met at an event, do your DD, take your time and have a solid legal agreement

5. Network like crazy, it will pay you back 10x, I promise you. If I can't solve something or I don't understand, someone I know can and will help

6. Ask for help. As long as you aren't an askhole, people will help you (to a limit) and ask for nothing in return. Don't be afraid to seek help

7. Foundations - is your mindset strong but flexible? Are you ready for the endless rejections and challenges property will bring?

8. Respect Investor funds - treat it better than your own money. Ensure your deal analysis and process is shit hot, so you are protecting their investment in every way possible and reducing risk

9. Your team *(Broker, Accountant, Solicitor, Lenders etc.)* need to be high performers and understand how you operate, your goals and what's in it for them. This will streamline your entire business, save and make you money

10. It's so easy to compare ourselves to others, especially on social media. This can become toxic, and harmful. I've been there, and it will only harm your mental health. Focus on you and your journey, don't compare your day 2 to someone's day 2000

Jack Wicks

Jack is a property investor based in Surrey and has been since he was 22 years old. Jack enjoys all things creative when it comes to property deals and more recently focusing on recession proof and hands off property investments.

5 to 10-year guaranteed income producing property investments are the main priority. Finding them for both his company and other investors too.

Jack also has a passion for teaching others and more specifically young people who have been disregarded in the property education space. He now offers a low-cost monthly subscription to help them build a solid understanding of the industry with enough information to get started and making money.

"Enjoying life and having fun is the most important thing. Don't lose the first half of your life in the hope for a 'secure' second half. Make stupid decisions and go on holidays you can't afford as you will NEVER regret it."

FB – Jack Wicks
IG – @jackwicksuk

Why are you in property?

It's a proven wealth builder and if done right, the safest investment you can make. I fell in love with it due to the problem solving you are able to do. The diversity of property keeps it interesting for me too. I'm hyperactive and pretty sure I have ADHD, so I find myself getting bored quickly and property allows me to get involved in new things without a change of industry.

Finally, legacy. Being able to pass a property portfolio down generations to come is a great motivation to me!

Chosen Strategy?

It changes but we are focused on being recession proof right now. I have always been pretty happy with risk but now, with all of the legislation ruling in favour of tenants and after experiencing many issues with rental payments its essential to protect yourself.

People always say "single lets are great and cause you no hassle" but this simply isn't true, not always anyway. The biggest issues we have experienced have been from our single lets which is crazy when you consider the portfolio of over 100 HMO rooms. We had a great couple in one of our flats, paid every month and we even met them at the start. At 6 months they messaged me directly to say that the flat wasn't worth the money and they would be happy to pay £300 a month less *(around 50% less than agreed)* which we obviously said we couldn't do. They then decided to change the locks on OUR flat and refuse to pay the rent. 9 months down the line, £6,000 in rent arrears and court fees later they were out. Physically chucked out by bailiffs. Due to the tenants having a guarantor, we now have a lovely second charge on the guarantor's property which we will see at some point should she ever decide to sell!!!

Another experience was a couple again who had a child. 3 months in no money and no contact, agent had to put a Section 8 notice on the door (notice to leave), and we waited a month *(as per the law)*. No response, so then an abandonment notice needs to go on the door, guess what, another month *(as per the law)*. We eventually got in and they had literally left everything they owned, even their child's medical book! So, we had to go there and physically empty the place and dump their stuff, new carpets, new decoration and back on the market.

LOOOOOOOOONG!!!

So now my mindset has changed, it's no longer about quantity of money but the quality of life. People need to understand that to live a good life you need to wake up every day loving what you do and avoiding stress like the plague. More money doesn't mean you will live an amazing life if you are shackled to a desk or having to answer midnight phone calls. Life is bigger than the amount of money you have. It's about memories. I always think (really morbid but keeps me motivated) that one day, my parents won't be around anymore, one day I will be too old to get pissed every day of a 2-week holiday *(not far off this I think)* and so living your life NOW is more important than sacrifice for your future. Nobody is guaranteed one.

We source and acquire property deals that come with 10-year government backed and guaranteed leases. This means we can have the lease already waiting for us before we even buy the property, so we know our figures down to the penny. The leases include full management and maintenance which means it allows us to be completely hands off.

We also specialise in social housing and using the housing benefit element of universal credit to increase yields with single let property. 2SQUARED is the way in which we can house just two tenants in a house, but they can claim the non-shared one-bedroom rate which means we get that twice. We also make sure we are paid directly from the council. So again, recession proof, no non-payment issues and the icing on the cake is that we get to house those who need it the most!

Thoughts on property education and mentorship?
I've spent upwards of £50,000 on education, some good, some bad, some indifferent. It all comes down to what you do with it. Information is free now if you choose to look hard enough for it. Implementation of that information is what will bring you success.

I will always be happy to pay for a structured course or platform which will allow me to fast track my success. Another huge benefit is the network you build when you pay for these courses.

Make sure you like the person leading the course and aspire to be like them or have the life you aspire to have. You will need to take some risks on the back of advice given by them, so you need to trust them. The mistakes I made in terms of mentors and courses were due to ego, wanting the car and the house that mentor had. Forgetting the fact, he was some dickhead who would chuck his wife and kids in front of a bus if it meant more money or another car.

Ask around and get a balanced view of someone you are considering going with too. Remember, someone will always blame the course or the mentor if they didn't get results, very rarely will they just admit they did nothing to help themselves. Ask people why they wouldn't recommend it and ask those who have been successful what they did differently. Get a balanced view and go for it. 'Expensive' doesn't come into it if you genuinely change your life for the better, so try not to be scared by price, it usually means *(usually not always)* that it's simply a better course or mentorship and has stood the test of time.

How do I deal with stress?
This is something that my business partner Kevin Brittain and I have been talking a lot about recently. We have started 6 businesses in the last year and that comes with a lot of stress let alone doing that while locked down, having a young family etc.

Kevin runs to release stress, as I write this, he is on day 260 of running at least 5k every day. He's a mad man but it helps him clear his head. For me, I HATE running, high intensity weight training is my thing. I walk a lot too. I do a long walk in the mornings and listen to audio books. I then train in the middle of the day as its usually the time my energy and focus start to wane.

So, I think the point is, do exercise, whatever it is you enjoy the most. Eat well and SLEEP! Ignore the idiots that tell you to work 18-hour days and sleep less so you can fit more work in. Enjoy your life and don't take anything too seriously.

How do you decide who to JV with?

Quite simply you want to JV with someone who has opposing skills to you BUT the same goals and aspirations.

So, for me, I love talking, can you tell? Networking comes really easily to me and I seem to have a skill in connecting with people. I'm more than happy to put my opinion out there and I'm proudly open and honest.

Kevin, my business partner HATES all of those things. He is the king of systems and processes. He deals with everything in the background.

The combination is amazing, but we are both family men. Everything we do is for our families and as such we have a huge emphasis on enjoying every day and only doing what you love!

Secret sauce for sourcing/investing?

Focus on the money not the deals. Deals are everywhere. The real money is made when you have access to investments. Focus on connecting the money with the good deals. If the figures work on a deal brought to you by a deal sourcer, then stop looking at their fee, they just saved you an insane amount of time, all you did was buy the thing!

If you want a life which is free, you can't be 'on the ground' and 'hustling' every day. Leave that shit to the young lot who are still learning, they have time. I always think, if my business can't run when I'm not at home, it means I'm in a job. How can you make your business remote? Now more than ever you have an opportunity to operate a remote business as we've been forced to do so.

Stop thinking *"Well if I just go and do it, it will save time and money"* and start thinking *"How can I leverage other people so I can focus on my company growth"* While you are on viewings or doing your own refurbs you could be bringing in investors, opportunities and reducing costs which is ultimately a Company Directors job.

If you control the money, the deals will be everywhere. Everyone thinks money is hard to find or *"why would they not just invest it themselves"* change your mindset. Money is abundant, you only have to walk down your local 'millionaires' row' to realise quite how many people are out there with huge amounts of cash.

You will get bored of looking around piss stinking horrible houses I promise you. Focus on creating a business, not a job.

What has property allowed you to do? What has it given you?
Be happy! Sounds cringe but I was in a job, working at the airport and as close to depression as I'd ever like to be again.

Property has given me a true purpose in life. I can work from anywhere in the world which falls in line with our love for travel. I get to spend loads of time watching my son grow up and couldn't think of anything worse than missing huge parts of his life due to work. So, I don't!

Not just that but I have been able to help so many of my friends and families with the knowledge I have in property and business.

Should people invest in the North or the South?
The answer is and this is an answer I give to loads of questions, "it depends"

The north has great cashflow opportunities but (in general) low capital growth. The south has (potentially) huge capital growth but poor cashflow. So, if you need income, buy North, if you want long term investments or big lumps of cash then buy South. NEVER choose an area based on price. You can always find the money for the right deal so make sure it is right for you.

Jack is listening to Grime, eating a good Thai and drinking Rum, whilst reading Daniel Priestly (All of his books, but Oversubscribed is immense) in his Home office with his Wife and 2-year-old nutcase son!

Lloyd Girardi

Lloyd Girardi is a well-respected property developer, coach and mentor. In 2014 Lloyd started property developing with his business partner Andi Cooke. They went from a standing start with 1 buy-to-let property each, to a portfolio of properties worth over £20,000,000 using none of their own money to do so.

In 2014 Andi & Lloyd adopted the Build-To-Rent exit strategy on their developments. They learnt the hard way by making mistakes along the way. Together, they founded, White Box Property Solutions, one of the UK's biggest Property Development training businesses, showing people how they can follow in their footsteps and not make the mistakes they made to become a property developer using the build-to-rent or build-to-sell model Andi & Lloyd's personality, honesty and personal touch is what makes them different to any
other training business, creating the #whiteboxway, the pair take people from complete beginners in property development through to completion of their sites.

Property Developing is not easy but is very rewarding when done right. Lloyd Girardi will take you through the basics of how to get started in property development. In his talk he will show you inside techniques to find development opportunities close to your home, showing you that it is simpler than you may first think.

A live demonstration of what to look for and where to go. You never know… he may even find you a deal?

IG – @lloyd.girardi
YT/FB – White Box Property Solutions (LTD)
IG – @whiteboxproperty

Why are you in property?

Ever since I can remember I wanted my own business. My friends all went to University but it just never appealed to me. I'm sure you can relate to this feeling of wanting to do more with your life but just unsure what. That was me. I went travelling in 2005 and came up with what I thought were great business ideas. I wanted to be creative, I wanted to start something of my own. On my return to the UK, I was ready to start, or so I thought I was. That was until I needed to do something. I didn't know how to start. The easiest option was not to. I'm sure many can relate to this part, I got a job and worked for the next 8 years while my ambition of starting my own business faded.

That was until 4th November 2013 when unfortunately, my dad passed away from cancer. 56 days later my grandad passed away too. That was the kick up the arse I needed to live the life I had always dreamt. What was that life? My own business allowing me to have time, freedom and choices... not being stuck to an office chair with 22 days holiday a year. I love to travel, to drive nice cars, to live in a nice house, surrounded by my family. That is why I am in business. It just happens to be that property is the business I love. I didn't know I wanted to start a property business. I just found property investing interesting. Because of that, I found out more about it with my business partner Andi. We both wanted to become property investors, we quickly realised that you could do property with other people's money. We then discovered that we had some understanding of building, well Andi did. This was the start of us owning a property development business.

If I could start any business again, I would come back to property every time…why? I get to be creative; I get to build houses and know that I have provided a home for someone, I get to have the life choices I live for because I know I'm helping others.

What's been your biggest success in property?
Starting…

Too many people get caught up in shall I or shan't I, until you do it, you will never know if it was the right decision or not. Most of the time it is the right decision to do what you have always wanted to do. The reason is, when you are dedicated and passionate about something you will find every possible way to achieve it, even if you have challenges along the way. I wish I started sooner and I bet any successful property investor says   the   same   thing.

When I wanted to start a business but didn't know how, I didn't start. That was an easy get out for me at the time. Now, I wouldn't let that happen. I know how to start a business and even if I didn't, I know who to ask or find out the information to start. I've learnt so much from taking action.

So, my biggest success is starting. If I hadn't started in 2014, I would not have the £25,375,000 development portfolio that myself and business partner Andi Cooke have got today. Some of that are deals we are currently working on but it's still progression. Unfortunately, it was an unfortunate moment in my life that made me realise that life is too short. I started because I found out first hand that you don't control life, life controls you. That was my wake up to live it! I have certainly achieved many goals in my life to date, including the ability to travel. My biggest passion is travel, development has allowed me to share my love of F1 with travel and I have been fortunate enough to visit the Monaco Grand Prix 3 times.

All of this would never have happened if I didn't start. So, this is why my biggest success is actually making a choice and starting! It wasn't easy, it has been challenging, it's had its ups and downs, we've made and lost money on deals, but it's been worth it!

What property related tool/software/apps can't you live without?
Without question the biggest tool that we have in our armoury now is mypda.co.uk. My Property Developers Assistant. In our early days and

also not so long ago, we used to analyse deals on a spreadsheet, created by us. If you're like me, you will create a spreadsheet and then save it somewhere. I always forget where I saved it. I'm not the most organised when it comes to that. What MyPDA does is save everything to the cloud. Only you can access the information on your own log in. Every project we come across we can create using MyPDA and then do a Quick Deal Analysis (QDA) to assess whether the deal stacks up or not. From there we can save the project and come back to it later or we can proceed to a full appraisal. MyPDA takes a lot of information into account and also pre-empts you to fill in what you may have forgotten to fill in on your calculations so there no more spreadsheet creations. It's amazing.

The lite version is free to use and the Pro version is so detailed it will make any deal quicker and easier to appraise and save money in the long run.

What's your secret sauce for Finding Deals/sourcing?
I'm going to say it. I'm addicted to land sourcing and deals!

I get a kick from negotiations and making offers. Ever since we started, I love the process of hunting down a deal or negotiating to get the price right. On the other hand, I love to spend money too. So, it's not a case of me trying to save as much as possible to squeeze everything out of a deal, it's a case of buying right at the start.

My top tips on land sourcing especially is to treat it as a numbers game and not to get too emotionally attached to a site until you own it - "Buy with your head and not with your heart". Too many people get too fixated on a plot or building because it is local or it has a meaning or it's just available… You have to buy right. It has to be a numbers game. The way I find and analyse opportunities is like a manufacturing business. Let's take a car manufacturing business as an example, the car manufacturer doesn't build 1 car and then start on the next. They build a load of doors, engines, wires, interiors and then assemble is together in an assembly line. This is what you should do when finding deals. Treat it as an assembly line - use my 100/30/10 principle as a tip. Find 100 potential opportunities, take 30 of them and analyse them, choose the 10 you want to make offers on and offer on them.

Doing that every month will give you an advantage over many and help you win deals. What you are also doing by offering so much a month is building up a decent pipeline of opportunities and deals because not every one of those will be accepted because we are buying or offering on what works for us and not what the asking price is.

If you could share one message to every single person on the planet, what would it be?

"Activity Creates Opportunity."

This is a phrase that my business partner Andi created. There's no such thing as luck. Andi and I both believe this. People make their own luck – or, more likely, they make their own opportunity. Movie mogul Sam Goldwyn was quoted as saying, 'The harder I work, the luckier I get'. 'Luck' is the positive outcome of activity, the more effort you put in, the more opportunities are presented to you. It isn't luck, It's work. As Andi is fond of saying, activity is what creates opportunity.

Some people have said that we were 'fortunate' to get into developments. It wasn't fortunate that my dad and grandad passed away when they did; it was life. Unfortunately, life kicks you in the bollocks sometimes, but it's how you respond that reveals who you really are. Adversity can either knock you on your arse or make you stronger – it's your choice.

Before I started my own business, I never paid much attention to frequently quoted sayings, beyond acknowledging they were truisms people would parrot in support of their viewpoints. They were just words, but these days, having gotten into developments, having developed our business, more of these observations have begun to resonate with me.

That's why I've sprinkled several of my favourite ones throughout this book, the ones that mean the most to me, those which carry the most significance in terms of all I've learned on this journey.

These include two from Zig Ziglar:

"You don't have to be great to start, but you have to start to be great,"

and

"F-E-A-R has two meanings: Forget Everything And Run, or Face Everything And Rise. The choice is yours."

Another, this one by ice-hockey legend Wayne Gretzky:

"You miss one hundred per cent of the shots you don't take."

And from Richard Branson:

"I have always believed that there is no point in having regrets as you learn far more from mistakes than successes. Embrace a mistake and learn from it; don't regret them."

And the last, often attributed to Albert Einstein although no one is really sure if he ever said it, is worth repeating:

"Insanity is doing the same thing over and over and expecting a different result."

Don't wait until you're great – being great at something takes practice. It means you have to do it over and over so that you can become great at it. Start now and get perfect later. Otherwise, you'll never take that first step, and you'll regret never starting.

Don't miss your shot because you hesitated and never took it.

Do you know the wealthiest place in the world? It's the graveyard. How many unfulfilled intentions lie buried there? How many untold stories, unwritten books, potential inventions, and new businesses never started remaining under the surface?

If you want change, make it. Do something different. Don't let fear hold you back, if our fears didn't hold us back so often, there wouldn't be so many books on the subject. Susan Jeffers wrote *Feel the Fear and Do It Anyway*, on how we can turn our fear into confidence.

Don't be afraid of making mistakes but do be sensible. Learn from your mistakes but don't jump into the deep end when you haven't first learned to tread water. Start small, that might be a small site to start with, less than 10 houses. Keep it simple and learn the ropes.

Once you start, and stick with it, more opportunities will come your way. Andi and I receive development opportunities regularly because people know that's what we do, and because we created the opportunity for people to send us deals. *We created opportunity by taking action.* Start living the life you have always dreamt of instead of just dreaming about it. I dreamt of starting a business years before I did, but I didn't do anything back then to make it a reality. Now that I have made it a reality, I only wish I had started earlier.

Actions speak louder than words. Take action.

What's an unusual or weird thing you love?
It's probably not unusual or weird but I love whisky. I'm not a massive drinker but I love the social aspect of whisky. I love the idea of sharing a dram with a friend. Since starting my property business, I have been able to collect some amazing whisky's from around the world. I have a goal to have a collection of 200 bottles. I am over 25% of the way, I love the idea of knowing the story behind the bottle and sharing that with others.

Lloyd is listening to the beating sound of a hammer from his roofer, building his extension, whilst drinking Whisky (Macallan). He'll likely be reading Matthew McConaughey – Greenlights, in his favourite chair with his wife.

Saif Rehan

Saif is a part time Property Investor with a full-time job as a Management Accountant. He graduated from the University of Manchester five years ago and has always been stuck in a Graduate Position. He started researching into Property around three years ago with pretty much no savings to his name.

Saif wasted the first 18 months with the shiny penny syndrome, before he knuckled down and decided HMOs was where he wanted to be. If you then exclude 9 months of inactivity due to COVID, leaving 9 months of active developing, where he has converted two terraces into 4 Bed HMOs, three developments currently undergoing and another four projects starting in the summer.

Saif says he is fortunate to have an awesome client base that allows him to source and develop stunning homes. He never thought he'd be where he is today. Hard work and big goals really did push him to be the person he is today. He realised very quickly that he had no choice but to make Property work in order for my goals to be achieved as quick as he intended them.

IG – @saifrehan

Why are you in property?

I honestly didn't know the answer to this question a few months ago. I actually love the concept or principles of the property market and the secure returns it can generate on a monthly or annual basis. I originally got into this for the money.

I realised that every Asian Uncle that I knew who was doing well with their lives, all had one thing in common, they invested in Property. I thought at the time that if I had something to do with Property then I'd easily be getting on the path to have a good life. I soon realised this was quite true and there was so much to the world of Property.

Property has since become a vehicle for me, a vehicle that will be taking me to my goals. I have actually fallen in love with the Property life mainly due to how varied each day can be and the challenges we come across. Small things from driving around Warrington to figure out who can hire me a concrete breaker all the way to trying to find the Landlord of a Hair Salon closed by a COVID-19 Lockdown so I can issue and have a Party Wall Agreement signed. Varied right? Especially compared to my day job which is very stable and repetitive.

How do you manage your refurbishments?

Project Management is an area of Property that I like to think I excel at, and also, I help a lot of my clients with managing their own developments. I believe managing refurbs is all about managing people and managing resources.

There are two types of refurbs that you can carry out:

1. Appointing a Contractor who is responsible for buying materials and organising labour and you pay him for everything. Normally this option is slightly more expensive which is down to the contractor charging a premium.
2. Hiring a Trades team individually to make your own team so you can control the refurb that extra bit more, and potentially get a refurb completed at more value for money.

I personally like to hire my own tradesman to build a team for each of my properties. I'm a bit of a control freak and I haven't been able to execute developments well enough without being involved in the project management.

As an Accountant, I have a lot of experience of managing budgets, financial planning and how to make decisions on the back of the financial progress of a project. These are very transferrable skills that I've built up and ones that are crucial in my eyes to project management. I often get very shocked when I see developers not aware about the details of their builds or that the level of detail I am used to seeing has not been calculated, it doesn't surprise me why many projects are overrunning or even overspent.

Every project that I manage, usually has an excel spreadsheet backed up which tracks every penny spent, when I spent it and when I'm to spend money over the rest of the project. It's important to be always in control of knowing whether a project is running better or worse than your budget and how each decision affects this. I love tracking my projects individually for Materials and Labour, as I am normally responsible for getting matcrials to site. All of this detail allows me to learn and develop after every project. Every aspect of the project that I didn't budget correctly is perfected in time for the next project. I know how many pieces of timber and screws used for our current Office to 5 Bed HMO, so guess what happens when I have an Office to 6 Bed, 7 Bed or even 8 Bed? I apply the pro-rata on my materials and labour to the number of Bedrooms to give my budgets on my next project.

My trackers are then paired with an Asana checklist of my schedule ready for me to tick this off on every site visit. I can easily keep track of any revisions to the to-do list specific to a project. This allows me to focus on the details and snag my projects on every visit and add any small tasks to make sure they're not lost anywhere after decisions are made with my build team. I also like to keep a WhatsApp group with my Head Builder and his team to make sure we can all communicate together with the use of videos, photos and voice notes. Communication, cost tracking and constant snagging is the key to Project Management with Saif Rehan.

What (property related) tools/software/apps can't you live without?
I love Excel. Period. I run a lot of my business through Excel or Google Sheets. Whether it is deal appraisal, pipelining my developments and projects, managing my client list, or even using it to project manage a development.

When you really understand the power of Excel, the formulas, the systemisation it can build for your business at the click of few buttons you will never look elsewhere. Granted I am an Accountant and Excel may come slightly easier to me, but I really believe every business owner needs to learn the power of Excel and how it can really help their business.

I use Excel for my Property business, for my Accountancy role, and for my Clothing business. In every scenario it has saved me a lot of time.

What is one thing people misunderstand about property investing?
Property Investing has many different touchpoints and not the most typical that everyone perceives. For example, since my circle and Facebook friends have seen me get active in Property, they ultimately assume that I have millions in my accounts and constantly on a buying spree through Rightmove. However, it is usually far from it. There are so many strategies in Property and taking your time out to research and learn at what stage you can join the Property world is important. I still see myself at the start of my Property career - being three years into it, which has shown me how much of a long-term game this Property world actually is.

Do you think most property investors are completely honest on social media?
I think most of the good ones actually are but there are some sharks out there that only speak about the good moments because hey, that's what brings in the followers and likes?

However, I have found that transparency in the property sector is very rare to find but just as rewarding to share. I respect investors, builders or anyone on social media that is able to share the lows as well as the highs.

And in other moments I know of many people that are often selling themselves based on lies, whether it is fudged deal numbers or lack of experience in reality to what they are trying to show everyone that they know.

What differentiates you from your peers?
I honestly don't think there are many people as new to property as myself that look at the details like I do. I understand I'm nowhere near where I want to be, but I'm pleased at the systems I have in place to make sure I am doing all I can to be prepared on wins and losses. I am often contacted regularly to assist other developers on financial planning of their property businesses, deal analysis on future deals or even to take a new project as the PM. I love the detail and all the decisions it helps me make.

What do you do in your free time?
I play a lot of Golf, very little in lockdown or recently due to work being pretty crazy but I'm quite excited about getting back to this and networking with other investors. I don't have a lot of free time but I'm currently hustling to build up a future of working with lots of free time.

Who is really important to you in life?
Right now, there is nothing more important to me than my little family. I've not had an easy time with family recently which has put a lot of the responsibility on my shoulders so I'm only working hard now to make life for my family better and give my son, Ayaan, opportunities in life that I only really got to experience at an older age.

You can find Saif listening to Rap music, eating Fried Chicken, reading 50 Cent – Hustle Harder, in his home office in Sunny Manchester, with his little boy, Ayaan!

Hannah & George

Hannah and George have been in property for just under 2 years and in that time, they have sourced close to 100 property investment deals, raised £1.3m in private finance for their own portfolio which is worth in excess of £2m, launched several SA units and recently opened Dugard Construction.

Prior to sourcing George achieved a 1st Class Honors in Law at Sussex University but after carrying out an internship in China, he realised law wasn't for him and opted for a career change which saw him work as a Project Manager at a precinct in Australia. When George returned to the UK, he got his hands dirty as a plasterer which ignited his passion for property.

Hannah worked nearly a decade in the IT industry starting with a role at the London 2012 Olympic and Paralympic games before joining a global organisation carrying out Project Management and Account Management roles. She achieved a 1st Class Honors in Leadership and Business Management before recently escaping the rat race to join George full-time.

Starting as a team of 2 working out of Hannah's parents' house, Dugard Property is now a team of 5 with 2 additional job ads live and more in the pipeline.

FB – Dugard Property
IG – @dugard_property
YT – Dugard Property Business
W – dugard-property.co.uk

Why are you in property?

FREEDOM. We want to be able to do what we want, when we want, how we want. It's a very generic response but we love travelling (we actually met travelling) and are working hard to scale our business so we can be wherever we want in the world, for as long as we want, and still get paid.

Property is by no means as passive as people make it out to be, but providing you've built the right team and laid the foundations, you'll 'make money when you sleep'. I.e., as long as we provide a property refurbished to a good standard, attract the right tenants and have a handyman/builder on speed dial, whether we are in Wales working our backsides off or laying in the Caribbean for a month, we will still receive our rent payment.

Obviously, there are a load of other reasons too, such as:
- We own an asset that is going to grow in capital appreciation, not cash sit in the bank depreciating,
- We're building a legacy to hand over to our children,
- We don't need to report to anyone (no holiday leave requests!). If we wake up on a Monday morning and want a duvet day watching films, we can/will.

Why have you chosen your strategy?

When we first started thinking about getting into property, we quickly had to decide what our area would be. At the time, George was living on the Isle of White and Hannah was in Wales. You don't need to live where you invest but as we were starting deal sourcing, we needed to be in an area we knew well. Wales won the battle – not that there was much of a battle to be had!

Deal sourcing was our initial strategy as we saw it as a steppingstone to reaching our long-term goals. It allowed us to meet the right contacts, build a solid power team, expand our property knowledge, experience property purchases and refurbishments all whilst growing our own pot of money that we could then invest.

When deciding our area, we looked at what deals were achievable and BTL's were a clear winner in our eyes. Wales is blanket Article 4 meaning you either purchase HMOs with a license at a premium, or you face the battle over planning to convert a single dwelling into one. We're also aware that with the magnitude of regulations in place, this strategy can cause huge headaches. Not something we wanted to start with!

We fell in love with the buy, refurbish, refinance (BRR) strategy as you get the excitement of transforming a run-down property into a beautiful home as well as being able to recycle your cash! Winner.

What are your thoughts on property education/mentorship?

Although we offer training/mentorship ourselves, we're completely open that you don't actually need to pay for training. You can find everything you need online for free – but it will take a lot of time. Whereas a training course is time-bound, and everything is handed to you. So, it's weighing up your time v cost. It's also completely down to individual preference.

We didn't pay for any training when we started deal sourcing, but we have paid for training to learn about commercial to residential conversions and will probably pay for a lot more training going forward as we want to accelerate our understanding and progress. We also value our time a lot more now due to running multiple businesses. Note, there isn't any point in paying for training if you're not looking to implement your learnings straight away. Real learning comes from experience.

As for mentorship, you can find great mentors but ask yourself why you need one. Do you need a coach, someone to hold you accountable or a mentor? Do you know the difference? Mentors can make a huge (positive) difference when used correctly just make sure you do your research on the individual/company too. Specifically, mentors in property, does that mentor invest themselves? Have they done what you are trying to do?

How do you cope with the stress of Property?

Firstly, property is one big bag of stress! Accepting that from the outset helps. Refurbs overrun, period. Whether it's on time or cost, something will pop up. As quick as you want a purchase to complete, your solicitor can only go as quick as the seller's solicitor and if they're slow well then, you're going to spend the next few weeks chasing them. You think you've sorted your bridging finance then the lender drops their loan to value (LTV). We could go on, but you get the picture…

We're in the middle of reading 'The Subtle Art of Not Giving a F*ck' and there's one sentence that has really stood out: 'Problems never stop; they merely get exchanged and/or upgraded.' To put that into context, your builder phones you with a problem, he's stripped the 30-year-old thick wallpaper and found the walls are completely perished. The solution is to knock them back to brick, dot and dab plasterboard and skim over the top. You've solved one problem but now you have a new one, this is unforeseen and therefore an additional cost, so you're now eating into your contingency and/or over budget.

Coping with stress is all about solving problems, not avoiding them (even when you want to). But before you start brainstorming and thinking of solutions, take a step back, breathe, go for a walk, get some fresh air. You need to remove yourself from the situation to be able to focus and NEVER involve emotions.

When you do feel like you're stressed, take some time for yourself, exercise and eat healthy (so cliché but makes such a difference).

Generally, do you buy to hold or sell, and why?
At this moment in time our goal is to build our portfolio so we're buying to hold, although we will trade every 3rd/4th property to top up the bank balance (and cover any money left in deals).

Reason being we're building 'passive' cash-flow and as we're following the BRR method, we are purchasing properties where we're expecting very little money to be left in the deal so makes financial sense to keep the single-lets.

As we look forward to new strategies such as commercial to residential conversions, the numbers are a lot bigger, and therefore we would want to sell.

What (property related) tools/software/apps can't you live without?
Top 3: Asana, Google Workspace, DocuSign.

We're big advocates of automating as much as possible, outsourcing where you can, and storing everything in the cloud so you can access your files from any device and easily share them with your team.

Asana is super powerful and can be configured/adapted to your property business. We use it to track all viewings, offers, where properties are within the conveyancing process, who has actions etc. etc.

Is property a 'numbers' or a 'people' game?
Both! People have this misconception that you view a property, submit your offer and it's yours. If only it was that easy, eh.

It takes a lot of viewings, to offer on half, to be accepted on one. Especially starting out, as you're figuring out what you're looking for and how to analyse a deal, so you tend to be a bit slower getting your offer in and miss out. To secure our first deal it took something crazy like 40 viewings and 30 offers to get the 1 property!

Similarly, it's all about the relationships you build. Don't have an ego, don't tell an agent you have hundreds of thousands of pounds and want to buy a stupid number of properties in the next year. They will laugh and won't take you seriously. You need to be honest, build genuine relationships and follow through with your word. If you become known as the friendly person on a viewing, who takes an interest in the agent, submits reasonable offers and completes in a timely manner then you'll find said agent will start passing you deals as you make their life easier.

Do you think most property investors are completely honest on social media?

No! People are quick enough to highlight all the positives and good times but shy away from showing the negatives and the challenges (unlike us & Tej!). If we came across a page which was all rosy and perfect, we'd be sceptical.

What is your morning routine? Why is it so?

We recently started a new 'morning routine' as we realised, we were always feeling sluggish, found it hard to get out of bed and in general weren't coming up with new ideas regularly and/or felt a little demotivated.

Behold, a typical weekday morning:

- 6.30am wake-up. Alarm in another room so we can't snooze and brush our teeth straight away to properly wake us up!
- 7.00am exercise! We do a 30min HIIT session in our living room three times a week.
- 7.30ish – 8.00am ish quick shower & breakfast (likely to be smashed avo on toast with a fried egg mmm). We hold our 'priority meeting' over breakfast and set our key tasks for the day.
- 8.00am – 9.00am read. It depends on how we feel on the day, it's either an educational audible (currently the 12-week year) or a book we're reading at that time
- Work day begins…

On the days we don't exercise, it's swapped with a zoom call with our virtual assistant (VA).

Have Podcasts been important on your journey?

1000%. We love a good book but it's not practical. With podcasts you can listen to them in the car, on a run, sat at your desk, eating dinner etc. etc. so you can always be learning.

People are also more natural on podcasts, and therefore you get to understand them better, connect with them more. Conversations flow so it's likely unplanned questions will be asked, and you'll always pick up a few golden nuggets!

The Dugards are currently listening to Heart FM, drinking the finest glass of rioja, reading The subtle art of not giving a f*ck at home with Bella-boo. The best dog, ever.

Bronwen Vearncombe

Property Investor, #1 best-selling author and coach, Bronwen Vearncombe, has built a successful business over the last few years and been able to give up her full-time corporate banking job and find freedom.

In just two years she and her husband replaced their corporate income with property rental and left their jobs. Inspiring many people each year through her success, not only does she have a great property business, but she teaches others through her online learning platform established in 2017.

Just two years later they set out follow their dreams and specific adventures: John circumnavigated the globe with the 17/18 Clipper Round the World yacht race, and Bronwen followed working in the business and volunteering along the way. Travelling the world proved that they could balance a property business and adventure. In 2019 they spent 6 months working from The Whitsunday Islands in Northern Queensland, where Bronwen wrote her book Building Your Dream Life which published in 2020.

Bronwen is currently in Namibia volunteering at her favourite wildlife conservation group, Naankuse – a great place to escape the UK lockdown and continue to work from her laptop!

LI – Bronwen Vearncombe
TW – @bronwenv64
IG – @bronwen_pif
FB – @propinvfoundation
W – propertyinvestingfoundation.com

Why are you in property?

Property rental income has enabled me to leave the corporate rat race by giving me a regular monthly income. The freedom this gives enables me to follow my true passions in life and gives me choices. Choices I never had when I was trading my time for money in Lloyds Bank and the NHS.

What makes property such a powerful asset to you?

Property is such a great asset in the UK because of the demand for housing. If you buy in the right location, there is potential monthly rental profit as well as capital growth if you hold for the long term. So much more than if you were to invest elsewhere.

It's also a very rewarding business. For example, we are refurbishing older properties, creating lovely spaces for people to live in and in our work with councils, supporting families in need too.

What advice would you give a total beginner in property?

Get the best education you can to understand the risks and pitfalls that exist. Be very careful of the marketing tricks though. Start within your level of comfort and risk. Then grow as your knowledge grows. Consider a coach or mentor to hold your hand and give you confidence.

Surround yourself with positive people who are also making property their success. This is your support network. Read my book Building Your Dream Life and take a look at my website Property Investing Foundation – full of top tips and case studies.

What areas of property need the biggest change?

The whole conveyancing process is archaic and is not utilising technology to simplify the process. It relies on solicitors, many of whom still work in an old-fashioned way, often taking weeks to answer questions from a vendor's solicitor. Electronic ways are deemed not to be secure, but I know that with some focus things could be improved massively. It's hard though because the legal process isn't competitive enough.

Planning is another area which needs an overhaul in my opinion. Given in the UK we are not building enough houses for the demand, there needs to be a much simpler process and not just governed by what sometimes feels like the whim of the local planning head.

How do you cope with the stress of Property?

My way of relaxing is to do keep fit classes with a great local teacher – or even online. Must be live and with great music. If I can book classes in advance then it keeps me motivated. Yoga is great for relaxing too and both John and I love it. Brilliant for breathing and flexibility.

Then you can't beat a good long walk with a dog through the beautiful South Downs near our home.

Generally, do you buy to hold or sell, and why?

My aim is to buy for the long term and hold for regular income and capital growth. Buying and selling is a very different business and pretty risky as you are beholden to the market and local economics of prices.

After we left our jobs in 18 months we diversified from competitive HMOs into conversions and small developments. We used investors and joint ventures to keep our time available and to de-risk projects. Creating a trading business of guest houses for council emergency housing came from a potential commercial to residential plan. With experience comes alternative options and more opportunity.

3 Top Tips on raising investor finance?

Always get to know a potential investor really well before working with them. Consider a small cashflow loan to start with for say 4-6months so both sides can build trust.

Find out what a potential investor wants and needs before even suggesting any project you may have. It always needs to be right for the investor – not just you.

Never talk about interest rates you can give. This can put an investor off big time. Find out what they get currently on their investments and what rate they are looking to achieve and what level of risk they are comfortable with. I've offered lower rates for someone who might like to learn from the project and look over my shoulder.

What's been your biggest success in property?

Finding ways to solve problems, and there have been many! As I write about in my book, it's important to have a great support network, be honest and have alternative project plans – preferably two or three. Over the first couple of years, I worked hard to find investors and to build relationships with others. Making sure that I was thoughtful about the investors wants and needs and then finding the right type of investment that suited them.

Our new build development and sale of eight houses has been delayed because of Covid. We've kept our investors informed through monthly briefings and although it's costing us in additional build finance interest, none of our investors have pulled out.

What is one thing people misunderstand about property investing?

Many people believe that you can do deals with *'no money down'* and believe the marketing hype that many courses try to sell. Rent to rent is also sold as an easy way for people with no cash of their own to invest…but it's not the easiest of strategies in my opinion. Of course, it's possible…but you need a lot of knowledge and experience to convince a landlord to work with you.

Bridging Finance - expensive or very useful?

Bridging has been there as a backup in case finance hasn't worked or an investor pulls out at the last minute. Whilst building up experience it can be very useful but quite expensive and risky. If there are issues that mean you might need to extend the term, then there can be very high penalties. For a short-term project, it can bridge a gap whilst adding value, for example rectifying a problem such as subsidence or planning issues.

What differentiates you from your peers?

That's a hard question to answer as there are many different approaches to property investing. What others tell me is that it's knowing when to step back and allow others to support the business. We always wanted to do other things with our time – so when the Clipper Round the World yacht race beckoned…it gave us a timeline to work to and a focus to get our business to the stage where we could be more remote.

In 2017 – 2018 John and I travelled the world and ran our property business on laptops. John did the Clipper yacht race and I followed having my own adventures along the way. That was the turning point. It wasn't perfect and we've since got so much better at our back-office systems and processes.

We still invest and manage our guest houses, refurbs and developments from afar – returning to the UK to get new projects underway. Technology and applications such as Asana and LastPass make it much easier to manage projects and the people who support us.

What has property allowed you to do? What has it given you?
Realise what is important in my life and to have choices to follow the dreams I've had since childhood.

My passion is wildlife and conservation as well as teaching. I built an online property education business back in 2017 because I truly enjoy helping others learn. Having run a local mastermind programme for 10 people face to face in 2016, it dawned on me that, through using technology, the cost of a good basic property education could be substantially reduced. Plus, I could coach using Zoom anywhere in the world!

Then I wrote my book Building Your Dream Life whilst based in Australia in 2019. That was something I never thought was possible. Time and our success in inspiring others, along with a book writing coach made this possible.

Currently I'm in Namibia volunteering for a great conservation organisation. John and I have avoided the UK lockdowns and provided much needed support to this beautiful African country.

What's an unusual or weird thing you love?

As I've mentioned I'm passionate about wildlife conservation but I'm not a vet…however as part of my volunteering experience I was able to get very close to the animals. In particular health checks on two lions in the field at Zannier Reserve here in Namibia. Not only monitoring respiration, measuring their teeth etc. but also taking their temperature using a thermometer up the anus! I then went on to do similar checks with the vet for wild dogs, white rhino and cheetah too.

What's the best non-property investment you've made?

My Small Self-Administered Pension (SSAS). Transferring my company pension from my lengthy 21 years of corporate employment has not only given me the ability to choose how to invest it, but also to make sure it is protected for my two children in the future. That's the thing about pensions – most people don't even look at the annual statement and performance as they feel they can't do anything about it.

However, if you are an entrepreneur with a limited company, it is possible, with independent financial advice, to apply to HMRC to create your own pension pot. It has to be administered by a qualified company and there are very specific rules and regulations as to what it can be invested in.

Bronwen will be listening to AFRICA "Nowhere be like Africa, nowhere be like Home" Yemi Alade (feat. Sauti Sol) – (reflects the amazing experience we are having here in Namibia where we have been volunteering for a wildlife conservation organisation. Such wonderful people with hearts full of song). Likely eating fresh seafood if by the coast, shellfish and oysters with champagne, reading Race to the Pole by Ben Fogle and James Cracknell in Holiday apartments in the tropics with a sea view.

5 THOUGHTFUL QUOTES

"Di earnings are just fi di plus, Gratitude is a
must"
- *Koffee*

"Wherever you go, there you are."
- *Thomas à Kempis*

"Be kind, for everyone you meet is fighting a
hard battle."
- *Socrates*

"Fear is the path to the dark side. Fear leads to
anger; anger leads to hate; hate leads
to suffering."
- *Master Yoda*

"Choose not to be harmed, and you won't feel
harmed. Don't feel harmed, and you haven't
been."
- *Marcus Aurelius*

Richard Little

Richard Little has been involved in property development, land, planning & construction for more than 44 years. He is experienced in all aspects of the residential market, from single dwellings to multi-unit new builds and complex conversion projects.

Through his writing in sector publications, and keynote speaking at property and investor events, Richard expands upon the realities of property development. His experience of the highs and lows of the industry's economic cycles gives him first-hand knowledge of how to achieve excellent results within any wider economic context.

With a reputation for ruthlessly scrutinising every deal, Richard's main current business focus is on joint ventures, managing opportunity flow, as well as on land appraisal and acquisition.

FB – Richard Little
LI – Richard Little

Why are you in property?

My father started in construction and housebuilding in the 1950s so in many ways I was born into property. Growing up around construction talk and with frequent exciting visits to sites, the path to a career in the property sector was established in my early years. Whilst I did start my working life at 16 in an office for an engineering firm as a move to make my own way in a different sector - it only took 2 years to return to the energy of the family business.

As a housebuilder, now more commonly referred to as developers, we have been involved in property trading for decades with periodic lump sums bringing a measure of success. As with many housebuilders of longstanding trading has for many years. Only recently have many of us seen the benefits of holding property long term. Periodic, often sporadic sums of profit are fantastic however regular income from held assets gives housebuilders better cashflow and a more certain exit. As a family business we have the third generation heavily involved in our current businesses and the fourth generation already taking a keen interest with 'pocket-money' investments and site visits.

Generally, do you buy to hold or sell, and why?

As developers with a long history of trading we only started acquiring and holding residential property in 2014, which was a direct consequence of my son Brynley becoming more proactive in the longer-term strategy. Following trial investments over a couple of years during which we acquired 3 properties that were converted to provide 7 rooms and 9 studios it was quite clear that as a business we had no appetite to be hands on landlords, particularly with HMO rooms. The 2-year trial saw us source 3 properties direct from the owners, two of which were had financial issues and the third property had planning enforcement issues. We had control of 5 properties of which 2 were single lets and since then 3 have been sold with a fourth in legals as this is written. With a mixed experience of problem tenants and great tenants it became very clear to us that HMOs are a lot of work with relatively high ongoing upkeep costs.

Our move towards building and holding single let properties has been gathering momentum during the last year or so with plans to retain homes on all of our current and pipeline projects.

What's your secret sauce for Finding Deals/sourcing?

All of our deals between 1950s to 2020 have been direct to landowner/vendor. In the early days it was mostly word of mouth and introductions from family and business connections. It is relatively easy to source greenfield and previously developed brownfield sites, but the challenge often comes in connecting with the owners. The team use local planning authority documents and online resources to identify edge of settlement land which we generally take forward using land promotion with a pre-emption to purchase. The planning portal allows us to identify sites that are in the planning process, we get a full picture of any chosen area in respect of consent, withdrawn and refused applications. Also, the team keep an eye on market opportunities, not that we purchased anything prior to 2020 directly through agents.

We feel that it is beneficial to be aware of all opportunities in any targeted area that fit our criteria at the time. For instance, we will often be looking for sites that are capable of providing 10 to 100 dwellings, our preference is for new build rather than conversion. Market conditions changed in 2020 for us with sourcing through agents resulting in our first secured site which was on the market but not widely advertised as the agent approached their preferred connections in order to find a buyer quickly. The same agent then approached us with a second site which went in to legals early in 2021. Connection with agents and proving credibility of delivery is key. This is expected to provide a third of our pipeline in the early 2020s.

Without a third-party introduction we usually write to the owners, as listed on land registry, using a process of 3 letters - each one with a different message and call to action. We give details of our website in the letters which we know gets looked at more often than not. Owners also look at social media and google so it's very important that the public face is both respectable and relevant to the message. We are fortunate to be able to show a long history within the property sector which generally brings comfort to those we speak with.

What is your deal analysis process?

Once an opportunity has been identified and contact made with the owner/s we look to get to the NO quickly. With all the opportunities that come to us we use a 3 meeting and 4 appraisal system. Our meetings are generally direct with site owners and/or their agent, the first meeting concentrates on connection with a view to understanding any owner motivations. During second meetings we will discuss high level numbers in order to get a feel for price expectation. Our third meeting is where we introduce a proposed Heads of Terms. In reality, we do on occasion have fourth and fifth meetings in order to get a decision.

Our appraisal process is carried out around the meetings and is split in to four levels:

1. Initial assessment, where we look at land registry, flood risk, TPOs, access, land designation, market history, planning history and local restrictions. This may be done prior to any first meeting dependent on phone conversation, or more often after.
2. Planning assessment, this is a deeper analysis of existing planning consents; any planning history and/or planning potential. Generally carried out after the first or second meetings.
3. High-level numbers, covering potential developed values, all costs, profit and residual land value. Often, we will look at this level before or at the same point as the planning assessment. With many sites we can calculate the potential end value based on the site size rather than any specific design input.
4. Full-development appraisal, this in-depth analysis covers the key 9 pillars of development, demand, scheme design, planning, costs, deal structure, legals, funding, construction and exit. This appraisal is only carried out should discussions be going well and is an essential check before Heads of Terms are agreed. This part of our process is costly in time and money, and from experience

with others deals -something that many newer and established developers just don't do.

A definite NO for us is generally picked up at initial assessment stage and relates to specific site issues e.g., impossible access, TPO locations, flood issues and land designation. Other NOs relate to the site owner/s e.g., unrealistic time and value expectations. We are also very cautious if there are any more than 3 decision makers as from experience most of those opportunities are difficult to get through legals.

Whilst we don't want any no's, it's important to find any very quickly so we can channel resources to other opportunities as there are always a lot regardless

Is property a 'numbers' or a 'people' game?
From my own experience it is a mix of both as it is with most types of business. Creating great connections with people is essential in order to attract better opportunities, however, in my view some take too much time searching out and connecting. From an acquisitions perspective some opportunities come from our own network however, most come from identifying sites and reaching out direct to the owners. This is where the numbers game comes in. We process a lot of possibilities using our four levels of appraisal with an expectation of acquiring 5 sites from a 1000 direct to owner reach out. Most of the 1000 approaches do not get an answer and some are not proceedable due to planning issues and owner expectation, so the 5 deals come from c25 opportunities where we use considerable resources to further filter out.

We could use more resources looking at the identified sites more closely which would undoubtedly filter out many of them earlier however from experience we know that approach would cost us more money, so we take the view that investing less initially gets us solid results - so that's what we do.

How do you decide to JV with?
We collaborate in many cases with the owners of sites where it is advantageous to them to stay in the deal. This can work with the site

purchased in stages and/or with a lower initial purchase value with additional payments at agreed milestones though the project. Some of our landowners wish to have new homes built for themselves and/or to hold for rentals. Outside of landowners we work very closely with main contractors and management contractors who become delivery partners. We have limited experience of working with investors as partners and to be honest that hasn't as yet been successful as we've found it beneficial to buy them out due to various issues.

We do look at the key individuals and consider their values and character, and where possible we prefer to work with people where we have aligned values. In reality this is not easy particularly when dealing with a number of site owners and main contractors. With individual investors this is much easier.

What are your thoughts on property education/mentorship?
Personally, I've invested a considerable amount of money in education particularly into the world of investing, being traders, the nuances of investing have long been a mystery. The value can be there if someone is offering what you need, understanding what you need is the hard bit. There are a lot of offerings that are marketed and sold very well, unfortunately they don't always deliver value.

Key in my opinion is to speak with others that have been on the training previously and will give you a 'warts and all' review. Longer term and generally high-ticket mentorships can be extremely valuable to the mentees, if I'm honest they are often more valuable to the mentors. Of course, some people will achieve amazing results with the right mindset, lots of action and great mentors. Equally some people do amazingly well by consuming the low cost and free knowledge that is widely available and doing stuff, those people may do even better with mentorship however, we will never know.

The whole area of education and mentoring encourages strong opinions and ultimately yes there are people that really shouldn't be allowed to educate or mentor and there are people who would be much better off not investing in courses etc. but they mostly do with open eyes.

Richard is often listening to soft jazz whilst drinking red wine, reading Principles by Ray Dalio in his attic office, all on his own.

Adam Rana

Adam is a successful property entrepreneur, international business owner of multiple businesses and a business mentor in UK and Dubai. He rose to success in business in a short period of time, building a major successful serviced apartment business of over 22 apartments in a space of one year and generating six figure sums. Adam has since developed his property portfolio to over 40 properties across UK and Dubai.

His passion for property has led him to raise over £1 million in investor finance since 2019 and created multiple business joint ventures.

Adam's previous career in engineering at Jaguar Land Rover helped him establish many invaluable skills in leadership and development, which were transferable and enabled him to set up multiple businesses, since his first success venture in serviced apartments in UK. He left his well-paid job to concentrate solely on the growth of the businesses and property.

IG – @adam_Rana
FB – Adam Rana
FB – Holistic Properties

Why are you in property?

As a young child I was always fascinated by tall buildings and great architecture around the world in real estate, that led me to start investing in my passion and buying properties in the UK from the early age of 22. I am also passionate about investing in assets, and property is probably one of the greatest assets after gold, if done right. It also allows me to live a freedom-lifestyle through my regular income and increases over time in capital appreciation.

My ultimate dream is to go into building developments somewhere in the world.

Why have you chosen your strategy?

My main strategies in properties to date have been Buy to Let (BTL) and Serviced Apartments (SA). BTL has been a traditional, safe and passive income for me since 2013, it allows me to keep taking monthly rents and still benefit from capital growth by holding these properties for a long period of time.

The SA business has been a game changer for my life and family. This is probably one of the highest cash flowing strategies out there in the property world. I have built my freedom lifestyle, regular income, and a great brand through running a SA business. At the time of writing, this business has allowed me to live in Dubai indefinitely while earning daily income in UK (fully passive), a lifestyle I once dreamed of.

It's a pretty effective strategy if you get the correct knowledge and guidance as a newbie. Simply, we rent apartments around the UK and Dubai from landlords under a commercial management lease which is called Rent to Rent *(Guaranteed rent model).* We then let these units out on a short-term rental basis to guests (which is agreed in the contract and the lease) to make net profits up to £1,500 a month per unit, obviously it varies depending on the time of the year and location.

We also do a management only model where we profit share with the landlord and we get paid in a percentage to let these apartments on a nightly basis. The net profits can vary from £300 to £900 per apartment however this comes with less risk to the business as we do not make any furnishing or refurbishments investments like we do in the guaranteed rent model and therefore I would say if you're looking to scale your business quickly, this is the best way.

3 Top Tips of raising investor finance?
Network and network more! Attend all non-property events and if you're in a job tell your colleagues about your side hustle, you would be shocked at how many people have money sitting around in the bank!

When I was leaving my job at Jaguar Land Rover to fully grow my business, I told my colleagues what my new business is and surprisingly a lot of them took interest. Over time after leaving my job a number of my previous colleagues are my main investors. Through my one network of people, I raised £500,000 and potentially more in the pipeline. This is why telling people what you do is important and then to build a long-term relationship with them.

When you travel, go on holidays, go out on the weekend or even at your gym, tell people what you do. Obviously gauge the situation, but when there is a conversation tell them you help investors increase their wealth by investing in 'safe' assets such as property.

Tell people about your successful projects and the ones that were challenging! If you haven't done a project yet, show them what projects you can bring with numbers and how you can provide a good return on money.

How do you decide who to JV with?
The key for me is - do their values and principles align with mine? It is like having a friend but not treating them like a friend. We become friends with people because we are aligned and closely matched usually, and it must be the same in JVs. Otherwise, if you only go into it for money, you're heading for disaster. A partnership is just like a marriage, so it's best to choose a partner wisely to skip the painful divorce and I have learnt it the hard way by not understanding this at start of my business journey.

I also look at their life experiences in general, their wider circle and most importantly if I can proudly say in the future that we are joint venture partners. Depending on what you're looking for, I also tend to choose a JV partner with a secure business network, industry connections, client list, or specific credentials and this will drastically improve your chances of achieving long-term success.

Respect, both ways is important. Do not partner with someone just because they are satisfying your business needs, but you do not have respect for each other. The main purpose of forming a partnership is to achieve success as a team.

I tend to ask them what are their personal visions in business and life? It must be again closely matched with yours. You must create a win-win situation for you and the potential JV partner, before closing an agreement I ask if they feel like they're winning and happy with the deal.

Pros and Cons of your main strategy?
Serviced accommodation is not for the faint hearted however the returns and the reward is probably the best in the industry in terms of cash flow. There are a few challenges, mainly you must remember it will be a 24/7 business, so if you do not quickly build your automation, systems, and people around you then you are set up for 24/7 job that you may not want.

One of the toughest situations I was in was when we had to call the police at 2am to break up a 20-person party in one of our one-bedroom city centre flats. This was early in my days and that's why guest verification, having guest T&Cs to sign and holding a good deposit is so important.
There are lots moving parts in this strategy as its not property, but rather a full-blown hospitality business, so you need to nail every bit of the business processes, hire the right people, and expect to deal with some difficult customers over time.

When you scale up you can be hit by supplier issues as your cleaners and suppliers may not be able to keep up with your requirements, so you need to start working with some big players if you have more than 25+ units.

The pros outweigh the cons for sure, this is the reason we continue to do this as a main strategy and are now expanding internationally in Dubai. Serviced accommodation funds my financial freedom lifestyle, I can travel and live abroad whenever I decide to. It has profit margins up to 40% if done correctly and it's certainly satisfying to have customers give you positive feedback after all your handwork.

They say cashflow is king and this is a key aspect of this strategy. I used my cash flow to replace my corporate job income and now use it to invest in other property assets. I would recommend this strategy to anyone who has a passion for hospitality, customer service and loves meeting new people.

What makes you a good Landlord/lady?
I have been a landlord from the age of 23 which has allowed me to learn a lot over the years. The best advice I can give is treat tenants as customers as you would in your job. I create a high level of 'tenant experience' from ensuring all the admin is done on time, clearly and communicated well at each stage of the letting process.

We manage our own properties under our management company; therefore, we have created a strict vetting process, however I have been using the same process since when I was 23 which has allowed me to have great tenants to this day.

Main points I consider when looking for a tenant:

- Good money management shown on bank statements
- Good credit history and no CCJs
- What are their long-term life plans? gives you an idea of what type of person they're and if they will have rent issues
- Are they fair and honest in the first stages of referencing? even 'small' acts of dishonesty are bad indicators

Do not mess around with the regulations and safety requirements. I also ensure myself and my teams have all the safety standards up to date in line with all the regulations.

Tej Talks

Keeping in touch throughout the tenancy is a great way to be a good landlord, check up with a simple text. Do regular inspections which has helped both us and the tenants in improving the quality and notice maintenance issues early. We also tend not to increase rents as it allows us to keep good tenants in our properties.

The main priority is to make the tenants really feel like this is their home, this is achieved through working effectively and efficiently, regular communication and making sure they have everything they need i.e., working shower, boiler is serviced and in full working order.

What are your thoughts about education/mentoring?

I am a true believer in mentoring and coaching; this can be in the form of networking with new people who are a level above you or through paid education. I am myself a successful mentor in property and other businesses. Through my knowledge and experiences that I have gained, I can share insights and support many aspiring individuals out there. The main reason I still take mentoring is I'd rather learn from other people's mistake and not repeat the same mistakes, essentially get to where I want to quicker from learning from others' experiences. Mentoring takes time and as an individual you must be a driven and ambitious person to go down this route, a mentor will only guide you and coach however you must take action to be successful.

I personally invest in education and mentoring regularly as it continually grows me and opens up more connections for me and as a result my income and my wealth grows continually.

I spent around £4,000 in serviced accommodation mentoring over a year which helped me scale my business up effectively and quickly in line with my vision.

I am regularly spending over £1,000 a year in my personal educational growth through mentoring or masterminds.

Adam will be listening to house music or hip hop, eating a healthy mix grill in a Lebanese restaurant, reading the Chimp Paradox *(for the 5th time!)*. You'll find Adam in Dubai Marina, but in Birmingham UK during the summertime!

Sarah & Rob

Maygreen Investments was set up in 2016, after sitting in a pub beer garden discussing how Rob and Sarah wanted to create a business that would replace their salaries and give them the freedom to decide when, where and how often they worked. In Maygreen's first year of investing, they went from 0 to 7 HMOs, investing over 200 miles away from where they live and carrying out large renovations on all of them.

Their passion lies in the creative side of designing their properties, creating their brand and building a sustainable, ethical business model. They strive to create a business that means more than just the numbers. Delivering outstanding projects to house the most vulnerable in society where they can truly feel worthy of a great place to live is now a big motivation for Maygreen.

They're a married couple so balancing running a growing business and a young family has its challenges, but they wouldn't swap it for the world. There's nothing better than achieving big goals with the one you love most!

Srah and Rob strongly believe in working with a mentor to elevate your success, so it's an honour for them to be included in this book to share their advice. Having an experienced mentor has been a game changer for them and the business. They now mentor their own group of mentees, helping them build successful property businesses like Maygreens. Many of them have now created design led property portfolios that focus on quality and generate an income stream that supports their life goals. To play a part in this process is a huge privilege and passion of Maygreens.

IG – @maygreeninvestments
W – maygreengroup.com

Why are you in property?

We are creative people so the main attraction to property is being able to create incredible, inspiring spaces for people to live. We both have business and finance experience so being able to combine our love for design and creativity with building a sustainable business and an income stream is the perfect match for us.

We as people spend 90% of our time indoors and that figure has increased at the time of writing as we fight our way out of the coronavirus pandemic. Our belief is that by creating functional, inspirational spaces that foster social communities, we create a positive impact on the lives and mental health of our customers*.

Using a property portfolio to build an income stream has given us a level of freedom that we would not have enjoyed in a 9-5 job or even, other types of businesses. We choose how and when we spend our time within the business and our personal lives. Sarah is an Aussie and Rob is a Brit. We will always be dividing our time between the UK and Australia. So, building a location-free business that provides us with freedom is very important. Property is part of that, along with systems, processes and the right people.

We treat our tenants like customers, their rent is the lifeblood of our business so it's critical they feel valued as customers. Our customer service is measured by how we treat our tenants. If our customer service is on point, we retain them for longer and minimise voids.

Why have you chosen your strategy?

We specialise in HMO's for two reasons:

1. We can exercise more creativity with the design of an HMO because it's more desirable for our tenants who are individuals of a younger demographic than the tenant profile of a BTL which typically needs to appeal to families and couples who prefer a more neutral interior.
2. A good HMO provides a much higher monthly cash flow than a BTL therefore, needing fewer properties to create the income we want from our portfolio.

We have two different customer (tenant) profiles, some of our properties accommodate young working professionals who want to live in a high specification co-living property with the best facilities available to them. This customer profile is often looking for like-minded people to live with, so creating a community in the property is paramount to us. Our professional customers tend to be a little more transient, they like being able to move into a property without having to set up bills, council tax etc. They are looking for convenience which is part of the service we provide.

We also have properties that accommodate vulnerable young people who have had a tough start in life. They have full time support within the property by a trained member of staff who lives there 24/7. We are developing properties for those most vulnerable in society without compromising on the quality, design or finish. These properties are on long commercial leases, so they provide a strong commercial platform along with a positive social impact.

HMO's are becoming more heavily regulated which is pushing the rogue landlords out of the market, this is another attraction to us. We relish the challenge of a big project where we can strip a property back to its bones and rebuild it as a safe, compliant place for people to live and love. Competition is fierce in some areas of the UK so ensuring our product is ahead of the competition and competitively priced is essential for us to remain successful in the HMO market.

Tell me about your biggest failure in property so far?
We spent a large sum of money with a 'property mentor' who had a very loose association with the truth. Looking back on that time there were red flags, like some of the advice we were given to not follow legal rules and regulations and to cut corners wherever possible (this was not the approach we took).

This 'mentor' was a great salesman and he convinced us that we should use his build team who shared the same values as him and cut corners on three of our projects. After lots of heated arguments, withholding money and lists of snagging that went into the hundreds, we got the projects finished to a satisfactory standard, but they have cost us a fortune in maintenance over the years.

We learnt a big lesson during that time. Always do background checks on anyone you plan to do business with. Regardless of whether they come recommended or not. If we had checked companies house, we would have discovered the 'mentor' was a banned director. If we had asked to see the builders previous work or speak to their previous clients, we would have discovered there was very little track history, and the quality was not up to standard.

There are lots of sharks out there, be cautious of everyone you are looking to work with.

What are your thoughts on property education/mentorship?
Despite having a bad experience with a mentor. We still believe that working with a credible mentor is a very powerful experience. Having regular accountability with someone who can be your sounding board and can guide you around some of the pitfalls (in property these can be very expensive!) is invaluable.

We've worked with lots of different mentors who have (mostly) provided us with the skill and confidence we needed to build our business in the speed that we have. We think we would have always made a success out of property; it just would have taken longer on our own.

We look at our mentors as non-executive board members. They are paid to advise us and help us grow the business but do not have a stake in the company. Now we have our own group of 1-2-1 mentees who are looking to start or scale their HMO businesses and we take this same approach with all of them.

If you want to work with a mentor, here are some important checks to make. Check they have experience in the property strategy you want to carry out? Can you see actual examples of their projects and are those projects representing quality? Do your values align with theirs? Speak to other people who have had **success** by being mentored by this person. Check for red flags on Companies House.

Finally, no matter how credible a mentor is, they aren't going to do the work for you. Don't start working with a mentor or sign up to a property course expecting that that in itself will make you successful. Don't be a course junky. Choose a strategy and focus on it until you become the expert. The biggest learning is from doing. Listen to your mentor and implement their advice. The quicker you implement their advice and do the work, the quicker you will learn and be successful.

Should people invest in the North or the South?
Before deciding on the area, you want to invest in, what is your strategy? Are you looking to create monthly cash flow to replace your salary by building a property portfolio? Or do you want to generate pots of cash by buying and selling (flipping) properties or developments? How far away do you live from the north or south? How much time do you have to dedicate to property? If you decide to invest far away from where you live there are some big challenges that come with that. The more time you have, the more likely it is you will make investing remotely a success. It's important to have answers to these questions first before you decide where to invest.

In the last 5-10 years many investors based in the south (including us) have seen investing in the north as a great way to make their money go further because house prices are significantly cheaper while achieving high returns from rising rents in the north. Cities like Manchester and Liverpool are experiencing London style regeneration which we believe is nowhere near the peak.

Because of the recent influx of small-medium sized property investors developing property in the north for rental purposes, competition is fierce. HMOs are prevalent in most cities and saturation is becoming more of a problem. All you need to do is look at the quality of rooms in the north compared to the south on Spareroom.com and you will see the quality is far higher in the north. Vendors and estate agents know that a run-down property on Rightmove is attractive to remote investors so it's more and more difficult to find properties that offer true value. If you're expecting to consistently recycle all of your money out of property in the north by adding value and refinancing, you are going to be disappointed. These deals are hard to find and not the norm with property prices still being low in comparison to the south.

That said, the north is still and will continue to be a fantastic place to invest. If you're looking for realistic returns on a fraction of what it would cost to develop an HMO in the south, the north is a great place to start. My tips for investing in the north are, do your due diligence if it's an area you're unfamiliar with. Make your product stand out from the crowd. Deliver a great service to your tenants (customers). Don't be greedy - make your rents fair and competitive to minimise voids. Lastly, if you're investing remotely, your team on the ground especially your builder and letting agent will make or break your success.

What (property related) tools/software/apps can't you live without?
We honestly don't know how we would manage without the software and tools we use, and most are free. Slack and Asana do most of the heavy lifting in our business. Asana is an incredible tool for managing your own team and your builder. It's a prerequisite for our build team to be able to use Asana as it's the only way we can effectively manage all the ongoing refurbishments, as well as all the maintenance issues that come with managing a large portfolio.

Instagantt is a fantastic tool that links to Asana and enables you to create gantt charts for your refurbishments. We have a weekly zoom call with our build team to review progress on site and instagantt works brilliantly for this purpose. Slack is the best communications tool we have ever used. It's super simple and allows you to categorise conversations into channels so it's clear what conversations need our attention and which don't. We have slack workgroups with our internal team, virtual assistant, our lettings team and our 1-2-1 mentees who all love using it to connect with each other and contact us privately.

Other great tools for productivity are Cold Turkey which blocks distracting websites for periods of the day when you're looking to get into some deep work. Time Doctor for managing and monitoring our VA's (based in the Philippines) work. They login to the system each time they start work so we can see when and what they are working on. We can see if a task is taking longer than it should and there is never any question of the hours worked when it comes to payroll.

We couldn't survive without Google Suite. All of our documents are created using Google's tools and central drives. All of our systems and processes are saved in google drives and access can be given to the team members that require them. Our VA's work remotely so making life easy for them by having a centralised set of tools and storage has enabled us all to be more productive in growing the business.

How important is interior design? Any tips?
We believe design is an incredibly important part of any property refurbishment or development. More than that, the level of importance you place on the design of your property directly reflects on you and your company's brand values. In our experience, when you focus on quality design, your end product attracts a quality customer who values the space and respects it as their own. Reducing damages and maintenance and increasing customer satisfaction and retention.

That said, we still need to build a sustainable business model so budgets play an important part. Luckily, these days, there are plenty of cost-efficient products you can source to make your project stand out. It takes time to build a cohesive design but places like Pinterest and Instagram are incredible resources for inspiration. Kitchen companies like Howdens now do fantastic laminate doors and worktops in modern colours that are a million miles away from their cheap looking predecessors. H&M home, Dunelm, Ebay and Iconic Lights are favourites of ours for sourcing interiors and lighting within budget. John Pye auctions offers heavily discounted products from desirable brands like made.com and is great for saving money on big ticket items like sofas and lighting. Our go to supplier for HMO bedroom furniture is Landlord Furniture Company. Their products are durable, look incredible and best of all, they deliver, set up the furniture and remove all packaging from the property. Compare this to furnishing a house with IKEA furniture, where you have to build everything from scratch and deal with mountains of packaging. You'll never use IKEA again!

A huge amount of effort goes into styling our properties to a professional level before the photography. Why? Because the photos, videos and 360 tours become the content that is individual to you and your business. This content is the building blocks of your brand. We can't stress how important this final part of the process is. We have built a brand around quality design. All anyone needs to do is look at our Instagram feed or website and they will instantly see what we stand for by seeing the visual content we use for all marketing. Additionally, having the rooms styled means when prospective tenants come to view your property, they start envisaging themselves living there. Making that emotional connection with the property helps to convert your viewing to tenant applications. Design isn't all about colours and finishes either, how a property functions is just as important. In an HMO, facilities are vitally important. Are there enough laundry facilities? Can you move them away from the kitchen in a utility room or other area? Is there enough kitchen worktop and refrigeration space for the number of tenants?

When we start the design process of an HMO, we start by thinking about how we can optimise the space so the tenants build a community. Our belief is that if we create great communal spaces, that will encourage tenants to socialise, form friendship groups and consequently, love living in the house even more. That means more tenancy renewals and a better income from our investment. Think about cinema rooms, co-working spaces, games rooms, chill out rooms and well-designed outdoor spaces with BBQ facilities. By prioritising the design and tenant experience within your HMO's, you will always stand above the competition, now and in years to come.

Currently listening to Techno Techno Techno and Haux, eating Sarah's home cooked vegan mushroom wellington and a delicious vegan feast, reading black box thinking by Matthew Syed and The One Thing by Gary W. Keller and Jay Papasan, preferably on the white snow-capped swiss mountains in Zermatt or on a beach in Australia with our little family of 3 and the cast of Friends (for the lols obvs.)

TJ Atkinson

TJ Atkinson is a Property Investor and Property Entrepreneur and Property mentor. TJ owns and manages Buy To Let, Commercial properties and Rent to Serviced Accommodation properties in London & Kent. TJ also specialises in a three niche, low entry property strategy known as Rent-to-Rent Serviced Accommodation, Rent-to-Rent HMO and Deal Packaging, where he also coaches and mentors others to use as a foundational strategy to get started in property investing. He truly believes anyone can get started in property by utilising one or all of these three-low entry, low barrier and low competition strategies.

He actively works with new and experienced investors to explore opportunities to create strategies to increase their profit through his Borrowed Property Strategy Program. Tj offers an intensive training and mentoring program. His reviews and success amongst his student are testament to his training style and desire to see his students succeed. Tj is a much-requested property and income creation speaker across the UK. He regularly hosts the 'Breakthrough Property Events'.

He is a best-selling Amazon author of 'The Borrowed Property Strategy: How Anyone Can Earn An Income From Other People's Property', and Untangling Success: 6 Key Principle to having whatever you want which you can order on Amazon.

TJ Atkinson spends his spare time coaching young entrepreneurs in his community, travelling and reading and writing crime thrillers.

FB – Tj Atkinson
IG – @tjalife
W – tjatkinson.com

Why are you in property?

Freedom!

I know everyone in property flippantly says freedom, but in truth, I got into property looking for the best way to leverage my time, which to me is my definition of freedom.

I wanted a vehicle that could pay me in perpetuity but required minimal effort, which would therefore permit me to have the freedom to pursue other ventures.

All my life, I had always wrongfully assumed that in order to make serious money, you had to work 24/7, you have to 'be in' your business, with no breaks, no down time. This was a lie, but a very often misconstrued belief for may new entrepreneurs.

However, the only business or vehicle that seemed to offer the freedom I sought seemed to be property investing. I have quickly learned, that although no business is devoid of effort and property investing is NOT passive, it is certainly one of the most leverageable propositions out there. Meaning on the assumption that everything goes according to plan. A property will pay out a consistent monthly income and offer increase capital appreciation whilst been managed by a property manager.

I wanted the freedom to work if I wanted to and the freedom to take days off if I wanted to and property allows me to do so.

What advice would you give to a beginner?

Be cautiously pessimistic with a high dosage of optimism, until your confidence is developed, through experience. Baseless optimism is delusional and dangerous. In many circles we call it faith. In business, this is called reckless.

I say, property investing is not easy, there will be various challenges. This might not be what you want to hear. It might be more digestible to hear, that property investing is easy, and you will succeed without any problems, but that would be far from the truth.

Guard your heart from disappointment, by acknowledging that there is a chance of failure. Not because there is anything wrong with failure, but simply because most people are not well equipped enough to bounce back after a setback especially at the beginning of your journey.

Failure has the capability of crushing your dreams permanently, however, by managing your expectations, when you experience a level of failure, you will not be crushed because you expected it and had hopefully put contingencies in place.

This might be the most negative thing you read in Tej's book, but it will eventually show up as the most valuable piece of information you will receive in property.

Write down your strategy and write down possible hurdles or problems and then write down possible solutions. This chess strategy means you are prepared for each and every contingency.

Nothing will go as expected and that is the joy of property investing. Double your expected time scales on projects, increase your waiting allowance for mortgages and investor finance. Always think a few steps in advance so you are always ready to implement plan B, if plan A is not working.

3 Top Tips for raising investor finance?
Raising investor finance is not difficult. It is not easy, but it's certainly not difficult. It requires strategy. Most people fail to successful raise funds for a multitude of reasons.

Bear in mind. Investors want to invest, and they are looking for ways to ensure their funds are outperforming our dreaded interest rates. Investors are always looking for opportunities and instruments that will increase their wealth. Your job is to position your proposition in an attractive manner, ensuring the prospective investor is able to visually calculate returns, measures risk and understand possible (multiple) exit strategies.

Before, we further delve any further, please remember that not every person is suitable to be your investor. An investor relationship is like a marriage and regardless of whatever document or agreement that you sign, you are still responsible to them and will have to ensure that they feel safe and secure. This is why you should also be selective with who you allow to invest in your projects. Some investors are a nightmare to work with, some are controlling, and some will require constant reassurance and babysitting. This is why courting your investor is important. Get to know them on a personal level, understand their ethics, understand their attitude.

Raising investor finance is multi-faceted, but it's centralised on these three things:

- Put out consistent content, that demonstrates your experience and ability, ensure that your values and action are congruent
- Experienced and inexperienced investors only buy into people and part with their funds when that have a level of certainty about you
- Visibility, demonstration of experience and congruency are all quick ways to build confidence and certainty in an investor's mind

Why have you chosen your strategy?
I chose Serviced Accommodation as my go to property strategy for the following reasons:

- Serviced Accommodation via Rent-to-Rent offers investors multiple opportunities to secure a property income with a significantly low financial entry point. For example, we have successfully secured properties with less than £1000 and go on to generate circa £500 per month in profit
- Low risk strategy – By utilising rent to serviced accommodation, it allows us as investors to significantly reduce our risk exposure, meaning we are able to return the property back to the owner should we need to, or the property is no longer required

- The hospitality industry is 20 billion pound a year market, and we only need to acquire a small part of that market to make a significant income for ourselves
- Quite often in property you do not get the opportunity for a trial run. By utilising the Rent to Serviced Accommodation model, you are able to trial run a property but most specifically a location and if it is profitable, then you are about to scale up or even purchase a property to use for serviced accommodation
- Deal analysis is easiest in this strategy simply because we have excellent comparable data to gleam information and data from. Hotels have excellent data at their fingertips to adjust their prices and we also have access to this secondary data to build our Serviced Accommodation businesses

Which books do you find yourself going back to after the first read?
'What to say when you talk to yourself' by Shad Helmstetter is my go-to book.

I am firm believer in self-development before any self-education. I don't want to sound too airy fairy, but your attitude and your perspective will determine your altitude but most important your acceleration.

Whenever I start to have doubts in my ability, I find myself reading this book again to assess where that doubt or fear is derived from. Fear in most cases is irrational and many cases (which most people don't know), it is best to sit back, and assess where that feeling is coming from, discover the root cause and detach it from the source so that irrational fear is completely destroyed. Most people push fear aside and this is good, simply because you have not allowed it to stop you from taking action, but long-term growth involves destroying the fear.

In the first chapter, Shad explain that your infantile upbringing and conditioning almost always resurrects itself in later life. For example, if you come from a good home, you are told YES 50,000 time before 18, conversely, in the same home, before 18, a child is told NO more than 160,000 times. Therefore, evidencing why some people have self-doubt, self-belief or confidence issues. I think this is a must read for everyone, especially anyone who wants to get into property investing.

Dealing with your belief system will determine your risk level, it will determine your propensity for action.

TJ is currently listening to anything by Drake or Beyonce, eating Jollof rice and chicken. He's probably reading The Confidence Code by Katty Kay & Claire Simpson, in his home office with his nieces.

Davinder Sanghera

Davinder Sanghera is a property developer and investor with an investment portfolio of £2.5million.

A Mathematics graduate, Davinder worked at three Tier 1 investment banks for 5 years in NYC and London. As a treasury trader, Davinder regularly transacted multi-million-dollar deals with constant interaction with banks, brokers and clients to mitigate against risks and execute the best deal.

Not feeling fulfilled with the corporate role, Davinder invested in a BTL London property to create a secondary income, which led to leaving the banking industry in Feb 2017.

Since going into Property full-time in January 2018, the focus has been on pursuing a HMO (House of Multiple Occupation) strategy where 2 bed terraced houses are identified in key areas to renovate into 5 bed HMOs. These are then rented to either students or young professionals.

SpotTheDave has raised over £1million from Private Investors, most of whom have reached out on Social Media.

Davinder is passionate about Ethical Wealth Creation, Sustainability and Learning Languages. Fluent in 3 languages; English, Punjabi and Spanish, the goal is to be a polyglot.

FB – @spotthedave
LI – Davinder Sanghera
IG – @spotthedave

Tej Talks

Why are you in property?

I believe Financial Literacy and Ethical Wealth Creation are super important. Property is just one of the tools that allows one to create wealth in an ethical manner. Once one is the Property grind, learning about interest rates, calculating the ROI and Cashflow increases financial literacy. I can't say I'm passionate about Property per se. It's the thing I've been slightly more successful at than anything else I've done career-wise. I only started watching Homes Under the Hammer and Interior Design programmes in my 30's, after I took the leap into Property. It's definitely not something I grew up with or was exposed to as a child. My Grandad, who's one of my role models owned a few investment properties and I saw the retired life my Grandparents were living and still live and that's what I aspire to have.

The running joke is that I can't even unscrew a lightbulb. When I see a problem, most times I look at Who can help me in solving the issue at hand? Not How can I do it. It's resulted in me learning how to manage people really well, mainly because I'm useless and I have no idea how to fix anything.

Before Property, I was in investment banking as a Money Markets trader, and I had very little control of my time. I didn't even know why I was doing the tasks set out other than my manager was dictating they had to be done. Whereas Property makes complete sense to me. I understand Property on a Macro level for example how interest rates effect Property Prices, what political and economic factors can affect market activity.

The main reason I invest in property is to reclaim my time back. If I invest in assets now, my future me will be time rich and wealthy. In my former life as a trader, I traded my time for money. I started work at 07.30am, ate lunch at my desk and spent 10-11 hours in an air-conditioned office. During the winter months, I wouldn't even see any daylight. That's not the life I wanted to live. The people around me were bitter, had ego's and overall weren't nice people. I was terrified of becoming like one of those dinosaurs. A part of me still has that trader aggressive mentality.

As quickly as I had got into Investment Banking, I made plans to get out. This calculated decision took me 5 years to achieve. In part, because I had two amazing women managers who showed me what successful women can achieve in a male dominated trading floor. Yet, when my role models stopped becoming my role models, it was time to make a change. I believe in life; one must always be going forwards not backwards. Perhaps one can side-step from time to time. But it's essential to be moving forwards for your goals. Therefore, a big part of me knew that if I left banking, my renumeration would decrease significantly and I was used to living a comfortable life with 12+ countries visited per year. That's when the idea of investing in a BTL and Passive Income came to like a ghost chasing me in a dream.

After buying my first BTL, the amount of comfort and security I felt knowing I had some income coming in whilst I was sat at home with a broken wrist was amazing. Lack of income can cause great anxiety and I was fortunate that after leaving investment banking, I didn't have this as my London BTL was cash flowing a decent amount.

Property is super challenging. There's always a fire to put out. However, if done in the right way, outsourcing tasks to the right people can free up copious amounts of time and headspace that can be spent working on things one is passionate about. For me, it's Learning languages and Sustainability. My goal is to be a polyglot. I'd also love to be making an impact on scale within the Sustainability sphere. I'm currently in the beginning stages of this. So, watch this space!

Why have you chosen your strategy?
I invest predominantly in HMOs. I was led down this route as I wanted to invest in high-cash-flowing assets. What I didn't know at the time was how this strategy isn't passive the way a BTL can be. When deciding on my strategy in 2017, I wanted the highest ROI with minimal time input. I failed to consider the mental energy required too, something that is not spoken about at all.

However, after having set up these HMOs and having had them running in their 3rd year, I'm looking at ways to make it so hands off and passive.

I've always utilised a letting agent to source and manage my tenants. Yet as I'm younger and am only focusing on my own small portfolio, at times I've been slightly better at sourcing tenants and filling empty rooms.

I have a Virtual Assistant to manage the financial admin, something I wish I had started a lot sooner. Passing on the nitty gritty has been great for reliving stress as I am able to have a high-level view on the financials as well as drill into any bits, without actually doing it myself.

How important is interior design? Any tips?
When designing an HMO, the key is to maximise the space of the property so that it flows and all rooms are being utilised effectively. My back to brick renovations results in a blank canvas, where even the stairs are ripped out. This ensures new compact stairs are fitted, usually in the middle of the house and the en-suites can be tucked behind the stairs. Every square inch of space is maximised!

All of my 5 bed HMOs have a joint communal kitchen and living room together. I personally prefer to do this rather than a separate kitchen and separate living room. I think it promotes socialising. Therefore, I always put the kitchen in the darkest part of the communal area, essentially as one enters the communal area on the ground floor, the kitchen is first and the living area towards the end where the patio doors open up to the garden. This is slightly odd as most times the kitchen extractor needs to be ducted out to an external wall and if the kitchen is in the internal dark part of the property, it can mean ugly white casing running along the tops of the kitchen cupboards. However, I've found the flow works so much more. Tenants watching TV and socialising in the living part of the communal area don't get disturbed by those walking past to get to the kitchen.

My 5 bed HMOs all also have a breakfast bar area or an extremely large island. On the very rare occasion I've popped into my HMOs, I've noticed my tenants utilising the breakfast bar area for working and having group zoom calls, as well as dining.

If the space allows it, I'll put in another dining table set. But I'm not too fussed if that's not possible.

3 Top Tips on raising investor finance?

1. If you don't already have a network of high-net-worth family and friends you can tap into, then getting out on Social Media is a game changer
2. Just be yourself and keep highlighting what you're doing, the trials and tribulations you're going through and the successes you're having
3. One thing I failed at in the beginning was identifying whether the person I was speaking to was in fact going to lend me their capital or had the same goal as me: building their asset base. Using the traffic light method when meeting potential angel investors allowed me to figure out pretty quickly whether the person was indeed a lender:
   Green = would definitely lend their capital, even if it wasn't to me
   Amber = would maybe consider lending
   Red = wouldn't lend, is most likely a money borrower too

I spent too much energy trying to convert the Red's when I should've just asked them how they were funding their projects and moved on to the Amber's and Green's. Amber Angel Investors have allowed me to build up my property business. Amber's are those that have never invested privately before but are silently watching. When presented with an investment opportunity Amber's have reached out themselves to indicate their interest. You'd think nothing could go wrong with a Green Angel Investor; however, I have managed meet Green's and they then decided not to invest in me. This was with two Green investors that even met me at my HMO projects. This is then the perfect opportunity to re-evaluate your pitch.

I realised pretty early on, these investors weren't interested in the numbers or the deal at all. They were interested in me and wanted to understand what my values and morals are. Nowadays, I end up talking about the values my Punjabi Grandparents have instilled into me more than the property deal.

The key is to be your authentic self. There are some people you're not going to vibe with at all. We come across these people all the time.

What is one thing people misunderstand about property investing?
The hard work continues after the tenants are in.

Bad tenants can break you mentally, voids will impact you financially and baller investors with 80 properties are sometimes totally comfortable with 50% of their portfolio being empty.

That's not being a savvy property investor.

That's being a muppet.

I personally know Property Investors who are so obsessed with trying to achieve a certain rent per month, that they'd rather have their rooms empty for 3 months than reduce the rent by £25 pcm. Whilst they're too slow to adapt and change, I've knicked their tenants and would've filled my rooms three times over. It's important to look at property investing as a long-term strategy. A £25pcm reduction on 3 rooms isn't going to break the bank. But 3 rooms empty for 3 months at £525pcm is! Do the maths!

Is property a 'numbers' or a 'people' game?
I believe it's both. An investment has to make sense financially. The purchase price, purchase costs, refurb costs, GDV, ROI are all key aspects to factor in when assessing an investment. Don't forget to factor in the interest costs of a private loan. Projects almost ALWAYS go over budget and run over time.

The people aspect in property is extremely important as people are the tenants that generate the income. But there are also so many other relationships involved that lead to running a successful property business. Letting managers, Sales agents, tradesmen, solicitors, accountants, a community of other investors to share the pain and of course, angel investors which allow you to buy properties in the first place.

Having great relationships will enable you to grow the property business even when the numbers may not be growing.

Things always go wrong, there are always challenges and being able to share the tough times is important, therapeutic even.

When you feel overwhelmed, what do you do?
In 2020, I felt overwhelmed, anxious, and sad for a good portion of the year. Things that made me feel better and get out of the slump were:

1. Walking meditation. I discovered a walking meditation and now I use my Headspace app to walk and meditate
2. Walking or running. Even if it's only 20 mins but getting out of the house was important
3. Sharing the struggles with my best friends. I have a great support network of childhood friends. None of them are in property and they've known me for decades. Being able to be real with these friends and being vulnerable was comforting. I would aim to have a call with 2 friends a week whilst on my walks, especially during the time when meeting up in person was forbidden
4. Sharing the property struggles on social media. I've had rodent infestations, broken fences, builder issues, but sharing about this was therapeutic as loads of others had been through the same if not worse struggles. It's
5. Saying no to things that weren't in line with my truth and putting up healthy boundaries in business and personal relationships.
6. Listening to books on audible as I've lost the practice of reading. I can smash through a book a week by listening at 1.75 speed and listening to 15 mins here and there whilst I'm getting ready in the morning or getting ready for bed.
7. Therapy: I did both group and individual and I learnt a lot more from Group therapy and got to connect with some awesome people.

8. Yoga/Stretching. I try to find the time to stretch even for just 10mins a day. When my neck niggles or my lower back is feeling sore, a good yoga session can sort me out. So, I pop on a session on YouTube and smash it out.

Davinder will be listening to personal development books on audible or Electric Dance Music and some J Balvin. Likely eating home cooked Indian food *(Invite her over, she'll bring bottles of bubbles ;-))* in lockdown London but dreaming of a new country to hit up now that she's surpassed 50 countries.

TEJ'S TOP 10 TIPS FOR PRODUCTIVITY

1. I use the following tools to make my life easier, streamline my operations and save time; SearchLand, Hammock, Asana, HubSpot, Google Sheets, LaterMedia, Canva, Pablo, Audacity and Adobe Premier Pro & Audition

2. Read the book "Deep work" by Cal Newport, I aim to follow the principles in there and ensure I have 'no internet' focussed time to get work done, like writing this book. It's hard when we have so many incoming things, and we have to be reactive sometimes i.e., if a deal comes online, but we need time for deep work

3. Use a 'Pomodoro timer' to get yourself into zones of focus throughout the day, it's so simple but it works incredibly well. You'll increase your productivity quickly with this

4. 'Do Not Disturb Mode', my phone goes into this when I turn it face down. So, when I'm working on important tasks, I do this, so I don't get any interference or temptation to scroll social media

5. Take breaks! Not just daily, but bigger breaks like a long walk, a day off, finish early one day, start later another and do what works for you. Burning out is not fun, or cool, ignore the (often American Silicon Valley) types who say that it's okay and part of business. Mental health should be a priority

6. Sounds can be really effective in helping you focus, whether it's music, white noise, classical vibes or 'focus playlists' (Headspace app has lots of these), whatever works for you, give it a go. My noise cancelling Sony headphones are one of my best investments, they really block out the world. Plus, when I'm having a Burna Boy party they really get the vibe started!

7. What you eat, you are, what you do, you become. Eat healthy foods, not as a diet but as part of your everyday lifestyle. Exercise regularly too. I made these things my 'non-negotiables' when I started business, I promised myself I would do these two no matter how busy or hard life was otherwise. It's done well for me,

hence why people call me *'Caramel Thor'* when they see me. HAH.   Just   kidding   ;)

8. When working at home, have a clear physical and mental separation. For example, only take work calls, or be on social media in the 'office', when out of this room you are not 'at work'. Make the areas distinctively different, we aren't all fortunate to have a separate room, but do what you can to break it up and also not let business bleed over into personal time. Easier said than done!

9. When creating content for social media, learn to repurpose or hire someone to do it for you. Every minute counts, it's annoying and inefficient to be creating the same content over and over, or not using one across different platforms/types. e.g., one 10-minute video could become a podcast, 1-minute clips, IG reels, IGTV, YouTube, screenshots/photos and a blog, over multiple platforms of your choice across many different days

10. Enjoy yourself! All the tips before are meaningless unless you're doing something you like. "It doesn't feel like work when you love it" sounds cliche, but it is true. I, and all of the guests in this book love Property, which means our productivity is naturally higher than those who don't. If you don't, then find what you really want to do

Stephanie & Nicky Taylor

Stephanie Taylor and Nicky Taylor are sisters, business partners and unlikely Co-Founders of HMO Heaven and Rent 2 Rent Success. Property has been life-changing for them and now they're passionate about sharing the ethical way to get started in property without having a huge amount of money to start.

Their journey has taken them from overworking and financial uncertainty to starting their own businesses in which they have attracted contracts worth over £2 million in HMO Heaven, their award-winning HMO development and management company. Bought their own multi-million-pound property portfolio of blocks of flat, commercial properties and HMOs with a focus on bringing beautiful, affordable homes to market. And, Created the Rent 2 Rent Success System which has helped hundreds of people achieve success.

They debunk the myth that you need large sums of money to get started in property through their inspirational Rent 2 Rent Success Podcast, YouTube channel and blog. They've been featured in Entrepreneur Magazine, The Telegraph newspaper, Property Investor Today and many others. Their book Rent to Rent Success: Our 6-step system to get you started in property without buying it is a number #1 best-seller with over 130 5-star reviews.

IG – @stephanietproperty
LI/FB – Rent 2 Rent Success (Secrets)
YT – Rent 2 Rent Success Secrets
W – rent2rentsuccess.com

What makes property such a powerful asset to you?

Property is a powerful asset because of the speed with which you can start and the fact that it's the norm to buy property assets with other people's money. Whether it is mortgages, private finance or joint ventures, *in property, it's not your resources which limit you, it's your resourcefulness.*

The biggest property investors and developers are investing with other people's money. And you can too.

I spent decades *not* investing in property and believing that property and business success was for 'other people' when in fact it's available to anyone who wants it. I started investing in property at the age of 45 and am amazed by the fact we've been able to build a multi-million-pound portfolio in a few years, starting with little. But what if we'd started 15 or 25 years ago. As the famous saying goes "Don't wait to buy property. Buy property and wait."

Have an established way to give too, as that makes your success so much sweeter. We love B1G1 who make it so easy to give to charitable projects all over the world through the work we do every day in our businesses.

Why have you chosen your strategy?

We have two main strategies now
1. Rent to rent (R2R)
2. Multi-unit blocks.

Rent to rent is a cashflow strategy and buying multi-unit blocks is an asset-building strategy. I'll talk about them both.

We started off with rent to rent. It's a property strategy that most people have never heard of. Those who do know about it often regard it with suspicion. When I first came across it at the age of 45, I thought:
'This can't be right', 'this sounds like subletting', 'surely it's not legal', and *'why have I never heard of it before?!'*

It sounded too good to be true. Now, after building our rent-to-rent business and helping hundreds of others to do the same, we know it works, and is both is legal and ethical.

What is rent to rent?
We truly love the elegant simplicity of this business model, the heart of it is:

- You rent a property, usually for 3-5 years.
- You pay the owner or letting agent a guaranteed rent and usually you take on paying the bills.
- You rent the property out to tenants as an HMO or SA for a higher rent than you're paying the owner.
- The difference between the rent you receive from tenants and the rent you pay the owner or letting agent after deducting the running costs is the profit that you make for your business.

It's an incredibly efficient business model, as it:

- Requires little money to start up.
- Means you can be profitable within a few months (most businesses are not profitable in the first year).
- You have consistent recurring cashflow (most start-ups do not have recurring revenue).
- You have the names and addresses of your perfect customers (most businesses have to find their customers).

Rent to rent was the perfect model for me getting started, because I had the confidence I could do it. Buying and developing properties felt out of my reach at the start. Managing a property seemed lower-risk and something I could do. As a mum, I knew how to manage a household and I'd managed demanding professional roles, so I had the courage to start. I saw people managing house shares very badly and not caring. I felt I could do it better simply by adding care. I was inspired to do it in a way that would be a win-win-win - a win for our landlords, a win for our housemates and a win for us. That's where the name of our business comes from. I chose HMO Heaven because we wanted to transform HMOs from hellish to heavenly. We're so proud of the service our team provides for landlords and housemates and the fact HMO Heaven has over 70 5-star reviews on Google.

So how can you do the same thing in your business? This strategy works well for beginners who want to get started in property with little money. It's also a great strategy for experienced investors who are buying and managing their own properties, who'd like to leverage the opportunity to increase their cashflow for little investment compared to the big deposits needed to buy properties.

The best way to get started is to learn more about rent to rent. There are lots of free resources online and we have a free Guide and Masterclass to help you get started as well as The Rent 2 Rent Success Podcast, YouTube Channel and blog.

Rent to rent gave us property experience, confidence, consistent cashflow and the freedom to escape our 9-5s. The cherry on the cake is it helped us to buy properties too and that's how we found our second strategy which is buying multi-unit blocks.

Multi-unit blocks are blocks of flats. Typically, it's big houses which have already been converted into flats. It's ideal when the properties are not in good condition and all the flats are on one freehold title deed for the whole building.

We fell into this strategy by accident. We missed out on a succession of HMO properties because a lot of people want to buy HMOs in our area. What we found in buying our first multi-unit block is very few people want to buy them. Even fewer people are interested if some of those units are commercial units (even if it's only one!). Of the few interested, even fewer meet the requirements for commercial funding.

All of this means that

- Per rental unit prices are lower (a rental unit is a flat or studio so there are 6 units in a block of 6 flats, for example)
- Competition to buy this property type is lower
- Sellers are more likely to be interested in a creative strategy which gives them certainty as so many deals fall out of bed when lenders give a 'down valuation'. This is where a lender values a property at less than the purchase price agreed between the buyer and

seller. Creative strategies typically mean the buyer won't need a big deposit or a mortgage at the start.

And multi-unit blocks just keep on giving because they also:

- Save you on conversion costs as the property is already converted. Therefore, you do not have to worry about architects, planning and building regulation applications as you would do in a conversion.
- Give you economies of scale which make all your costs lower.
- More likely to significantly increase in value in a short time. The reason is that when lenders value multi-unit blocks, rental income is a fundamental in their valuation. Therefore, when you increase the rent for a commercial property, you increase the value of the property. And that link is much stronger than it is for residential buy to let property. This comes to the fore when buying unloved properties which can be improved by a simple refit and redecoration.
- Title splitting bonus. When you buy multi-units on one title there are lots of ways to add value and one is to split the titles so you can sell the units individually. What I mean here, is that if you buy a multi-unit blook of 6 flats on one title you can only sell it to someone who is willing and able to buy 6 flats on one title. If you split the titles so each flat has its own title you can sell the flats individually. There is more demand for one-bedroom flats than for a block of 6 flats and, as we discussed earlier, when you sell one flat the price per flat is more than when you sell six in one transaction.

There is so much jam in the multi-unit block cake!

Let me give you an example of the economies of scale. We bought a 12-unit property in March 2019 and paid under £32,000 for each unit including buying costs, and the rental income of each unit is £400 - £600 per month. To buy 12 equivalent rental properties (ie a studio or one-bedroom flat) in our area individually would cost from £70,000 per property, so you can see it's an over 50% 'discount' for buying a multi-let. And we have lower management costs of the units all being in one place and lower maintenance costs as we only have one roof rather than twelve.

The property price was £375,000 and when we bought it the gross rental income was £37,000 per year, when full. At purchase, the lender's valuer, who are normally very conservative in their valuations, valued the property at £500,000. And that was *before* our refurbishment. Our post-refurbishment gross rental income is £66,000 per year. And following the refurbishment and increased rental income we forecast a substantial increase in value which will allow us to refinance and pull out all or most of our initial investment and invest again.

This strategy works well for beginners and for more experienced property investors. Look out for flat conversions all on one title which need some improvement. Depending on your experience, and risk appetite, choose the number of units that best suits you. For example, you could start with a house converted into two or three flats, get some experience and move on from there.

At the beginning, I'd didn't have the confidence to think we could buy a 12-unit property, attract private finance and succeed in securing traditional commercial lending finance. It's been amazing what's happened for us since we first started in rent-to-rent HMO property management.

Once you've set your goals, whatever is right for you, get started! Nobody ever wishes they'd waited longer to get started with property investment.

What advice would you give a total beginner in property?
Start by working out exactly what you want from your life and what resources you have to get started. So few people do this. Doing this early will turbocharge your success. I spent decades on the treadmill being in a sweat, working hard, and going nowhere. The contrast to what I've achieved in the last few years of intentional focus is marked. I've gone from professional level procrastinator to consistent action taker and I wish I'd understood the simple way to do this much sooner.

Tej Talks

Ask yourself the following questions:
- Where do I want to be in five- or ten-years' time?
- Why do I want it?
- What resources do I already have (or could easily get) to get there? This includes time, money and knowledge?
- What else do I need and what first steps could I take to get it/who could I ask?

Once you know where you want to go and why, use the answers and make your plan. Set your goals and take daily or weekly actions to reach them. It sounds so simple, yet it's so powerful. If you can work with someone experienced who can show you the fast-track it can really speed up your progress.

Remind yourself daily of your goals. Set yourself up for success. Keep taking the steps, keep working the system, and you will get there. All you need to do, and this can sometimes be the difficult bit, is believe in your own success, believe in yourself, get out of your own way and follow the plan, even though it might feel uncomfortable at the start. As Les Brown says *"It ain't over, 'til you win!"*

Keep going!

Generally, do you buy to hold or sell, and why?
We buy to hold because we're thinking about legacy. What I love about what we do is how much more we're able to give.

Our mantra for business and life has become believe bigger, be bolder and be a gamechanger. Believe bigger is a reminder to get out of your own way and honour our potential. It's human to look for problems, especially in oneself, so it's important to consciously focus on believing more is possible and acting from that belief. Being bolder is important because many of us let fear of what others will think stop us from taking the action we want to take. Being a gamechanger is about using the abundance we create to become a gamechanger in your own lives, in our families lives, in our community and in our world.

We choose to buy property to hold to create a legacy that will live on far beyond us. To our family and beyond. My son, Alex, is now in his thirties and I'm so proud of him. I often wish I had known this world sooner and been able to bring Alex up in a world of love and abundance rather than love and scarcity. Now we understand the world of abundance it's a joy to be able to share it with Alex and guide him in realising how much wealth he can grow and how much he can give.

It's been so thrilling to be able to share with Alex our knowledge of property over the last few years. He conscientiously saved for some years and has bought his first home, turning down our frequent offers of financial help. It needed a back to brick renovation, so it was a baptism of fire for him! With his own property in the bag, we're excited about what the future holds for him in terms of building on his assets and growing what he has and what he can contribute. It makes my heart sing to know that I can help guide Alex to be able to achieve financial independence whilst also being able to support his family (if he chooses to have children) and leaving a legacy that lives beyond him. It's a gift most people won't ever achieve. For Alex I want to leave the knowledge for him to grow his own wealth rather than leave the wealth without the knowledge assets.

Beyond Alex, we want to have assets in trust for causes we believe in. We want to continue to make the impact we can make when we're no longer here. We have set up a SSAS (Small Self-Administered Scheme) pension and will add additional structures to enable this to happen as our portfolio grows. Bringing old buildings back to life that have been here for centuries before us and will be here for centuries after us, reminds us that we are custodians, to do the best we can and pass on the baton to future generations.

How diverse is the property industry?
Property does feel like a mainly white male industry. We're often asked as Black women, whether we feel people underestimate us. Yes, sometimes they do. I underestimated me for decades too!

There have been times when we turn up to meet a builder or an architect and they've been surprised. I'm surprised too, by the assets we now own, the developments we do and the knowledge we've learned. What makes me feel delighted is hearing from other Black men and women that our story made them realise it was possible too and inspired them to get started. The property ownership rate is just 29% among Black households compared to 63% of households owning their property in England and I'm passionate about helping to change that.

Money flows. And I think most of us would be shocked by just how much money has flowed right through our fingers when we weren't intentional about it. If you live and work in the UK, it's likely that over a quarter of a million pounds has been given to you in the last ten years.

I say this because the average UK salary is £24,500 which is almost a quarter of a million pounds over ten years. Of course, some of that is paid in taxes, but of the remainder you do have control over; are you happy with how you've managed the money that you've worked for?

There are so many ways to get started like we did, even if you feel you don't have enough money, time or knowledge. I regret the decades I wasn't intentional with my money and I wasn't investing. Now I love to help others get started much sooner. Back yourself 100% and take your first steps.

Stephanie is listening to Put Your Record on by Corinne Bailey Rae, drinking lime and soda and eating raw cashew nuts whilst reading Becoming by Michelle Obama. On the roof garden of her apartment in Sienna with her adorable pet dachshund Susie.

Nicky can be found listening to Cheerleader by OMI, sipping a strawberry daiquiri and eating a freshly caught lobster and monster king prawn seafood platter. Likely reading The Louder I Will Sing by Lee Lawrence, in Hellshire Beach, Portmore Jamaica.

AJ Shome

AJ started life as a technology fanatic and in his early work life forged a successful career in software sales at one of the world's largest technology companies.

After building this foundation, he leveraged a lot of the skills and experience from this sales career and started Founthill in 2014 focusing on creating value through land sourcing and planning. Right from the outside, the real ambition for this business was to grow this into a significant and respectable new build development company in London and the South East and over the last few years he and the team have made great strides along this journey. Currently Founthill are working to deliver a committed pipeline of close to £40m GDV and hope to double this by end of 2021.

AJ loves all things personal development and is always looking at new opportunities to grow and push the boundaries. He also has a huge passion for travel, having been to over 120 countries and is relentless in his pursuit of his rather large bucket list.

Whilst still a bit of a social animal, nowadays he tends to spend much of his spare time with his wife, 3-year-old son and 7-year-old rescue dog "Ramsey" who has also become the firm's mascot!

W – founthill.com
EM – aj@founthill.com

Why are you in property?

Ever since I was young, I have been drawn to being an entrepreneur and recognised that property, through all its diversity, is the perfect platform for living this out.

Initially the low barriers to entry and the wide support and knowledge available across the property industry allowed me to dip my toe in initially, but then I soon recognised how varied this sector goes and that is really is an entrepreneur's playground and I was hooked. There is something for everyone in property and there are limitless possibilities, so I thought if I'm going to pick an industry to be in then it might as well be this one!

Growing up I had come from a low-income family that was often faced with financial uncertainty, and so I have always been fascinated and transfixed with building wealth, so my family and I don't have to face these issues in our future. I found that property can deliver for you on all levels of the wealth hierarchy such that you can have cashflow income from rents, you can make large intermittent profits from developments and you can hold high value, appreciating assets that will secure your family's livelihood for generations, all within one sector.

I also love the networking and connection to others that property gives you. I think this was probably the key thing that really opened this area up to me and keeps me motivated. I also think it's also an industry where you can do good in the world and deliver on one of the most important aspects every human being's life, the place they call home.

Why have you chosen your strategy?

Since starting in property, I knew really early on that I wanted to become a developer and I had little interest in being a landlord. Jumping straight into new build developments can be quite risky when inexperienced and is very cash intensive. However, the real break for me came when I found a mentor who honestly changed my life.

He taught me that the real power in property development comes from being able to create value in land and planning first. Being able to source

Tej Talks

land opportunities and gain planning permission has a lower barrier to entry when done creatively and so this provided an ideal steppingstone to getting into the larger developments that we are doing today.

There aren't many people out there that do land and planning very well and so we have tried to excel in this space to ensure that our developments already come de-risked through planning gain and the intimate knowledge of a site that we build up before we go into the build phase. This has been a crucial factor in building a sustainable development business and has accelerated our progress because we now control our own pipeline of development sites, whilst not being at the mercy of the open market.

What advice would you give a total beginner in property?
Be strategic, have a plan and then go and find the best mentor you can to help guide you to execute on that plan. Property is full of niches and creative new strategies, but it is important to go deep into whichever area you set your sights on, otherwise you're not differentiating. It's worth trying to be contrarian in whatever approach you take and don't follow the herd, that's were low margins and risky deals live. Also, don't go chasing shinny pennies! Property is a long game, so pick your area of expertise wisely and stick it out for the long haul.

Don't underestimate the value of hard work, the more you can do to set yourself apart the more successful you will be. Look at what your competition are doing and ask yourself, am I doing things smarter than them or am I working harder. If not, then don't expect anything more than mediocre results at best!

What are your thoughts on property education/mentorship?
I made a complete U-turn into property from a successful career in Sales and Technology and I wouldn't have been able to do that without enrolling in a Mastermind programme to start with and also networking week in week out with other like-minded property people. Building my network in the earlier days was absolutely invaluable and is one of the most important things you can do to help you develop and become successful in this sector.

As mentioned, the biggest step change in our business came when meeting my mentor and good friend Paul Higgs. Paul had an extraordinary background in development with some of the largest developers in the country but is an entrepreneur at heart and also has a keenness to help others. He unlocked a whole new world of possibilities for me personally and within our business and taught us things that have set us apart from other developers, even those who had many years more experience than us! Finding a good mentor can be tough, but it's likely to be the biggest game changer in anyone's business or property journey if they can find the right one.

Generally, do you buy to hold or sell, and why?

I would say that I have done things in a very roundabout way. Being based in London I have tended to flip and sell properties always. Plus, I mentioned, I'm not really that drawn to being a "landlord".

However, this has meant that I have often followed cycles of "feast & famine" waiting for development to cash out before I see any income from developments. In most cases it is advised to create a "cashflow base" first and then go onto do more profitable yet lumpy development deals.
I didn't take this advice though and probably regret not doing more to hold onto properties and generating that cashflow base earlier. I'm currently building a portfolio of single lets to provide this consistent cashflow and I guess the advantage of doing it this way that I now have a bigger pot of capital now to allow me to very rapidly build this base.

3 Top Tips on raising investor finance?

Always focus on how you will protect the downside of an investment and prove this to the investor at every opportunity. Have integrity in everything you do and build a reputation for always doing the right thing. Always imagine it was your money that was being invested and act accordingly. Don't put all your eggs into one basket. Make sure you have a plan B and ideally keep a pipeline of investors because individual circumstances can change rapidly, and you need to be prepared.

How do you find an area to invest in?

We tend to work in specific boroughs where we know the planning authority and local policies really well. Some councils are notoriously hard work, so we tend to avoid looking for deals in these places. From a development perspective, it's really important to understand the demand for certain properties in that area. We tend to focus 'mid-market' family housing in commuter areas with connections to London for this reason.

The numbers need to work for us - so a detailed analysis of the comps and the average £/sqft (Price Per Square Foot) for an area is crucial. Given the ever-increasing cost of builds, it's never been more important to ensure that the sales prices are high enough to ensure the project is viable but of course still affordable, so the units fly off the shelf.

We also need to operate quite locally as we can't be expected to travel too far between sites when we get to the development, as we try to keep as much of the build team together as possible.

Should people invest in the North or the South?

From a development perspective, the south is generally more viable because of the higher capital prices in contrast to build costs, but of course the cashflow is very poor. Some parts of the North still offer exceptional yields and so I would look to those regions more for single let cashflow opportunities.

What's your secret sauce for Finding Deals/Sourcing?

Working hard, being patient and never giving up! In property its always best to be contrarian and not go where the masses are. Try to be one step ahead and get in at the crest of a wave or find a sustainable niche.

Deals of all types are out there, it really depends on what you are focused on. In Land specifically in the early days it was all about trial and error, whilst building up our experience. After some time, you start to get a sense of what works and what doesn't – but I don't think there is much substitute for experience and being persistent.

How important is interior design? Any tips?

It's absolutely huge. We've blown the ceiling price on a number of property sales over the years and I believe that staging and interior design was key to that. Plus, my wife is a passionate interior stylist, so I'd be in trouble if I said anything different!

I also think that when designing houses in the planning stage, you really have to try to understand your target buyer right from the start and design the houses to meet their demands. Often you have to do this is several years from when you are actually going to be selling the houses and the temptation is to leave this until it's too late to do anything about it. So, we make sure we now bake this end user design into our process right from the start.

Simple things can make a huge difference, for example remembering that kitchens are often the most important room in the home and designing them open plan with large family areas attached. Or in the current climate, ensuring that you include a good-sized study can swing someone into buying your property rather than the development around the corner.

Is property a 'numbers' or a 'people' game?

Naturally I'd expect most people to say it's a combination of both and I would tend to agree, but I would say to be really successful in property it is really more about being effective in "business". A great business requires so many things such as control of the numbers, strong relationships, effective marketing, motivated staff, efficient processes, smart use of technology and so on. That's a game all in itself and so your results often depend on balancing all aspects of running a business.

It's also incredibly important to understand your own individual strengths and preferences. Personality assessments such as Myers-Briggs or Wealth Dynamics have been absolutely game changing in helping us to understand the type of activities where we are in "flow" and how to build teams where each individual is playing to their strengths.

We focus a lot on ensuring we have the right person doing the right jobs. Some people are much better sitting behind the spreadsheet managing risks and others want to be out there with people all day everyday growing the pipeline. Both are incredibly important, but it's just very important that people do what they are best at and we come together as a team to make it all work.

How diverse is the property industry?
The diversity of the property industry is what makes it so compelling. There is something for everyone and you get all types of people making a success of it across a very wide range of niches. The industry is always evolving and there are more and more creative strategies that are being uncovered all the time.

In this particular moment in time, more and more diversification is being driven out of the changes to the high street, the impact of the Covid-19 pandemic and the government's policies that are being put into place to boost the economy and reform the planning system. This creates opportunities and those who choose to ride the wave can become very successful in new sectors of the industry as they unfold.

Do you think most property investors are completely honest on social media?
Not really, but I don't really pay too much attention to social media! I'm always a bit wary of anyone who is 'over promoting' themselves and their achievements in property. I've seen a lot of "smoke and mirrors' being used in many of the attention-grabbing headlines and there is not much to keep people accountable. Particularly if they have seemingly done things overnight. Property is a long game and the most successful people in this industry realise that.

When you feel overwhelmed, what do you do?
Often just work my way out of it! We experience lots of crisis moment in our business and I think as a team we generally flip into 'action' mode and don't stop until we get it solved. A good morning routine helps you to keep it together and I have been meditating for some time now, so that certainly helps.

What is your morning routine? Why is it so?
Wake up 5:55am
Drink pint of Water
20 mins – Run / X-train / HIIT
20 mins – Yoga / Weights
20 mins – Meditation
Ice Cold Shower
1 Hours with Family before starting work

I also do an 18:6 fast every single day with lots of green tea during the 18! This routine helps set up the day and allows me to get this out of the way before my son wakes up.

The other thing I'm pretty focused on is increasing my overall healthy lifespan, so this routine has specific benefits in this area (read Lifespan by David Sinclair or The Telomere Effect by Elizabeth Blackburn). Health is really the most important thing in life and increasing healthy lifespan means you have more time on this planet to see, hear and do the things you always dreamed of.

Who do you look up to/ who inspires you?
Tony Robbins – Life and personal development – he is still my favourite personal development coach and is an astonishing human being who has a real connection with people.

Sam Zell / Wiliam Zeckendorff / Candy & Candy – Inspirational Developers who think big and are true contrarian visionaries

Richard Branson – Entrepreneur – His attitude to life is just an inspiration along with his ability to enter a new sector and dominate through connecting with the modern consumer in a way that stuffy old corporates can't.

What differentiates you from your peers?
Hard work - Putting in the effort today that others won't, so tomorrow we can do what others can't. Commitment to business improvement and development – we have quarterly business reviews, strategy days and

lessons learned sessions throughout the year to ensure we are always getting better at what we do.

Resilience – Never giving up. We have become very good as a team at overcoming challenges and problems which crop up and being able to solve complex problems to the satisfaction of all parties has become our hallmark.

What's the best non-property investment you've made?
I would say that I invest heavily in life experiences. Life is for living and I never feel remorse for anything that has helped me to experience more in life. Having never left the UK as a child, as an adult I have been fortunate to travel to over 120 countries and have had a life full of "bucket list" experiences. I see this as an investment in helping me to keep an open mind and retain my hunger to experience more in the world.

I also believe that books and audiobooks are without doubt the best value investments in the world. It is incredible that you can consume the knowledge that has sometimes taken the author a lifetime of work, for less than a tenner and in a matter of hours. I just don't think you can find anything more valuable than that.

AJ is currently listening to Progressive house music, eating Crispy Duck Pancakes whilst reading another business biography, on an airplane with his wife, 3-year-old son and their beloved dog, Ramsey.

Tej Talks

Stuart Scott

Stuart is a multi-award-winning property developer, serial entrepreneur and speaker.

He won the highly prestigious '2019 UK Property Developer of the Year' and '2018 UK Property Investor of the Year'.

Stuart is an innovator who has helped pioneer change in the UK HMO market and is at the forefront of #TheColivingRevolution.

Prior to property he headed up innovation teams designing products & experiences for the world's biggest brands. Stuart has built and sold a number of businesses including a creative marketing agency and a product design company.

FB – The Co-Living Revolution Company (Group)
IG – @stuartscott.coliving
W – theco-livingrevolution.co.uk / co-livingspaces.co.uk

Why are you in property?

Myself and my wife are serial renovators who caught the development bug a long time ago. When I was building my 2 companies, we invested in buy to lets on the side and loved the process of adding value and transforming buildings. Back then we did pick up the tools and loved every minute of it, however, these days I let the builders handle that side of things.

When I sold my company, I had a vision to transfer my skills of innovation, design and customer experience into the property sector. This approach led to us pioneering the evolution of co-living in the UK back in 2015. Although we focus on high performance and high yielding properties, we are on a wider mission to create social impact and drive positive change in real estate.

Why have you chosen your strategy?

I lived in HMO's growing up in Brighton and I had a great time. I am still friends with many of the people I lived with in those HMO's and it was pivotal in creating my social circle of lifelong friends. Back then HMOs were very basic, and we certainly did not have the facilities and environments on offer today, however the principles of social lifestyle and collaboration are as strong now as they were back then.

I decided to focus on the HMO market as it was an industry that had not had any major innovation for some time. There is a reason the industry has such a bad reputation and that is down to old school landlords cutting corners and providing a substandard product. My hope was that by launching a new type of product on the market I would disrupt those landlords and help drive a wave of change as everyone upped their game. My timing back in 2014/15 was perfect as I was on the crest of a wave evolving the next generation of professional HMOs into Co-Living.

Co-Living has such potential to provide a better way for people to live in urban areas. Every product goes through ongoing evolution and this change is great for both the customer and the market. We have an opportunity to genuinely improve people's lives by providing spaces for housemates to socialize, work, collaborate and relax.

Tej Talks

Generally, do you buy to hold or sell, and why?

I like to blend both buy to hold and buy to sell. Every year we always sell at least 1 turnkey Co-Living property and use the profit to pay down debt earlier. I think it is important to have a strategy that provides additional liquidity into the business.

Should people invest in the North or the South?

Ahh the classic North South debate! There are 2 key reasons why we decided to invest in the South. Firstly, I grew up in Brighton on the South Coast and wanted to make an impact in the area I felt most passionate about. I did not want to spend a large portion of my life building a portfolio only to sell off those further away in the future. Secondly my strategy is to blend both cash flow and capital appreciation. Although more expensive to buy and develop in my location, it provides a strong capital appreciation trend that will ensure healthy lump sums available in the future if needed.

How important is interior design? Any tips?

Design is a huge factor in creating a product that both attracts new customers (tenants) and retains them longer (occupancy) as they enjoy the experience. In property there is such a focus on interior design, however this is such a small part of the overall design process. When we design co-living our creative process includes brand experience, communications, onboarding, product design, bespoke design, technology, customer journey and customer research. As Steve Jobs famously said, *"It's not just how it looks, it's how it works"*. Good design will lead to higher rents, higher occupancy and higher valuations. Good design will give you a strategic edge in the market.

How do you manage you refurbs?

We use cloud-based project management software along with spreadsheets to track project progress and budgets. We have also developed templates to create more detailed 1st and 2nd fix appendix documents that give the contractor/builder more information to quote and deliver design-led co-living.

What is your morning routine?

I was never a morning person before property. Over the years I have started to value getting up early and ring fencing the first hour of the day for strategic work. It allows you some quiet time to work on the business rather than in the business. The important thing to remember here is that you are planning, not doing. It is time to think about new concepts, ideas and plans to move your business forward. The doing (tactical work) can then be planned into your calendar. Some of the best strategies come from quiet time and a notebook to sketch thoughts down and work through some ideas.

What makes you a good Landlord/lady?

The key skill is empathy and a customer centric mindset. We are providing a service to customers who will stay or leave based on their experience. We run regular user research studies to gather insight and customer data. For many years' landlords saw tenants as problems and not customers. Customers need to be understood and the relationship nurtured. You are not just selling a room; you are selling a package of facilities and service.

What advice would you give a total beginner?

Learn by doing. Make sure you do your due diligence first and then get your first Co-Living HMO prototype onto market to measure feedback to continually improve the product you offer. Decide on your location and the criteria you are happy with for stacking deals. Once you are happy with the location, minimum ROI and cash flow you can focus on getting out there and finding the right sites.

What are your thoughts on property education/mentorship?

In my previous businesses we always had non-exec chairmen who are basically consultants providing mentorship to owners of companies. These mentors would be people who have done what you are looking to do and can help you fast track your progress. When I moved into property full-time, I had no issue paying for training to help accelerate my growth. I have been part of 'board' style groups, masterminds and 1-2-1 mentoring.

I was put off by the *'get rich quick'* and *'you don't need any money'* side of the property training industry and this always made me wary of training. I was shocked how many people offer training when they had only just learned the strategies themselves. Over the years I have been asked to mentor many people and I have always said no so that I can laser focus my time on developments. In 2020 I finally launched my Co-Living HMO Training company called 'The Co-Living Revolution'.

We host Discovery Day events to learn about HMO's & Co-Living along with our flagship 6-month Co-Living Mastermind programme. On the mastermind we cover the step-by-step blueprint to create your own Co-Living HMO spaces along with sharing key suppliers, products and contacts to design the high-quality end product. I wanted to create training and mentoring that was niche to our expertise after many years of pioneering Co-Living HMOs in the UK. Everyone wants to know how to get ahead of the curve, outperform the market, attract more customers and create the best product available.

We don't outsource this; we innovate the ideas that become HMO trends and share exactly how we did it. That is our USP (Unique Selling point) and it is what I have done my entire professional life. I'm not just training; I am upskilling landlords with universal methodologies and approaches that can help them ADAPT to a fast-changing HMO market.

Stuart will be listening to Groove Armada, reading about Self-Builds whilst eating BBQ in the garden with his Wife and daughter.

Marc Turnier

Marc is the Founder and Managing Director of Arcvelop. A chartered UK Architect, he has worked at some of the UK's most renowned and largest architectural practices, Foster + Partners and Allies and Morrison, where he delivered landmark mixed use, commercial and residential schemes from £50m to £150m GDV across the World.

In recent years Marc has worked as Design and Development Director for various high net worth Private Equity Property Companies in Central London, focusing primarily on commercial and residential conversions of medium to large value-add schemes ranging in value from £0.5m to £20m GDV.

Through Marc's experience and expertise in design-led conversions, Arcvelop offers the unique opportunity to combine first-in-class architectural design and development into investment projects, working with a growing number of Clients, Investors, JV Partners and its own growing portfolio.

Arcvelop now has a breadth of current projects across London, Kent, Yorkshire, Lancashire and the North East.

FB – @arcvelop
PI – @arcvelop
IG – @arcvelop
W – arcvelop.com

Why are you in property?
Innovation, Ambition, Pride, Family and Investment.

These are the five elements of why I choose to do what I do. I grew up dreaming of building a life which my business could revolve around.

Like many people, my core objectives were also to achieve design freedom, lifestyle freedom, travel freedom.

Property made sense for me, I'm entrepreneurial and I enjoy designing. I'm logically creative. Impulsive on some decisions and risk adverse on others.

It's a myth that Architects are well paid. In fact, the reality is, Architect's work extremely hard, with a lot of extra (unpaid) hours. It's one of the negative sides of the industry.

Personally, I take great satisfaction from taking a derelict property with loads of character, stripping back the fabric, exposing the details and re-designing a new proposal within the existing constraints and confounds of the building.

'I like ruins because what remains is not the total design, but the clarity of thought, the naked structure, the spirit of the thing' - Tadao Ando

What makes property such a powerful asset to you?
Property is the 'safest' investment vehicle to building sustainable wealth. It's certainly not a 'passive income', however, there are situations whereby I have created wealth with doing very little...which one could argue is wealth created passively. The wealth created from investing in property can far exceed the amount of time one would need to save.

The easiest way to explain is through an example. In 2016, I was earning a gross salary of £50,000 a year. I was proud of it, at the age of 26 I was the Design Director of a successful property company managing a portfolio of developments worth around £50m GDV. After tax I would take home around £36,000 per year.

In the same year, I also invested my money into a freehold block of five flats, it looked good on the spreadsheet, there were some risks, I took on five existing tenants, and had small cosmetic refurbishments/improvements to do. I added some parking spaces at the front and re-rendered the outside. In two years, I was able to refinance the building, the surveyor valued the block at £140,000 more than I purchased it at. I could refinance and take out £100,000 whilst keeping the flats. Wowzer. Light bulb moment.

Even if I had saved every penny from my job for the last two years... I still would have been £28,000 short of the investment return. Now, not every deal is like this, however, there is the potential with property to make your money work for you. This is a very powerful asset over the long term.

What is your biggest success in property?
I have a couple of personal success's I'm most proud of.

The first would be establishing and growing my business, Arcvelop, creating strong client relationships whilst also working with investors designing our own developments. This success is far from complete, the company has a long way to go, however, I once considered this a bit of a 'pipe dream' whilst navigating my route through architecture and learning my craft.

"Success is no accident. It is hard work, perseverance, learning, studying, sacrifice and most of all, love of what you are doing or learning to do."
- Pele

The second success would be building my portfolio and business alongside working. It really was like running two jobs at once, however, I can say it's given me the opportunities to invest in larger projects, a steep learning curve of experience and the ability to continue building intergenerational wealth for my family. These are my best success' to date; however, I'm always looking to the future to find the 'biggest' success.

How important is interior design? Any tips?

Interior design is one of our core values. It's incredibly important in our company's vision. It generates new business, it creates sales, it visually sets us apart from competitors, it's the branding image of our company. Our branding and interior design style was intentional from the beginning.

"Architecture is really about well-being. I think that people want to feel good in a space …on the one hand it's about shelter, but it's also about pleasure." - Zaha Hadid

Within the property industry, we have seen a large increase in 'Instagram-able properties', the bar has well and truly been lifted within our 'property ecosystem'. This is no bad thing. For years previous, student accommodation, professional HMO's, buy to let's, commercial conversions, social housing could be painted magnolia and sold for the top profits. Now we are seeing that to operate within the top 5%, you need to be designing properties over and beyond what was previously expected. There is competition, and it's ultimately raising the quality of accommodation for the end users (the tenants).

This process will displace the landlords who give property investors a bad reputation. It will organically replace the run-down accommodation where opportunities are presented.

So, if you enjoy producing well-designed accommodation you're going to do well, it not, you may be forced to up your game!

How do you manage your refurbishments?

Whilst banging my head against a wall, usually.

Strong communication, problem solving, people management and don't forget the contract or the contingency.

Tell me about your biggest failure in property so far?
Like everyone, I have many. Some are property related, others not. I thought I would give a couple of examples.

Growing up I competed at national level in swimming, I trained 9 times a week (6 evening sessions, and 3 morning sessions), It was a tough sport and dominated my life at a young age. I breezed through local competitions, the 'Yorkshires' regional competitions and the North-West winning golds at every level. Eventually, I got to the Nationals and I soon found out I wasn't the best or the fastest. I came 4th in one of my events, it was good, but ultimately, I had failed my goal.

However, looking back, it taught me a lot. The relentless training, pushing myself to be faster, mentally focusing and preserving in a competition. Sometimes winning and sometimes failing. The mindset which I developed from it has helped me much more than the medals.

In property my biggest failings have been from not acting quickly enough, not trusting my instinct and mistakes made through the experience of managing small and large developments. There is no avoiding it. This is still an on-going process, and I don't believe you ever stop failing.

"I want to be able to look back and say, 'I've done everything I can, and I was successful.' I don't want to look back and say I should have done this and that." - Michael Phelps

Which books do you find yourself going back to after the first read?
'*The 4-Hour Work Week*' (4HWW) is the bible I go back to. It changed my whole perception of working and how valuable my time is work. It was one of those light bulb moments. Prior to reading the book, I was often working 70–80-hour weeks for a large corporate Architecture practice which wasn't personally fulfilling. The 4HWW pushed me to think about achieving more by using less time through outsourcing, systemising and creating new habits in order to achieve freedom. Ultimately, it made me rethink things.

At the end of each chapter, the book takes you through a series of challenges/tasks to interrupt the way you currently work and think. These could be as simple as changing your approach to emailing people back or creating a mobile lifestyle. The book is appropriate for everyone interested in changing their lifestyle, business or how they currently operate in their career.

It's a book I enjoy cover-to-cover, regularly re-read my notes and I truly believe it has had a large influence on my career and setting up my own business.

My other choice has to be 'How to win friends and influence people' by Dale Carnegie. This book really deep dives into managing people and bettering your communication. Loads of great nuggets and real-life examples to take into any business or different life scenarios.

3 Top Tips on raising investor finance?
My three top tips would be:

1. Create a profile online, network and showcase everything you are working on. The earlier you do this, the better. You never know who's following your progress
2. Tell everyone what you're doing. Everyone has a degree of interest in property, even subconsciously, as you're dealing with people's homes
3. Be transparent, honest and upfront. People really appreciate these values

What differentiates you from your peers?
We keep it simple. We combine architecture and development for our investors (as the name suggests). We have an in-house team of talented Architect's trained at the most successful practices in the UK, who integrate first class architecture and interiors into each investment project.

"Architecture should speak of its time and place but yearn for timelessness." - Frank Gehry

We pride ourselves on adding value through our vision, expertise and creative design solutions. We're also property investors, so we know how to work within a budget!

You can find Marc sipping on elderflower tonics (occasionally with gin), listening to 80's dance classics (traveling whenever possible!) but most likely working between London and Valencia, whilst simultaneously trying to read and learn español. Hola!

Rich Liddle

Richard was a Military Officer, helicopter and jet pilot for 21 years, and is also a successful property investor and developer, with a passion for providing homes to those more vulnerable across a spectrum of needs. Graduating from Newcastle University in 1998, Richard joined the Royal Navy as a helicopter pilot and saw combat around the globe, including the invasion of Iraq in 2003. He has been on operations in Libya, Syria and multiple times in Afghanistan where he was involved in many multinational operations.

Three years flying Search and Rescue helicopters covering the West Coast of Scotland proved some of the most exciting, dangerous and challenging conditions ever seen; 212 live rescues included rescuing fallen climbers from Ben Nevis, sailors from sinking boats and even the swift movement of premature babies in incubators between remote Scottish locations in order to save lives.

He even bought a development building while deployed to Afghanistan using only a satellite phone to secure the deal. This took remote and challenging investing to a new level!

Richard is an advocate for the eradication of homelessness within the ex-service and veterans' community. With the Supported Living Gateway, he hopes that the whole Supported Living Sector can benefit from improved communications and smoother relations between providers and developers, collectively working together to provide homes and spaces to improve everyone's future.

Richard enjoys travelling and spending time with his family. His lasting claim to fame is his role as an X Wing pilot in the Rogue One Disney movie that is part of the recent Star Wars series.

FB/LI/IG – Rich Liddle / Supported Living Gateway
W – supportedlivinggateway.com

Share one message to everyone on the planet

I am a great believer that our time on this planet is short. Having spent over 21 years in the military and over 10 years deployed on active combat operations I witnessed more times than I care to remember the speed at which life can be taken away from us. Time is the greatest gift, but it is also the quickest to be taken away.

We all have ups and downs; we all have days of feeling low, but we have to remember how lucky we are. We have been given a great gift, and it is up to us to use that small scoop of the universe that was given to us to the maximum, use every ounce and enjoy it. Every person on this earth dies, it's a guarantee along with taxes, but not everyone truly lives. As Michael Schuller once said; "the bad news is that time flies, the good news is you're the pilot."

We can't make more of it, but we can make more of the time we have.

Live hard, live free and enjoy every minute.

Best non property investment made

This is an interesting one as I have a passion for watches. I know many people and especially men have the same passion as sometimes it is the only piece of Jewellery a man will wear but my passion stems from my childhood which is an interesting story that leads to this investment.

So, I was born in Bahrain as my father worked in the oil industry in the 70's. During this time, he acquired an 18 karat rose gold Rolex Day Date watch. Now this thing never left his wrist and as he came back to the UK and retired it still never left him, he would garden in it, on occasions leaving it in the flower beds where it had come off as he pruned his roses, he would fix the car in it and to him it was just a watch.

From an early age my brother and I were fascinated by this and always asked to wear it as we sat on his knee, we would put it on and let it dangle on our wrists like an Arabian price, the weight of the gold making it hang down. This obsession was with us throughout our childhood and it was something that brought us closer to my father, being part of his love and passion for this watch which went with him everywhere. It is ridiculous to think of all the things he did whilst wearing this solid gold watch.

So, this image and thought stuck with both my brother and I as we grew up and both to this day have a passion for vintage and classic Rolex watches.

A few years ago, I was involved in a project to commission a Rolex watch specifically for the military, very limited numbers and only available to a certain group of people. While I was involved in this project, I got the opportunity to wear a classic Paul Newman Rolex Daytona watch from 1977, my birth year. I realised I had to have this watch and dually convinced myself with one of my favourite quotes by Richard Branson; "If you see an opportunity, say yes and figure out how to do it later", and I had an opportunity to buy an extremely rare watch, at an exceptionally good price (still 5 figures mind) and it was from my birth year. I committed that day to buy it and would find the cash by hook or by crook.

I did find it and I still own that watch to this day, I, like my father, wear it for its beauty, it was never bought as an investment, much like my father's Rolex, it was bought as I loved the history and story. That watch now is worth over 1000% of what I paid. Not only the best financial investment but also the best sentimental one, and one I will hand to my future generations.

Why are you in property?
For me property was about one thing and one thing only… choice.

I began as an 'accidental landlord' back in 2003 when the small terraced cottage I owned and lived in was rented out as I deployed with the military to Iraq for the invasion of a country, we were declaring war on. When we were given the order to deploy on Operation Telic, we had no idea how long we would be away from home, so I moved out of my home and rented it. As I was sat in the blistering heat of the Iraq desert, I used to smile each time I would see a little rent payment drop into my account.

This sparked what would become a lifelong passion for property and passive, alternative income.

The reason I turned this first incident into a more professional thing was due to the path I was being led down in my career. I was a military helicopter pilot on the front line and spent a long time deployed and away from home. Having done this for a number of years I realised how fragile this was as a career, many of my colleagues had to retire from flying due to medical issues and numerous other things, we were subject to extremely stringent medical examinations and tests every year and it didn't take much for your flying certification to be revoked. Even though I loved my job, I realised I had to have an income of equivalent size should I for some reason not be able to continue in this very specialist field.

What is your deal analysis process?
Deal analysis for me is the most critical area yet I find so many overlook this aspect. Deal analysis is generally done when a deal is found or seen and this usually kicks off the process, but this is far too late.

In the military we had a saying, 'train hard, fight easy', meaning we practise and practise, we work on all emergency scenarios and simulate everything time and again, so our reactions become second nature. This training ultimately means on operations when we are confronted with a real situation our reactions are second nature.

I apply this thinking to deal analysis. The more you do and practise, the faster you become, and also you become more accurate. It also allows one of the most important skills to be developed, the ability to dismiss a deal quickly and move on. I see all too often people trying to make a deal a deal because they are blinded by wanting to make it work. Another thing I am passionate about is what I refer to as a 'strategic knowledge base'. This is the key data surrounding your area and can take a while to do it but once it's done and stored in your head it only needs to be refreshed every 12 months maybe. This involves big picture things like governmental plans for the region, the strategic housing and market assessment for the area, the councils plans. I would look through the planning departments projections for the region, find the average price per square foot for all pockets of my region. I then plot all of this on a 1:5000 map on a wall and this becomes, or forms part of my strategic knowledge of the area. The next thing I do which again people tend to pay lip service to, is get the boots on the ground. I walk an area at different times of the day and just feel the atmosphere of the region. All of this before I have ever entered any details on a spreadsheet. Again, a good old military saying, 'time spent in reconnaissance is seldom waisted'.

Why have you chosen your strategy?
My current strategy in property is that of supported living. Having been a landlord for a number of years I have seen the ups and downs, the good tenants and the bad, the CCJs and the court cases. These are all part of the territory and part of the journey.

I always wanted to give back and help those less fortunate, or maybe down on hard times and I witnessed a startling reminder of how quickly things can change during my last trip to Afghanistan in 2011. Two colleagues of mine who were at the pinnacles of their career, ultimately professional and people I looked up to, went from this elevated position to the brink of homelessness within what seemed like the blink of an eye. They came home with crippling PTSD and saw family lives crumble around them, domestically and professionally they fell so quickly, and I couldn't believe my eyes.

For this reason, I delved deeper into the world of supported living which ultimately not only enables me to assist with housing some potentially vulnerable tenants, but it also allows me to be far more hands off. This is all down to the nature of the leases which I strive to obtain on these properties where they are handed over fully to the care companies on long term leases, so they can provide the support and wellbeing to the tenants as well as a home.

It was this reason that myself and four others established the Supported Living Gateway which is designed not only to make it easier for the property investors to get into this strategy by providing the right communication and contacts within the organisations but also it made it easier for the care companies and housing associations to find properties which fitted their needs. This ultimately leads to a very solid business model as well as enabling the moral box to be checked too, which is something, we should all spend a little more time on helping those around us.

We spend a lot of time in business saying don't look back and keep going forwards, learn from the past but don't look back, however if we all took a look back every now and then and offered a helping hand to those behind to bring them up to our levels, we would all ultimately progress both further and happier, and that is what supported living is to me, it is my chance to help those that need it the most.

Rich is currently listening to old school hip hop from the west coast of America and all things 80's to relive his youth, he loves the history of music and the growth of hip hop and gangsta rap is a fascinating story of entrepreneurial mindset, grit, determination and never giving up.

(Rich: I love an Indian, and not just you Tej!) but he has a soft spot for a really spicy curry. It is a meal which not only tastes amazing but always seems to be more sociable than others and just evokes a happy feeling within Rich. Property has given him the time and ability to spend more time with his partner Aimee and 2 children, their passion is for travel and adventure.

Andrew & Mary

Andrew and Mary are qualified architects with over 20 years combined experience working on award-winning projects in the UK and Australia ranging from single family dwellings floating in the Thames through to airports and London underground stations. They have taken their design skillset and applied it to their property portfolio to create high-quality spaces on a budget, that their tenants are proud to call home. Their background in architecture makes it easy for them to quickly assess an opportunity and maximise its potential, increasing the tenant experience as well as the profitability of a project.

Their design ethos focuses on creating 'healthy happy homes' with the end-user in mind. They priorities greener energy homes, with a strong sense of considerate design to maximise great user experience for healthier happier living. They put design at the forefront of everything they do and believe that good design can save money, increase returns and create considered beautiful homes without breaking the bank.

They invest in HMOs in Leeds and are scaling into larger new-build residential developments and commercial conversions. They also have experience with Serviced Accommodation and the R2R sector and like to get creative with deals having secured projects direct to vendor via probate and under lease options.

IG – @elitedwellings
FB – @elitedwellings
EM – contact@elitedwellings.co.uk
W – elitedwellings.co.uk

Why are you in property?

In 2015 we quit our jobs and went travelling around the world for a year taking in 16 different countries in 4 continents and have never looked back since. It's very difficult to go back to a 9-5 job, trying to climb the corporate ladder after that type of experience. We want to visit every country in the world and have visited about 50 countries so far but there's still a lot more to see! In order to do this, we realised that we need to be able to earn money passively, without trading our time for a salary. Whilst nothing is truly passive, we can choose when and where we work on our business, and the returns we generate for the work we do is significantly higher than any salary would pay us.

We are qualified architects, and so our skillset in design, construction and project management, along with our desire to create beautifully designed homes meant that property was the perfect option for us. Sometimes you can be too close to something to really see its potential, and we originally looked at multiple different ways that we could earn money to support ourselves from email marketing to selling tea. Our background is in commercial architecture and we worked on developer led projects that needed to generate a profit. It wasn't until we stepped back a little that we realised we were already in the right industry, it's just that we needed to be the developer.

Why have you chosen your strategy?

As mentioned above, generating income is the priority from our property portfolio; meaning cashflow is the most important factor for us. We love the security of Buy to Lets (BTLs) but in our experience the monthly cashflow is low (£250+) and we felt we would need to build a large portfolio to meet our targets. We started with a Serviced Accommodation strategy, and whilst the monthly cashflow was great (average £1000 a month), no matter how systemised we were, it was a business that required too much of our time.

We ultimately landed on Houses of Multiple Occupation (HMOs) because of their ability to generate similar cashflows per property as Serviced Accommodation with less time spent on management and we

Tej Talks

could use a smaller portfolio to support ourselves financially compared to BTLs

What advice would you give a total beginner in property?
The Elite 3 Ps: Patience, Perseverance and Practice:

1. Everyone says that property is not a get rich quick scheme but, we don't think people truly understand that until they start. It will take time and patience to reach your goals but, quitting won't make it happen any faster. It's important to focus on the small steps you can make and when you are just starting out, try to do one thing every day to ensure you are moving your business forward. Eventually the compounding effect will bring you exponential growth and the rewards that you want.

2. It took over 90 viewings for us to obtain our first property and when people hear that number their jaws usually hit the floor! Most people will give up long before they have viewed that many properties and ultimately it was perseverance that kept our business growing. There will be many obstacles throughout the various stages of being in property and you have to find a way to overcome them. If it was easy, everybody would be doing it.

3. Every project you do will be unique in some way, no matter how many times you have done the strategy before. There is a very steep learning curve when developing and investing in property and the more you do, the more you grow. We build our confidence with every property we develop, and every mistake is a lesson learnt for next time. Practice is our education.

Generally, do you buy to hold or sell, and why?
We buy and hold our properties as we want to build a portfolio. Monthly cashflow from rent is more important to us than chunks of cash because our goal is passive income to support our lifestyle. Despite this, we know there may come a time when we need to sell a property in order to release funds and increase the pot of cash to help the business continue to grow so it's not a hard and fast rule. We are also driven by long term

Tej Talks

generational wealth over short term profits which is created through holding property for many years.

On average property values double every 7-10 years so when you take into account compounding, that's an 8x increase by the time we hit the average UK retirement age. In theory, a £100,000 house will be worth £800,000 which is a far bigger profit than any flip deal.

How do you manage your refurbishments?
As we are architects, we self-manage our refurbishments. We learnt very quickly that specialist tradesmen generally carry out work much better and faster than a 'do it all' tradesman or contractor and bringing trades in for short burst helps to keep them motivated and energised. Through our expertise we can work effectively with the people we hire as we are able to communicate with them and understand their needs and how they work.

We produce a full set of drawings including things like layout plans, electrical layouts, wall finishes, floor finishes, drainage routes, kitchen and bathroom elevations and setting out. This is supported by a detailed specification document listing exactly what products we want to be used and where. This is issued to each of the trades, so they know exactly what is expected and quotes are submitted before any work starts. By communicating clearly, the quality we expect and overseeing the projects ourselves we can be confident in the end product we produce. This may change in the future when we hope to spend more time abroad but at the moment it is the best option for us.

What's your secret sauce for Finding Deals/Sourcing?
We have a few strategies for finding deals but, our secret sauce is that we have systemised them with our Virtual Assistant (VA). As one example of this; we have trained our VA to scrape property data from various desktop sources to find suitable properties for sale on or off the market. They now have the knowledge and the ability to analyse them at a high level to see how many rooms we can achieve, what improvement opportunities there are, and what the estimated ROI might be based on our average room rates in each of our target areas. They then alert us to

view any suitable properties so that we only see warm leads. We also have a similar process for direct to vendor leads that culminates in our VA sending out the letters for us using templates we have pre-written.

Hiring a VA is a great way to expedite your business growth and is definitely something you should look to do early. Our VA is based in the Philippines and is paid £2.50 an hour which seems crazy low here in the UK but, is a good wage for him. At the beginning, they require more of your time as they get up to speed but, once they have learned the processes, they can save you hours. It's a great feeling going to bed and waking up to work being completed for you!

How important is interior design? Any tips?

For us, interior design is so much more than placing colour on walls and adding soft furnishings in a room. Interior design is about the overall space and how it comes together to form one considered whole. As architects we have a duty of care in providing great spaces and prioritise creating places where our tenants feel happy, healthy and proud to call home. Looking at it from an investor perspective, good design can ultimately increase the end value of your property meaning more money can be withdrawn at refinance stage. Alongside this, higher quality, well designed. spaces attract higher rents and better tenants. Higher rents = better cashflow and better ROI. On the flip side, getting the design wrong can be a real turn off for tenants and leave you struggling to fill your properties.

However, before you start throwing lots of cash at your properties and installing all the brand names, the real skill lies in doing this whilst maintaining a budget.

Here are some rules we suggest you try and remember when you are designing your next project:

1. Maximise space wherever you can and reduce un-rentable spaces like corridors. Keep spaces like en-suites efficient to prioritise primary spaces
2. Plan your spaces wisely at the beginning. Check measurements on site and ensure all your furniture fits and co-ordinate sockets

to be located next to beds, desks, etc. The more you design, the more you minimise abortive work that will need to be redone

3. Understand your end user when considering the interior design, the look of a co-living space is very different to the look and feel of a buy-to-let house. HMOs have a greater scope for you to get creative whereas BTLs are generally blank canvases for tenants to stylise and make their own home

4. Be timeless and not on trend; try to avoid the latest fads and if you really want to use them, limit them to areas that can easily be replaced or updated when they go out of fashion

5. Be budget conscious and a savvy shopper. Creating great spaces does not need to break the bank but must improve the end value

Is property a 'numbers' or a 'people' game?

Both. When you are analysing a deal and submitting offers, you have to listen to your numbers to make sure you don't overpay/overspend on your refurbishment or buy a dud. It's so important you don't let emotions drive your investment decisions and are willing to walk away when the numbers don't stack. Property is an investment strategy so no matter how much you might hate maths, you're going to need to learn how to navigate a spreadsheet or two.

On the other hand, dealing with agents, vendors, tradesmen, etc. requires good people skills and an ability to build relationships. Our first HMO was purchased from a vendor who said they would 'never sell to a greedy landlord'. By listening to what he wanted from the deal, understanding his passion and woes, educating him about our business and how we operate, we were able to secure the property. If you can build relationships with people, then doors will open for you.

Is there a quote that means a lot to you? Why?

Mary's favourite quote is the phrase *'where there's a will, there's a way'*. It's a motto that we embody in our business and it helps us to get over any hurdles we face. No matter what challenge we come up against, we know we will find a way through it.

Andrew's favorite quote is *'everything you believe is a myth and that's a beautiful thing'* by Yuval Noah Harari. We create our own realities and ultimately our own limitations and by labelling them as myths helps us to realise that we have the power to change them.

Mary and Andrew are currently Listening to Harry Styles, eating 75% dark chocolate, Jay Shetty's 'Think Like a Monk' at home (but wishing they were abroad).

Laura Muse

Laura Muse is a Property Developer based in Sheffield, in her first year she raised over £4m of investment through the power of Social Media.

Her company I Squared Property which she runs alongside her husband James has grown from strength to strength enabling them to double their portfolio to 14 units in the first 12 months.

Laura specialises in raising private finance for their business. They are now coming to the end of their second New Build projects of 3 units, they managed to build and sell them during lockdown and it as funded by an Angel Investor. 2021 sees Laura and James purchase a 18 unit commercial property taking them to 33 units and also have some very exciting projects coming up.

Laura and James specialise in BRR, build to rent/sell and Commercial in Sheffield and surrounding areas as well as running a Lettings agency to help other Landlords with their investments.

FB – Laura Muse – The Social Propertypreneur
LI – Laura Muse
IG – Laura Musa

FB/LI/YT – I Squared Property

Tej Talks

Why are you in property?

In 2015 my world completely changed forever…

that spine-tingling gut-wrenching moment when you are told your only parent has stage four cancer and they think she only has a few more weeks left to live.

My mum and I had been best friends and partners in crime forever. I was brought up in a single parent home and the sacrifices my mum endured to ensure I had the best start in life are truly humbling now looking back now as a mother myself. We were told this devastating news in Dec 2015 and unfortunately by April 2016, after many months of chemo my mum lost her battle with such a cruel illness. During the time my mum was poorly I still had responsibilities in the career I had worked all my life to achieve (equine nutritionist). It still demanded me to be at work, away for weeks at a time, still attending sales meetings - I was consumed by the corporate hamster wheel and governed by the powers that be.

But really? Did I let this job take away them precious last moments with my mum?

Yes 100% I did. It is a regret I will have to live with forever.

People say it takes a life changing event for many people to see the light… I was one of these people. That was the turning point that me and my now husband James decided we wanted to create a life on our terms, our timetable and with choices. The only thing we knew that would make us money whilst we slept was property. From there an adventure started and I joined our property business in September 2018 and the rest they say is history…

What advice would you give a total beginner in property?

Mindset is king, queen and everything in between, having the right mindset will serve you well in the world of property. Many people I meet fail because they don't take the time to understand their current mental state, what works and on-going practice needed to be implemented every day, because when the going gets tough (which it will) you have to keep yourself on track. Keep pushing forward, overcome people's opinions (especially family or spouses if they aren't on this adventure with you), you need resilience which all come from you and your mindset.

We nearly gave up, we couldn't get a mortgage because we had sold our businesses to put everything into property, in hindsight it was stupid, but we had to make ourselves uncomfortable to get back to what we had and more not just in money but TIME! We tried many brokers who tried and failed, finally we met the one who we still work with today. But we could have given up and still been a slave to the JOB.

Don't give up. You're one more NO closer to Yes...and YES IS EXCEPTIONAL!

How do you cope with the stress of Property?

Wow... it's still a work in progress but it's about you. I work with my husband and that in itself was a learning curve, we don't have a job where we leave at 5pm and don't deal with it until 9am the next day. We live and breathe Property - is that right? Maybe not for a lot of people but we truly do love what we do. Stress is a part of the ride, my husband and I have a mind-set coach who we have worked with for many years helping us explore how to identify the triggers and how to manage the really stressful times in a variety of different ways, for me its exercise. Walking in the Peak District is my escape from Mum, Wife, Investor, and Landlord. Daily meditations *(which sometimes are every other day)* and journaling are what keep me sane so I can be the best I can be on that day. When it gets too much, I take time out, from 20 minutes to a couple of days or weeks because I've learnt and understand how I work and what I need to get back to my best and this is what works best for me. I'm not into the hustling until you die quotes, I think its bollocks!

Who wants to spend every hour of every day working? Life's too short, you have to live... and enjoy the adventure *(something I'm still working on myself every day)*.

Tej Talks

3 Top Tips to raise investor finance?

The number one question I always get asked is *"How do I find investors?"*

What people should ask is *"How can Investors find me?"*

1. Tell everyone what you do, from the school run to family, friends, past colleagues. The power in sharing what you do will open up the opportunities to start flooding in from places you would never expect, and the potential is limitless
2. Social Media – Posting consistently, being transparent and ultimately visible in Property groups and on your Profiles and Pages. Building up 'Know, Like and Trust' can be done incredibly quickly on Social Media. It took me 7 weeks to raise £600,000 from SM. Tell people what you do, how you can help them and giving social proof you are out there actually doing this not just talking about it
3. Networking – This comes in all shapes and forms, online, in person, property events, business events, every day is a networking day you just don't know it yet

What's been your biggest success in property?

We have done some incredible projects from building New Build homes in lockdown to acquiring an 18-bed commercial property for a substantial discount and many more projects in between but my biggest success in property is the time. We have created a lifestyle where I never work on a Friday, I have a mummy and daughter day every single Friday and have done so since 2018. I never would have been able to do this in a 9-5 job or in my previous business which again was a job.

We have built up our residual income to £5,000 net a month in 18 months and after the refurb of our last acquisition this will exceed £12,000 net a month, which doesn't take into consideration other build projects. This isn't me bragging, this is me sharing how property can change your life in a short space of time. Property has given us choices because of the income and that is our biggest success - time to spend as a family when we choose.

Do you think most property investors are completely honest on social media?
NO, NO, NO!

I have found myself subject to believing everything that I hear online, and unfortunately there are a lot of people making out that they have a lot more experience than they actually have, more assets, and the list goes on. Property trainers are the worst. I have had Property training and it was fantastic but then I've had property training where I have found out the person doesn't have as much experience as they said initially which when you invest a lot of money you feel like they have had your pants down *(Yorkshire saying)*.

Please research who you are going to work with from trainers to property traders, please don't hand over any money until you have proof and an iron clad loan agreement (which they have a means to pay out back if it goes wrong). We are complete transparent and everything we have done good, bad and when I've got it wrong it is on social media for anyone to see, if only more people were as honest.

What do you do in your free time?
I love the outdoors, being a horsey girl since I could ride at 5 years old and I take any opportunity to get outside in the countryside. I gave up horse riding in 2016 to start a family, but I have no doubt I will return to this lifelong passion when it is right for us but in the meantime, Hiking, Mountain biking, Wakeboarding, Diving or Skiing I'm ya gal.

What's an unusual or weird thing you love?
I don't know if it's weird or unusual, but I love caravanning… there I said it at 35 years old we love it and can't wait to get her out up and down the UK this year haha!

You can find Laura listening to 90's Pop Hits, eating toasted marshmallows, in her caravan somewhere in the UK with her fellow amigos James & Isabelle Muse.

Niall Scott

The co-founder of Scott Baker Properties, The HMO Platform & Asset Manager at co:home - a nationwide coliving operator. As a property development specialist, he focuses the majority of his time on building the Scott Baker Properties coliving portfolio, which first started in 2015 after attending a property investment training course.

Working alongside his business partner Matt Baker, in their first four years, they built a portfolio worth nearly £5 million, primarily funded by investor financing. With a passion for coliving and knowing the benefits that community brings, he also mentors coliving property development investors at The HMO Platform. They very much practice what they preach and it's their authenticity as a company that's allowed them to grow, connect and inspire others over the years.

Before property, Niall was working in customer service within the financial sector, and before that, he completed a degree in Horticulture. His connection and fascination with nature drives his passion for the need to provide sustainable living experiences within their coliving homes. He personally has a keen interest in reducing waste and educating housemates about how to reduce their consumption and live-in harmony with the planet.

Their team at Scott Baker Properties & The HMO Platform think alike too, and as a result of the company culture, they constantly look for solutions to problems. In April 2021, they launched Property Goes Wild – an environmental awareness campaign educating HMO & coliving property investors and developers about how they can help rebuild the UK's ecosystem and stop the decline in biodiversity.

LI – @niallscott
IG – @niallscott82
W – scottbakerproperties.co.uk

Why have you chosen your strategy?

I started investing in property in 2015, starting off with BTLs and then moving onto HMOs and now focusing on coliving. I became an entrepreneur as the corporate world was not for me. Property seemed like a good way of generating an income and building wealth as well as creating a more secure future.

It became quite evident when I started investing in HMOs there was, in my view, a missing link. Most investors were focusing on the property and what returns they could achieve, which is important, but there were very few thinking about the customers; in this case tenants. Having worked in customer service for a long time "the customer" was always a big part of any business, sometimes referred to as Know Your Customer (KYC), so this approach was surprising to me.

This mindset has resulted in a lot of areas becoming "saturated" with HMOs, but it's saturated with lots of substandard properties. What we refer to a beige box, these properties, whilst functional, are not appealing nor do they stand out from all the other beige boxes, hence the saturation. Because of this we have devised our Tenant First Method where we start with the end in mind. We refer to our tenants as Housemates and our demographic is mainly young working professionals. We ask them what they want from the property they are going to live in by surveying them to get their views. We spend time and effort on the interior design to create spaces for social activities, workspaces and chill time. We encourage coliving as opposed to just renting a room in a shared house, this not only helps with reduced void periods but also helps with their mental wellbeing. There are a lot of young people suffering from anxiety, depression and loneliness. Despite living in shared houses, they rarely spend a lot of time together which has an impact on their well-being. We encourage housemate led viewings, so they have more input in who they live with which increases the chances of them wanting to spend time together instead of alone in their rooms. At Scott Baker properties we aspire to be the leaders in shared living in the UK.

Moving from BTL to HMO was always the plan as HMOs generate higher returns and better cashflow (or at least they should do) which was a quicker way of getting out of the day job. However, they are much more complex and have lots of rules and regulations to be aware of. It is not simply a matter of splitting rooms up and building extensions to create more space; e.g., local authorities can restrict the conversion of family homes (C3) to HMO (C4) by implementing an article 4 direction. Local authorities can also dictate the sizes of bedrooms, ensuites and communal areas; above that which is set out in legislation. It is very important to know what is required in your area as it can result in fines, refusal of licences and empty properties. A investment property is only an asset when it is putting money in your bank account every month. Build teams also need to know the rules and have experience in HMO conversions and management agents need to be able to deal with the added workload which comes with shared housing.

What advice would you give a total beginner in property?
Don't be afraid to ask for help or to outsource the parts of the business you don't like or are not good at.

When I started out, I wanted to do everything myself and was convinced this was possible – despite having a full-time job at the time. I soon realised that was not the case! There are things I like to do, things I am good at and anything else should be outsourced. About a year into being a property investor I started working with Matt and things started moving a lot quicker with an accountability partner and someone who was good at the things I am not. From this Scott Baker Properties was formed and we now have several businesses and a team of about 15 who work with us. I could not have done so much without the team around me.

Of the team we currently have there is a mix of skills and experience from finance director, VA, accounts manager to marketing and project management. I am not a fan of spreadsheets so having an Accounts manager who really enjoys them is a no brainer for me. I also have a social media expert who looks after all the social media accounts for the company. Although I like social media, I am by no means an expert and lack the time to spend on it.

What has property allowed you to do? What has it given you?

I love to travel; it is one of my biggest passions I did a lot when I was younger and before I got tied to an office desk! Being in property has given me the freedom to be able to travel a lot over the past few years. In 2019 I went on a Safari in South Africa for 12 days with a group of friends which had been on my bucket list for as long as I can remember. That was one of several trips that year, so for me being able to do those trips without asking *"the boss"* for time off is very important to me.

Property also means I don't have to worry about how I will support myself in retirement, I didn't really think about this until my Father passed away. It was a wakeup call for me and got me thinking about my own future and how I want to live my life. Now I am in control.

Which books do you find yourself going back to after the first read?

I read a lot but one I'd go back to again and again is Think and Grow Rich by Napoleon Hill. It's a book to be studied rather than just read. This book was the one which really cemented the benefits of Mastermind to me. In this book Hill describes a Mastermind as: *"The coordination of knowledge and effort between two or more people who work towards a definite purpose in a spirit of harmony".* I have been involved with several Masterminds over the years and now run our own at The HMO Platform as we have seen how powerful they can be.

How do you cope with the stress of Property?

There is no denying property can be stressful at times and there are several things I like to do to manage those stressful moments.

- I have a morning routine which sets me up for the day and consists of a mix of the following – reading a personal development book, journaling, meditation, exercise, thinking time and affirmations. Select a routine that works for you and don't worry about what works for others; E.g., a lot of people struggle with meditation, therefore they should focus on something else. Personally, the worst thing I could do in the morning would be to watch the news before I have completed my routine. That would put me in the wrong frame of mind and that's not where I want to be. I do miss the odd day here and there but being consistent helps deal with stressful situations when they arise

- Talking it over – One of the benefits of having a business partner is being able to have them as a sounding board. Sometimes just talking it over clears any fog or uncertainty.
- Fresh air – get away from the desk and get out into nature. I am a country boy at heart and going for a walk in a park or open space is a good tonic for stress.
- Read/listen to Podcasts or motivational books – Reading or listening to a mindset or positivity book or Podcast is another way I find helps if I am having a bad day.

How do you find an area to invest in?

This is a question I get asked a lot and, in my view, it's not a straightforward question to answer. However, as with everything, I would suggest start with the end in mind and work back. Answering the following questions should help narrow down the areas:

- Who are your customers (housemates)? Are they young working professionals who need to live close to transport links or are they medical professional and need to be close to the local hospital?
- Which towns or cities are attractive to your target demographic?
- Which towns or cities have good employment options for your target demographic?
- Where is the demand for good quality housing?
- What's the budget?
- What lending options are available, E.g., is this a first purchase where lending may be limited?
- Is there access to additional funding, perhaps from family?
- What's the target income from the investment?
- How will a refurb project be managed? If it's a 5-hour drive and the intention is to self-manage – how realistic is that?

This is by no means a comprehensive list but by answering these questions it will become more clear which areas to start looking.

Niall is drinking Cabernet Sauvignon, reading The Wim Hoff Method whilst listening to A Star is Born soundtrack in South East London.

Tara Coley

Tara is a curly 30(ish), ex Financial Adviser, Mummy, ex-South London girl (now country bumpkin) and the other half to a pretty amazing man and mother to 3 kids. She is no stranger to being broke, to struggle and misfortune, she spent the first couple of decades of her life pretty poor. So, if that's your current existence- *SHE GETS IT* and is here to help.

Her fate changed when she fell pregnant with their amazing son 9 years ago. She was working in a banking job in central London, and just knew she wouldn't get to be the 'present' mummy she wanted to be if she didn't quit and find another way!

After a huge meltdown whilst staring at the pregnancy test, she set herself a pretty lofty income goal of creating £10,000 per month passive income through property investing in 18 months, her big WHY was so she could quit her job and be at home with her boy.

Her 18-month sprint to freedom saw her wildly pursue something that was pretty darn scary and at times felt unattainable. She did it, and yes it almost killed me. Hence why she checked out of London and live pretty simply in the country with roaming ponies.

LI – Tara Coley
YT – Tara Coley
W – taracoley.com

FB/PI – Wildly Simply Free

What do you do in your free time?

Free time was a foreign concept to me up until a decade ago. I was earning 6 figures in a corporate banking job in the City, I had a large office overlooking Oxford Street, yet still, I was struggling to reconcile how I would ever slow down enough to start a family with my husband who *desperately* wanted to.

I tried to persuade him we should wait a few years, or at least until I 'slowed down' a little. But I knew deep down there wasn't a clear path of how to do that.

A few months later, I stared at the positive pregnancy test and burst into tears. They were tears of frustration. 'FLIP!'

I knew I wouldn't be the Mummy I wanted to be. I knew my current job would mean I'd have to drop my kid off whilst it was dark, and pick him up after dark, *(I'm not judging any Mums who do that by the way)* but my goal was to be there for my child's *'first' everythings*...their first word, steps, solid food etc.

Getting my time back was the only worthy goal I wanted to make, but how?!

I got an email invitation to a property conference and decided to go, dragging my hubby along with me. I observed first-hand the testimonials of many people who had replaced their income relatively quickly through property investing having gone on some courses and implemented what they had learned.

We were broke from our wedding, but I asked my husband if he didn't mind trying to do a few courses to figure out how we could change our financial position.

The courses were good; and gave me the tools I needed, but the implementation was very hard.

Tej Talks

I embarked on a plan to quit my job and replace my income through Property, I had 9 months of pregnancy, and 9 months of maternity leave, therefore 18 months to make it happen. I promised myself I would not give up.

The goal? To create £10,000 per month passive income through property. I had just shy of 18 months to hit it. My biggest problem? … No cash to buy property. Thankfully I found a few people to back me and my strategy, they invested in me. I used 'buy refurbish refinance' which allows you to recycle your money so you can buy another and another and another with the same pot of cash. I bought on average a property a month in London for a year.

18 months later I handed in my notice and quit my job. It was the best day of my life. I burst into tears.

I spent the first few years of my sons' life going to baby classes, meeting up with NCT mums, swimming classes, having picnics, doing a lot of cycling whilst building my property business each day with the support of a mother's help.

My Son is now 8 and we've since moved out of the 'big smoke' in search of a slower pace of life in the countryside. We live in the New Forest, close to the coast.

I've learned to slow down a lot, I spend a lot of time, cycling, in coffee shops, hanging at the beach, reading, pottering around the house, baking, and just doing mummy and property stuff combined.

My Portfolio is now valued at approximately £12,000,000 and we have a very strong cash flow covering our living costs, and the expensive needs of our growing family *(as we've gone on to have lots more little people!)*

I deliberately started my Facebook group 'Wildly Simply Free' to encourage myself and other people to *Wildly* pursue their dreams and goals, live *'Simply'* and get *'Free'* in time location and bank balance. You can join here. bit.ly/wildlysimplyfree

3 Top Tips to raising investor finance?
1. Get an investor pack together, this should include everything they might need to know about you/your deal and what's in it for them
2. Get confident in your numbers – create worst, mid and best-case scenarios
3. Know the process of how to protect your interest and theirs

What differentiates me from my peers?
I find a lot of property investors/developers are working very hard in pursuit of financial independence, and many seem to burn out. I was there in the first few years; I cried every month. But I had a moment where I realised that I have got to enjoy the journey and create balance.

These days I tend to be doing the complete opposite. I buy 1 property a quarter and work a few at a time. I just want a simple life and that is what I am drawing closer to.

How diverse is the property industry?
This is an interesting question; I can only share my personal experience from what I've seen of diversity in Property. But as a woman of mixed heritage *(my father being of Trinidadian descent and my mother Scottish)*, I can honestly say in my years of heavily investing in property I have not seen a huge array of people from the BAME community investing in property, and even fewer in Property development. I often find people are very surprised when I tell them what I do.

Having grown up near Brixton and being a born and bred 'South London Gal', plus the product of an inner-city school *(that didn't have the best reputation)*, most of my dearest friends growing up are from either a Black African/Black Caribbean background.

There was one commonality between us all, our families did not have a lot of money. I have seen first-hand that the findings from the recent 'resolution foundation' study are indeed true. People of Black African ethnicity have on average one eight of the wealth of their white counterparts. People from Black Caribbean Backgrounds prior to Covid had just £1,000 in savings. Whilst people of White ethnicity had £197,000 in savings.

Lack of accessible cash is a huge reason for the lack of diversity in property, however, I believe there are so many other reasons too. Injustices of the past, lack of being able to easily access higher education due to income, therefore, lack of being able to compete for those higher-income jobs.

I have come to the conclusion that because investing in property is cash intensive it is not as easy for a person of the BAME community to step into as easily as their white counterparts who statistically might be able to tap inheritance/family with savings to help them get started.

Those people of Diversity that I have seen do very well in Property, often do so in the lower cash-intensive strategies such as Rent2Rent, this is clearly due to lack of start-up cash.

I am very aware that the main reason I am where I am today is that I have been able to work with investors who have backed me financially, and now we're in a position where we can choose whether we do or we don't work with investors. Obviously, there are always exceptions to this, but I would love to see this change.

What has property allowed me to do? What has it given you?
I don't have the desire to be glued to my phone posting across social media platforms all the
hours in a day, I spend the longer school holidays like summer and Easter travelling around Asia with the family. I used to mentor but have completely paused that to free up my time.

The goal is to continue to free up my time and be a present Mum, so I have more time for other things. I am on social media but mainly in my FB group. My time is mainly spent continuing to build our wealth and inspire as many as I can, but as a mother of 3 kids, I'm just mindful to not get caught up in doing too much. Then missing the stuff that really matters in the process!

Property has allowed me to help more people and give me the life I want. I've helped many mentees get Financial Independence. I've also had the privilege of opening a Women's refuge for women fleeing domestic abuse, my husband and I both work from home and are hands-on with the kids which is a dream. Plus, we travel a lot, normally 3-4 months I year. I would not be in the position I am now without property. We continue to move towards more commercial type developments most recently a B&B to 6 flat conversions and find this means we need to do less work/ apply for less lending/ deal with fewer builds for a greater return.

How I can help you? My boomerang programme literally contains everything I use to implement the BRR strategy successfully and has helped me build the wealth we have, it took me ages to put together, it really is what I believe to be the best out there, and what I wish I had access to when I was first starting out. You can find out more about it here, http://bit.ly/taracoleybrr we will offer a 30% discount to any reader that wishes to buy the programme just email support@taracoley.com and quote this book in the subject line.

Tara is in her beach house in Thailand, eating Jerk chicken with Rice and Peas, and Plantain and Dumpling, listening to I'm Still in Love With You by Sean Paul, with The hubby with a Mojito in hand.

Lidia and Alex

Alex started his successful career in property finance working for the largest specialist mortgage lender in the UK for several years. He worked his way up and then decided to have a complete career change by joining one of the world largest technological giants. Alex worked in a leadership role for a number of years, building a solid foundation and skill set in procurement, project management and sales before becoming a full-time property developer in 2020. He is a wizard when it comes to re-configuring a property floor plan and knowing exactly how to make the best use of every inch of space. Alex project manages all our developments making sure the projects are delivered on time and on budget.

Alex is passionate about cooking, fitness, travelling and spearfishing. His dream is to beat the world's free diving record.

Lidia has a wealth of experience in housing, law and finance gained from working in the banking sector as well as one of the largest affordable housing providers in the south west. This has been invaluable for the growth of WCB Homes particularly securing mortgage finance, dealing with the legalities, negotiating property deals and ensuring they complete on time. Lidia enjoys looking for derelict and unloved properties to transform into beautiful homes. Lidia is passionate about interior design and loves bringing together affordable elements to create perfect interiors. Lidia is a professional bargain hunter and is known for delivering some fantastic refurbs on a shoestring budget.

Lidia is passionate about yoga, salsa dancing, travelling the world and food.

FB – @WeCreateBeautifulHomes
IG – @wecreatebeautifulhomes
WS – wecreatebeautifulhomes.co.uk

What makes you a good Landlord/lady?

We really think gone are the times when landlords could get away with faded magnolia walls, pay as you go top up electric meters in each room, mouldy ceilings and stained divan beds with flee infested mattress. The tenants deserve so much more!

We treat our tenants as valuable customers, and our business model is heavily focussed on user experience. We place our customers' needs and aspirations at the heart of everything we do. Our design-led approach provides unique customer-centric spaces for people to live, socialise, work from home and feel like home. We provide comfortable beds, memory foam mattresses, desk spaces, functional lighting, an abundance of storage space, super-fast business broadband, full laundry facilities and cleaning services. Our tenants also benefit from generous communal areas such as lounge, kitchen, home-office, hobby room, separate laundry facilities and well-designed outdoor amenity spaces.

Going paperless alleviates problems like lost documents and slow payment processing. Online forms, digital tenancy agreements, and mobile and auto-pay options for rent payments are convenient for tenants. Our tenants also appreciate the ability to quickly and easily submit maintenance requests and schedule repairs online.

Customers also like to feel appreciated, listened to, and rewarded on occasion. If they're good tenants who keep the place clean and always pay their rent on time, we always find a way to thank them for it, whether it's a gift voucher on the anniversary of their tenancy date, or a small birthday gift.

Just like loyal customers will spread the word about brands they love, happy tenants will share their rental experiences and promote your properties for you.

The systems we use are:

- CRM – Click Up, this is for tenants, investors, suppliers, project management etc
- Inventories – Smarter Inventories

- Lendlord – for managing our portfolio
- Go Tenants – Tenancy Management
- Xero – accountancy
- MileIQ – for business mileage

What's your secret sauce for Finding Deals/Sourcing?

We use different types of marketing, Facebook Ads, leaflets, direct to vendor letters, social media. We found that in our area 'we buy houses for cash' type of marketing doesn't work. The average house price in our area is £380,000 and people are naturally cautious of any 'cash' promise, often thinking it's con.

Our best strategy is to get the agents do all the leg work for us! They have established brands, huge marketing budgets, access to portfolio or tired landlords, sales and negotiations skills, insider knowledge and much more! Why compete if you can work together. We found that building strong working relationships with local agents have brought us more off market deals than direct marketing. It works both ways, where we get to hear about any potential deal first, and the agent is guaranteed a fast and hassle-free sale.

We now have a few agents on board who understand creative strategies and we are in the process of setting up a lease option and an assisted sale deal.

Another great way of finding deals is using social media. We frequently post on our personal profile about what we do in property and we've recently had 2 DTV deals coming directly in our inbox.

Do you think most property investors are completely honest on social media?

There is no way to know for sure.

I think many property investors use social media to build their brand, attract investors and JV partners. Most mentors or property education courses teach you to have a social media strategy, outsource social media management, repurpose your content across different platforms, target your message based on the outcome you'd like to achieve.

Most property investors use social media as free marketing tool. They strategise around their message, plan their content weeks in advance, use different scheduling platforms to post at specific times of the day and across multiple platforms. These accounts are very easy to spot; non-engaging, non-personal and repetitive.

One of the indicators for me personally, that someone may be overexaggerating their achievements is when a property investor is 'smashing it', every. Single. Day. Sellers are throwing themselves and their below market value properties at them, solicitors are completing in 14 days (possible, but this is an abnormal solicitor behaviour), tenants are behaving, investors are queuing up to give them funds, and of cause they gone from zero to a multi-million pounds business in 12 months.

I only follow property investors on social media when I can feel their authenticity. When they share their daily struggles as well as successes and when they are not afraid to admit their mistakes. Some of our investors explicitly said they've spotted us on social media and made a decision to invest in our business because we share the good, the bad and the ugly. I think authenticity and honesty on social media, particularly in the property world, is rare, but there are some amazing property investors who I hugely respect and follow for being open and honest.

What differentiates you from your peers?
I think few things. I am hugely ambitious, determined, very positive and I believe everything is possible, you just need to find a way. I came to the UK with £100 in my pocket and I hardly spoke the language. Fast forward to now, our property portfolio in Bournemouth is worth £1,900,000 and our ambition is to grow it to £10,000,000 in the next 3 years and start investing in other people's businesses to help them grow and become successful.

It didn't happen overnight of course - many sleepless nights, huge setbacks, trials and errors, cowboy builders, unexpected bills...but you will never find me dwelling on a problem or feeling sorry for myself. If something unexpected happens, I instantly switch to a solution mode. I am naturally very positive and happy person, I embrace imperfection. That doesn't mean that I don't push myself to be the best version of myself, but I never compare myself to others. There will always be someone smarter, wealthier, funnier, you can easily go down a rabbit hole of comparisons and find all the things wrong with you and your life. I am just happy being me and grateful for everything I have.

My greatest believe is, if you can dream it, you can do it! But of course, you have to put in the leg work too.

3 Top Tips on raising investor finance?

- Social Media. Most of our investors found us on social media. The key here is to be consistent, honest and authentic. People invest in people (obviously the deal needs to stack up too!). If you can get the same return on your investment with 10 different people, you are likely to invest in someone you resonate with, who shares the same values and who is similar to you. We like people who are like us. If you are not on social media, sharing your journey, how do you expect investors to find you or know that you are looking for funding? In the last 18 months we've raised over £600,000 of investor finance through social media alone
- Friends and Family. People who are just starting out in property often overlook who in their immediate circle may have savings. We've raised a significant amount of money through friends and family. Think about it, you are helping them grow their savings. What would they like to do if they could earn that extra pot of cash? Go on a family holiday? Buy a new car? Sign up for a training course? Or buy a new garden shed? Make it your duty to help them make this happen! When you think about it as helping people, you will find it much easier to start those conversations that we dread when we are new to property and looking to raise finance
- SSAS Networks. SSAS investors are always looking to grow their pension pots. Join SSAS community online, or locally to you. Build your network of them and use them as a lender. We found

working with SSAS trustees so much easier compared to bridging or development finance.

If you could share one message to every single person on the planet, what would it be?
"If we really love and believe in ourselves, everything in our life works"

Over the years I realised that best way to win ourselves is to appreciate how special you are. There will never be someone like you.

You are a big deal!

Make doing things you like and enjoying your life a priority. It's about proactively creating a life you want instead of living the one you think you are stuck with.

For many years, I thought people like me, having come from under-privileged background, are just not destined to become a business owner, or a homeowner, or being able to positively impact on other people's lives. I was making excuses for myself, blaming my past for where I was at that point in time. It all changed when I attended 'Unleash the Power Within' with Tony Robbins and his words 'Your past does not define your future' made me realise that I need to re-wire my brain and train to think differently.

Every single person is born with a unique and valuable gift to share with the word. Take the first step and most answers will reveal themselves through doing, not thinking. We live in the world of limitless possibilities. Your reality is created by what you focus on and how you chose to interpret it, if you really love and believe in yourself, you will create the life you want.

Lidia will be listening to New York Mambo Mix, eating a Thai Green curry whilst reading "How to win friends and influence people", on the beach watching the sunset drinking mojitos with Alex.

Kevin Edge

Kevin Edge is the rarer form of property development entrepreneur: one whose experience and portfolio was built on the foundations of long, cold, physically testing work on the construction site.

More than 30 years ago he started work as a bricklayer, working his way from the ground up to form his own design and build company. Since forming Civic D&B more than 25 years ago, he's managed more than 150 property projects, amassed a multimillion UK portfolio and honed and refined an intricate understanding of project management and the planning process. Recognising the advantages of formal training in interconnected disciplines, he has qualified to level 4 as an Accounts Technician and to PG Cert level as a Project Manager.

He has worked extensively with private investors and as a JV partner and has a clutch of property development awards to his name, including Deal of the Year at the Property Investors awards 2016 and Deal of the Year and Development of the Year at the Property Investors awards 2019. He was runner-up in Property Entrepreneur's Property Entrepreneur of the Year 2019.

His expertise has been shared in assorted construction and property press, on podcasts and on the BBC. He is now a board member of Property Entrepreneur.

W – founthill.com
EM – kevin@founthill.com

Why have you chosen property development as your strategy?

Property development was an obvious route for me because of my background; I've been in the housebuilding industry for getting on for more than 30 years, and I've run a design and build company for about 25 years. That means not just that I've got all the practical and project management skills that mean I understand every part of what goes on on-site, but I've gained a lot of contacts, from potential investors to local authorities, to tradesmen I can trust to meet the right standards.

With property development, you're usually working on a reasonably clear site. That makes a difference. With renovation projects you're more likely to encounter unforeseen issues; with new builds you can conduct soil checks, topographical surveys etc. before you purchase the land, so you can assess any remediation and land issues that need costing, which are your biggest uncertainties.

Property development is definitely a step up, and I've done a lot of studying to make that step easier – you need a wider knowledge even with decades in the industry. I'd definitely recommend real experience, education and, if possible, mentoring - because there are high barriers to entry. Financially you've got a lot of fundraising to do, which means there's a greater risk if you don't know what you're doing – you could easily come a cropper! It's a long process, which means a long wait for any reward. And developing a site requires expertise regarding legislation as well as building – and we're seeing more and more regulation, a push for higher standards and energy-efficiency levels. If you don't know the processes – even the hoops you have to jump through to get utilities set up on a new site - you can't see the pitfalls or the problems that could lie ahead. My background puts me in a strong position.

The reality is that property development adds value. You're adding value to the land itself. There's a clear, quantifiable gain, something which is less clear in renovations and conversions. Importantly, you know you're also adding value to society, providing new homes which give options to the local community.

What advice would you give a total beginner in property?
First, I think you need to know that this is really hard work.

Don't underestimate the amount of effort and knowledge required.

It can take many years to become an overnight success.

With that in mind, you need to put in the effort to get the knowledge. Read as many books on the subject as possible, so you understand the battlefield you're entering. Visit property networking events so you can learn from people already on the journey. Some of them will be willing to talk to you directly and give you the benefit of advice based on years of experience. Contact property developers – even if that's people you see profiled in a magazine – reach out and see if they'll take a little time to give you advice. Listen to podcasts on the subject... In other words, do your research into the whole property development process.

Even if you think you're ready, think you've got the money to make a start, I'd tread carefully. I'd probably avoid property development as a route initially, because it's such a long wait to see a return. Development is a profit activity, it comes in lumps; you need to have an existing income or cash reserve which will see you through from start to finish, because you don't earn anything until the very end. That's after the bank, the investors, the bills, the suppliers and the contractors have had their money. Which could be two or three years down the line.

So, you need to be sure you can do this. Look at the details of other deals before you start. Stockbrokers do what's called paper trading, testing their methods. Run dummy test investments and get good at it. It's harder than you might think!

Start any potential property deal – even the fictional practice ones – with a really high-level assessment – the sort of thing you can fit on the back of a cigarette packet. If it looks viable, start working down into the detail. Look for template spreadsheets online to get started, but don't rely on one alone working for you. Research and compare templates, see what's different. This is vital background work, because you need to understand what the numbers really mean, the impact they each have. Everything from all the various costs of works through to interest rates on various financing options. Overlooking something seemingly innocuous, or getting your figures wrong, can have massive impacts on viability and deliverability. If that's all working, if you're running the numbers and making accurate assessments, it may be time. But get your cashflow sorted before you take any risks.

What are your thoughts on property education/mentorship?
I think education is essential in property development. You're dealing with very large sums of money and a substantial amount of risk.

The biggest risk in property development is in the ground; if the site isn't right, the investment isn't right. It takes knowledge to make that assessment. Now, I've got decades of on-site project management and hands-on experience to call on, and there's no better lesson than boots on the ground and learning by doing. You learn from the mistakes of others – and you'll probably still make them yourself. And then you've really learned the lesson!

Increasingly, in running my D&B business, I found that my competition comprised of the people who used to work for me; I'd been mentoring almost inadvertently, by spotting potential and talent and investing in their learning - to benefit them, the business and our clients.

But years of practical site experience doesn't mean you still don't have a lot to learn.

So, take your time to get the right education. Don't go straight to a mentor; you need to know the basics. There are some really good courses and networking events out there. I learned from loads of sources, lots of people, before I was ready to take the next step up. Take a year to do your research and learning.

I spent a few years looking at different people before choosing the property development trainer I decided to invest in. It was definitely worth it. A mentor can guide you along the way. There are SO many things you won't foresee, without that insight. You'd find yourself with a problem and suddenly have clients looking at you for an answer. And in property development, any time that a property is standing there and you're wrestling with a problem, it's costing you money. So, choose a mentor wisely, someone with proven industry experience, a strong track record. Be sure that anyone you choose has the expertise in the knowledge gaps you want to fill.

What are the pros and cons of property development?
I'll get the cons out of the way first:

Firstly, you've got to raise or directly invest a lot of money. Then, you won't see any of it back until the very end of the project, which might be two or three years down the line. What's more, all the risk is in that last bit of profit, the bit that's yours. Because, whatever happens, the bank will get their money first, then the investors, and you've had to pay all your contractors, subbies, suppliers etc. If there are hold-ups or problems on site, the cost is coming out of your pocket first. You only get your money when everyone else has been paid.
I think it's worth building a property portfolio first, to cover your income on a month-to-month basis. With BTLs, for instance, you get cashflow. There's less risk, fewer variables, and the value of most property generally goes up.

But the pros of property development are really positive, for me at least: You're working from the ground up – and most of your risk is in the ground. That means you can make decent assessments early and either dodge the risk entirely, or plan to mitigate that risk, as appropriate. If you design your site and your properties right, you can add value. You're starting with a clean slate, so if you design something that's attractive, in the right location for the right market, and you manage it correctly, there can be significant profit.

You're getting to create something from nothing. That's a remarkable feeling. Buy-to-let can feel a bit loveless, I think, but with property development you get to leave a legacy. You're making homes for people, for families, for generations to come. You're making a real difference.

What are your three top tips in raising investor finance?

Firstly, think about it from the investor's angle. Be aware that this is someone's real, hard-earned cash - treat it with respect. Don't treat it as being as important as your own money – it's more important than that - you can do what you want with your own money! Do your due diligence and make sure you're offering a shared opportunity, rather than it being all about you. Show would-be investors how you have arrived at your numbers, in detail, show you have done your homework, show them how you have assessed the risk factors. Not all deals are good investments, so make sure yours are.

Secondly, be visible and accessible. Online, on social media, at events, within the industry - so people can see you are likely to be looking for funds. It can take time; a lot of our investors are people I have known for many years and they have taken their time to watch what we do and see how we get on before making contact.

Thirdly, start building your contacts well before you need them. It's all part of building your profile and raising awareness. So far, we've worked with people we've already known through past work and networking. But that's a limited pool size. In principle, there is a lot of cash looking for opportunities – you need to make sure you have a robust plan for any opportunity you present, because your reputation is on the line.

With all that in mind, when you're raising finance, make sure you are clear you understand the financial rules – FCA regulations, for instance - and follow them. They're there for a good reason - to protect both investors and fundraisers, to keep everything clean and clear. Give your investors regular updates on how the development is going; you can even offer a combined earn and learn. But no matter how involved they want to be, you need to be transparent, open and communicative.

What is your deal analysis process?
I use a multi-stage process. Any deal needs to go through one stage to get to the next.

1. I start off with a really high-level, basic sums assessment to see whether it's worth looking at. Ballpark, headline figures.
2. If the opportunity passes that initial assessment, I start factoring in specific costs to each area of the project, based on past experience. This is a thorough analysis based on multi work sheets and working off of our most recent market costs from our on-going projects.
3. If it still looks healthy, it's time to put an offer in to the landowner.
4. Assuming that offer gets accepted, there's a deep layer of real market costing well before we get to site. I'll analyse timescales and the cost of time. I'll check with all the necessary suppliers and skills to get the latest market costs at that exact moment. All of this is entered into Excel. We've created a series of sheets, which we created in-house and use on every project; we understand them intimately. They account for time and the cost of time. That helps us set a contingency figure as well; it's tight, because we've been so thorough and accurate with our costings, and we've had enough time on site to know the real costs of lost time and when it happens.
5. So, we've got our checked, working numbers, which create a budget for the project. This will be checked at least monthly throughout the project, to check there's no overspend, that everything is as it should be. You need to watch every number – you treasure what you measure! Cost-to-budget reconciliation all the way through is vital.
6. Before we start, we'll do a cashflow projection, to establish what we need and when, and where it's coming from at what time, and when it needs to be available.

The biggest cost I see missed off people's deal analysis process is the cost of time. People forget time carries a cost. Time erodes profit – starting from day one. So, it needs to be factored in and monitored closely all the way through.

How important is interior design? Any tips?

The right approach to interior design is absolutely crucial. I ran a design and build company for 25 years and a lot of our success was based on the quality of the interior design. I employed a skillful in-house interior designer, because people want a home not just to live in, but one which adds value to their lives, their lifestyles; they want a house that solves problems, not one that has irritating niggles and problems. All of that comes down to functionality, livability and even sustainability as much as aesthetics. You've got to consider the way people use technology. Think about lighting and heating systems that can be really easily controlled by apps. Think about connectivity and the way people live their lives, the multitude of devices. Even the simple things like putting plugs, light switches and the lights themselves in the right place will make a difference.

It's important not to OVER-design an interior, in terms of fixtures and fittings, colours and textures, because people also want to put their own stamp on the place they buy, make it their own.

You need to work with really good interior designers; it's about finding the right touch, not intrusive or overbearing design, but considerate design. I would say, though, that I'd always dress a show home really well, to show prospective buyers what they can achieve, to let them imagine themselves in the space.

What is your morning routine and why does it matter?

I think it's important to have a routine. I think the power of habit is undervalued.

- I always start with 1L of water, to hydrate myself well.
- I'll always stretch the body thoroughly and do a few quick exercises.

- I've practiced transcendental meditation for 26 years now and I meditate every morning for 30 minutes, that's been a game changer for me.
- I enjoy my running, so I aim to run five to six times a week.
- I try to read 10 pages of a book every day. I read this technique in a book called The Slight Edge. It pointed out that anyone can read even the most daunting book a little bit at a time. I've read a lot of books this way!
- I keep a gratitude journal. Writing down the things I'm grateful for that morning. When you start thinking that way it's surprising the stuff you're pleased about, sometimes we miss the smallest details of how lucky we are, and life can pass us by.

I track all of this. It really matters to me to tick stuff off, to acknowledge that I've done these things. It builds up momentum and acts as an extra reward in itself. You might really not feel like reading those ten pages but making yourself accountable is satisfying. I think it was in 'The Seven Habits of Highly Successful People' that I read about private victories and public victories. Public victories are all very well, the stuff that people see that builds Ego, but it's the private victories, the things that nobody else knows about *(unless someone asks you about your morning routine!)* that build character, knowledge and gratitude.

What do you do in your free time?
I started learning the guitar. I actually bought one thirteen years ago and never picked it up. In order to cement the practice, I've just started tracking my playing. I practice every day. Everyone gives up early, because sometimes it's boring and you feel like you'll never get to a level you want to, but by tracking it, by doing 30 minutes, going through the mechanics, there's still a long way to go but, I'll get there! It's also a good way of switching off from work.

I've also started cooking from recipes, a few times a month. My partner always does the cooking, and she might not be enjoying me being in the kitchen as much... but I'm finding it really enjoyable exploring ingredients, finding out what works together, working from a recipe. I get to try something new a few times a month.

I love to travel, learning about new cultures and exploring the history of places. I started learning to fly a Paraglider, jumping off of a mountain with a bit of nylon sheet holding me a few thousand feet in the air. It's on hold for Covid, of course. But it's amazing, exciting, exhilarating, and I'm looking forward to starting again when we can. Ultimately, I want to fly the Himalayas unpowered…

I like to read. The greatest gift I've had from property has been the journey of self-development and the opportunity to be able to build my own library on the side of my home and fill it with books.

Kevin is reading The Geeta, drinking homemade Kombucha in the cave listening to Gilles Peterson on Radio 6.

Paul Million

Paul Million is one in a million in the property world. 3 decades in property, 25 years 'on the tools' and with an eye for design and a perfectionist ethos he has built, and runs, a portfolio of over 90 properties including 20 HMOs, some light industrial units, SA & over 60 single lets. With 10 upcoming JVs in commercial conversions to Co-Living, SA, Aparthotel, Supported Living and a £6m GDV newbuild site all under his VURV brand soon to be unveiled.

Paul is a beast of graft.

You cannot believe though, how much time he actually gives up for the members of The Property Thing network group he co-hosts and many others in the property community. He has recently been appointed the co-host of the Whitebox North East networking event too.

Paul is the master of the creative deal and has been doing NMD deals since the 1990s in his native town Darlington in The North East. A massive believer in Mindset, reciprocity, win/win and the power of the JV or 'Three-Legged Race' as he calls it. The power is in the people. He has more stories than you can imagine from years on the coal face and tells it how it is with great verve.

He enjoys snowboarding, hiking and wants to travel the world with his partner once he feels he has 'done enough'. Paul has a son, Jake, who is following him into Property at 19 already with an SA and a single let and two daughters yet to decide their path.

FB – Paul Million
IG – @paulmillion99

Where are you in property?

I'm not too much of a trumpet blower, apart from to say, "oy If I can do it, you can do it' BUT YA NEED TRAITS! So…. 50 Single lets, 20 HMOs, 4x (soon to be 8) SA, 5 Industrial Units, approx. 1/8th of this owned by my business partner.

Owned to Develop and in progress (all in generally 50/50 JV):
- 4 Micro SA included in the '7' figure above.
- 8 Bed Co-Living
- 8 Bed Co-Living
- 12 Bed Co-Living
- 8 Bed Co-Liv Mix with 5 x SA Medical centre Commercial Conversion

Into Planning soon:
- 12 Bed Co Liv Mix with 8 x SA or Flip Restaurant Conversion
- Co-Working mix 14 bed Co-Living
- 2 x Newbuild houses village location
- 16 Bed Co-Liv or 3 x 5/6 Bed Cluster flats under PD
- 20 Bed Co-Liv or 8 x Single Let flats Bank conversion

What makes property such a powerful asset to you?

Hard Money; Purposing, finding, buying, refurbing and building.

Easy Money; Collecting rent.

Free Money; Capital Appreciation. (The part that has alluded us Up t'North for so long).

I'm like a Croc in a river with the sound of migrating herds in the distance.

When will they cross? I dunno, but they will cross at some point. Meanwhile I'll make hay while it's raining with low rates and an ambitious, active perseverance.

If I stopped refurbishing and spending my rents on more property, I'd have an income with which to buy gold teeth. But I don't need to look like a Muppet so Ill crack on, for now, but travelling and snowboarding do beckon rather. I'm transitioning from spending my own cash to spending other investor's cash and leveraging other people's skills (Couple of JVs with builders) so I can live the life I want and still crack on. I'm building an enviable team to rely on. Its why I HOLD, not sell.

But I would like to buy, develop, sell at some point.

Why have you chosen your strategy?

I've got most popular strategies in there –

HMO / Co-Living: Higher income than Single-Lets and to be fair, I can experiment more and express design-led land-lording.

Serviced Accommodation: I'm not SO in love with this and never have been. Hence, I'm weighted more towards Micro-SA. Small units of beautifully designed affordable accommodation in lovely buildings that knocks staying in a hotel into the weeds - that compete with hotels for just over guesthouse money. If there is a sweet spot, It's here.

Industrial Units: Slow, steady, popular. Expensive to build but in numbers, can be cheap to buy. Low yields but VERY low maintenance & LONG landlord friendly leases.

Single lets: They provided a great platform and track record for further growth, but I did it for too long. I've got 12 or so supported tenancies in there so they yield better. Single-Lets are Golden Geese that lay quite small Golden Eggs but its regular, reliable & dependable. I have no voids at all, ever.

What advice would you give a beginner in property?

Grow a strong desire and bravery within you, but don't let it rule you! Use them to get to your goals. Like a Space-Hopper!

Design with your heart, rule with your head and use your strength to bully the right decisions for YOU.

You have to be resourceful, adaptive, a problem solver and a vehement b******d.

Don't take no for an answer but when you hear the word NO calculate why it's a no. Adapt around it. Keep on keeping on. Who is telling you NO and why?

Be equally qualifying of the word YES. Don't be Railroaded. Test stuff for yourself. Take your time but move decisively in a 'less haste more speed' manner.

Know enough about the orchestra to be The Conductor. Have a dabble on every instrument but BUILD the orchestra around you.

Don't jump into JVs willy nilly but JV you should, eventually anyway. Its where leverage is born, when you are ready.

'Shy bairns get nowt' and DO NOT be so egotistic as not to ask burning questions. Some Newbies know way more stuff than me in certain areas. I've got holes in my game. Everyone has. If you spend your time knowing everything you will lose.

Property is a Dichotomy Lobotomy. It can have you running round in circles like a dog chasing its tail. Fix on the horizon and move toward it herding cats as you go, with arms like Mr. Tickle.

Be interested.

Make sure you love yourself, are friends with yourself, trust yourself and trust your gut and let your Right Brain be as dominant as your Left. Creativity is King.

Help Others! 100% help others!!!

Leverage the knowledge of clever, successful people. We all know them or people who know them.

ASK them for help. A shoulder. ASK The Universe and the people in it. Successful people LOVE to help people who aren't yet successful but show the traits of those who are.

Go after it, one confident step at a time.

Be a Tortoise in a Tank, not a Hare in a Hyundai (or a Ferrari on finance).

Tell me about your biggest failure in property so far?
- Not taking a breath. Constant activity.
- Not allowing my fields to lie fallow.
- Not allowing enough space earlier to sit back and welcome more thought, creativity, professional relationships and effectively bigger and better deals in.
- Thinking property training and mentorship wasn't a thing.
- Not leveraging investors earlier.

You can do 10x as much in a three legged race with the right people.

What do you think of property mentorship?
It's not the dog in the fight it's the fight in the dog. It's how YOU use it.

I could write 10,000 words on this. I couldn't be a mentor I'd get too involved for which I don't have the time. I'm passionate about others success. How passionate are you about yours?

Mentee: "*£12k is SO much money.*"
Mentor: "*Okay Give me 5% of your net worth in 10 years' time then.*"
Mentee: "*F**k off that'll be £250k.*"
Mento: "*Okay give me £12k then.*"

I learned a myriad thing that will save me my mentorship fees 10x over. I'm about to claim £1,500,000 Capital Tax Allowances saving me £300,000 in Corporation tax over the next 10 years.

Thanks Mentor. I've got the kudos and confidence to JV with Investors and like-minded fruit-bats, in part, from being mentored. It aligned my Chakras. I also know many who have done and will do nothing with it.

It's the fight in the dog… but the dog needs training.

Paul will be listening to the radio, drinking Latte, reading Tribe of Mentors by Tim Ferris at home in his dressing gown like Lord Fauntleroy, with Toby the tortoise trying to bite his toe thinking it's a f***ing sprout or 'summet'!

Alfred Dzadey

Property and Business Entrepreneur.

Alfred comes from an engineering background, he studied MEng aerospace engineering at Hertfordshire university. In his corporate world days, he was a project manager at Jaguar Land Rover managing projects from as little as £2 million to £200 million for just under 5 years but now is full-time property investing. It was the only company he worked for coming out of university, great company to work for and he enjoyed every moment!

Now property investing wise, he is mainly focusing on buying properties that h can convert into high end six bedroom plus all en-suite HMOs for income in the West Midlands short term, with the help of private investors on loan agreements.

Alfred has managed to raise just under half a million so far and he is on the path to building a £4 million plus property portfolio by the end of 2021.

Long term, he wants to get into building out residential apartments (50 units plus schemes). He also hosts a property mastermind group and shares property educational content and vlog my property investment journey on my YouTube and on my Instagram. So connect with me on there if you haven't already.

FB – Alfred Dzadey Jnr
LI – Alfred Dzadey
TW – @alfred_dzadey
IG – @alfred_dzadey
YT – Alfred Dzadey

Why are you in property?

I have always had aspirations of being wealthy at a young age, so I took it upon myself to research how the wealthy people became so, and the common denominator was real estate/property for most of them. I then went deeper to understand why most people chose property over all the other asset classes. In most cases, it was because long term the increase in value over time outperforms other asset classes. Another big point is the ability to leverage against the asset, banks/people will lend against property because it's seen as having a fundamental bricks and mortar asset value and no other asset class offers this! You can't go to the bank and borrow money to buy its own stock or any other company stock so that should tell you what they truly believe in.

Another great thing is rental property can provide you income while you wait for it to appreciate in value over time. The simple fact it's a physical/tangible asset is also a selling point. The biggest selling point for me is that it's part of Maslow's hierarchy of needs, property is a *need* not a *want* in people's lives and therefore it will be here for generations to come! I can't say that about any other asset class, so for me this a great foundation to have when starting out in the investing world which you can then build on once it's stable. To summarise, these attributes convinced me this is the asset class I should start with as a foundation on the journey to building wealth.

What advice would you give a total beginner in property?

Start with the end in mind. Understand your why, goals and outcome, become very clear on what it is you are looking to get out of investing in property. For example, are you simply looking for income or are you in it to own property and get income from these properties?

Put a number against how much you would be happy to earn from each property because this will determine what strategies or tools you end up choosing to get you closer to your goals. I would then say to invest in some education either by investing your time to acquire the information or by paying for courses to acquire the information. If you have the money to be able to invest in your education this is probably the quickest way to acquire the information in a structured way, whereas if you go down the self-education route you have to put the pieces to the puzzle together, but there is no right or wrong. You just have to do what works best for you!

There are loads of resources available so if you don't have the money then tap into low-cost educational products e.g., books, property podcasts, property YouTube channels (like mine: Alfred Dzadey), follow the people who inspire you in property on the various social media platforms to follow their journey. A lot can be learnt if you are determined to put in the work and time to find the information and resources! If that is too much work for you then the paid courses option is available for you. Just do you due diligence on the course providers before selecting who to go with.

The next thing I would say is surround yourself with people actively investing in the strategy you want to do once this become clear to you. This was a game changer for me because being a part of mastermind groups/networks with people doing the same strategy as me made it easier for me to grow because I could always tap into the network if I had hurdles and someone within the group would have found a way to overcome it so for me this was a game changer in accelerating my journey.

Another point is work on your personal development, property investing is not just about buying property it has a lot to do with mindset e.g., being able to handle rejections, being able to overcome hurdles however big or small it may be, having the ability to persevere when things aren't going your way and having great self-belief because working on that mindset is equally as important as understanding how to invest in property.

Next point is taking massive action! I don't think I need to say any more than this but if you don't apply the information, you are learning then you are just wasting your time! Lastly, it's a journey and not a race so get started now and get perfect later. Don't wait to know it all before you make a move because you only truly start learning when you start doing!

Should people invest in the North or the South?

I flip this question around and say if you had all the money in the world what would your answer be. If your answer is the south, then your real problem is not having enough money!

If your answer is still you would go up north then your answer is likely based on your strategy I.e., are you investing for cashflow, capital appreciation or even both. This factor will determine what location you end up investing in because some areas will be better for capital appreciation e.g., London and the further up north you go you can get more cashflow but very little capital appreciation if any and the midlands is where you can look to maybe achieve both.

To summarise, start with what you want to get out of property investing e.g., capital appreciation, cashflow or maybe both then understand what areas work best for you and workout how to bridge any gaps you may have. Focus on the solution to the real problem/hurdle e.g., money, experience and how you can overcome them rather than doing things which don't align to your actual goals.

Who do you look up to/ who inspires you?

He is known as Uncle G, Mr 10x, GC, can you guess his name…Grant Cardone! I love everything about this guy. His character, courage, self-belief, his ability to think big, always wanting to level up and do more for the people around him. Grant is very outspoken, so I know he's not everyone's cup of tea but for me, he is my go-to guy! Everything he does I want to follow, his money mindset, his mindset of going big or bigger, his courage to go after anything he sets his mind to and his ability to sell anything is insane. I really resonate with him a lot because I think we are wired the same, I want to go big with everything.

If it's not scalable then I don't want to get involved - simple! I love the fact that he keeps it real and does right by the people. Some people will hear him speak and could find him arrogant but simply he just says it straight, no BS and goes against the grain. One statement he known for saying is 'rent your home rather than buy it'. He is trying to change the way people think, show them how the system is set to keep you broke and how to overcome this. He teaches people how to sell, handle objections, negotiate when it comes to business and lots more. This guy is truly the only guy I need to listen to if I need to get an energy boost, motivation or scale and go bigger with my goals. If you have not read his book 'The 10X rule' I would highly suggest you get it ASAP. This is for people who want more out of life rather than settling for mediocrity. Grant is your guy.

3 Top Tips on raising investor finance?

I have become known in the property space for raising money for my property deals strictly on loan agreements and offering a fixed return, so I feel I am qualified to speak on this subject. As I am writing this, I have raised just under £500,000 in private finance and by the time you read this it will probably be double. Tip number one will be to sell through and not direct. What I mean by this is not to go asking for money - you need to find ways to send out a message which says you need investors but you're not actually saying those exact words. This could be in the form of a conversation with a work colleague, family, friend, anyone you come in contact with.

The next time someone asks you how was your weekend? How are things for you? Say, "I have been busy speaking to people wanting to lend X amount of money on my project for a X percentage return on their money rather than leave in the bank where returns are ridiculously low, they see the benefit of investing rather than losing money leaving it in the bank". Then keep quiet and see what they say next - they could catch onto this or just ignore it. The more you do this with people you speak to the more you increase your chances of someone being interested in talking further and the ones who might not be ready could approach you in the future so just put yourself out there.

Tip number two is showcasing what you do - good and bad on your social media platforms because you never know who is watching and who might be interested in investing in you so put yourself out there so that people can decide for themselves if they want to work you or not!

Tip number three, when starting out looking for people to invest in your projects, you have to start from your immediate circle e.g., your family,

Tej Talks

friends and work colleagues. These are the people who should know, like and trust you. For someone to part with their money they need to tick off these three things so these will be the easiest people to convince when starting, especially if they can see evidence of you being serious with your property investment journey. Once you have done a few deals and in parallel have been sharing your journey on socials you will be approached by strangers wanting to work with you because they can see the success and see the challenges you have overcome. At this stage your experience makes them like and trust you and your social media presence makes them know you too because they have seen your journey.

Bonus Tip - The power of referrals, this only works once you have got an investor onboard. Once you get the opportunity it's like magic! I love it when my current investors refer me to someone in their network. It's the easiest investor you can get. In most cases, your investor has spoken highly of you already, they are already sold on the idea and they are ready to invest. All you have to do is have a brief chat and send documentations over and you have a new investor onboard.

What is the best non-property investment you've made?
This has to be in MYSELF.

I always have to bet on myself first. I have done this time and time again in my life. When I left secondary school to go into university, I had to take on a £25,000 student loan which gave me the opportunity to do my engineering degree and I had to learn and implement what was being taught to give me a chance to get a job coming out of university. I was adamant I would not leave university earning the usual graduate salary! People thought I was crazy and thought I should settle for the norm but I said no way especially when two of my friends had secured contracting jobs after leaving university.

A month after my last exams I was able to secure a £40,000 contracting job as a project manager. A year into working in the corporate world, I came to the realisation that working in there wasn't going to get me the wealth I wanted out of life so I called my friends who had also been working for a whole year and they all agreed there must be more to life than this.

This was the turning point for me to start looking into property investing as a vehicle to build my wealth. I went to a free 2-hour seminar, liked what I heard signed up to the three-day course and on that course, they were selling advance courses which again I liked what I heard, it was a total of £24,000 investment for the advance courses I had selected.

I decided I would invest again in myself by investing that sum and in return gain knowledge to go and build generational wealth. It was a hard decision at the time, I think I was the last person in the room to sign up because I had to sell it to myself first. This was basically me emptying my bank account to be able to afford this course but I saw it as another university degree, another opportunity to gain knowledge to empower me to build more. I saw it as one way or another money I would spend it on holidays because I love travelling too so why not pull that money forward and spend it today so that I can make more to spend more in the future. I also said to myself if I can't put £24,000 into myself how can I put that into bricks and mortar or even ask an investor to invest in my projects when I am not willing to do it for my myself. I was able to make that initial investment back in year one and was able to go and buy my residential home before going on to building a million pound plus property portfolio.

I am not saying this will happen for you if you spend this level of money on your education, but it will if you are determined to build a property portfolio, apply the information you learn and be resilient! You are your best asset so look after yourself before exploring other asset classes. If you want to evolve and do the things you want to do e.g., build wealth then you have to develop yourself first! This is how you get closer to building real wealth!

You'll find Alfred listening to Grant Cardone, drinking Pink Gin and lemonade, reading 'Who not How' by Dan Sullivan at home due to lockdown with his Partner.

TEJ'S TOP 20 BOOKS

1. Obstacle is the Way, Ego Is the Enemy, Stillness is Key – Ryan Holliday (yes, it's 3 books, *bite me*)

2. Tools of Titans – Tim Ferriss

3. The Chimp Paradox – Prof Stephen Peters

4. Never Split the Difference – Chris Voss

5. How to win friends and influence people – Dale Carnegie

6. The Secret Barrister (2x books)

7. Hustle Harder Hustle Smarter – 50 Cent/Curtis Jackson

8. Can't Hurt Me (Audiobook) – David Goggins

9. Principles – Ray Dalio

10. The Almanack of Naval Ravikant – Eric Jorgenson

11. Happy Sexy Millionaire – Stephen Bartlett

12. How to get rich – Felix Dennis

13. Deep Work – Cal Newport

14. A New Earth – Eckhart Tolle

15. Can't Hurt Me – David Goggins

16. The Subtle Art of not giving a F*ck – Mark Manson

17. Natives – Akala

18. Black Box Thinking – Matthew syed

19. Blink, Outliers, Talking to strangers – Malcolm Gladwell

20. Money – Rob Moore

Tej Singh

Do you think most property investors are completely honest on social media?

I think the property community (especially on Instagram) is really positive, open and honest. There's a difference between being dishonest and just not sharing things, I think most people just don't share certain things. I think most people are honest about the figures, timelines and deal details. However, I've certainly met people who were happy to chat shit and pretend on camera, but as soon as it went off... the truth came out. People are scared of being judged, or labelled, or being vulnerable in public - all of which I totally understand.

Being honest openly is not easy, but I really do applaud those who do it, who share the experience with us; good and bad. This is what's way more helpful than the positive, happy stuff; we learn from the challenges more than the celebrations. Compared to other industries (*cough cough FX*) there is very little 'stunting' in front of a Lamborghini with wads of cash pretending to be something they aren't. That would be quite fun to see, I did do a parody video with a friends Lambo, if you've got a sauce-mobile let me know I'll come over and make some more!

There are a select few, who do lie, shout the loudest and actually have superficial knowledge. Funnily enough they make the most money from selling their 'knowledge', with nothing to back it up. Always makes me think, how? Without any Social Proof? It's not entirely their fault, it's us, society. Believing in the get rich quick bullshit, not wanting to actually put in work, then cry after a course and say it didn't change their life in 4.5 days and they are still in a job they hate because they can't be bothered to do real work. Obviously though, there are lots of terrible and overpriced courses too. #Rant

I think there's also another select few who I don't really know what to call them *(at least out loud) who* are just haters. They have ideals in their head, egos, arrogance and an air of superiority and saviour-ism, and come together to berate, mock and hate on others. It's strange, most of them don't seem to be doing much in property… yet some of those they attack are really successful. Some are genuinely helpful, and help others avoid scams etc.

It's a funny world I tell ye!

What is your morning routine?
Out of lockdown it is:

- Wake up at 6-6:30AM
- Meditate for 5-10 minutes
- Read for 15 minutes
- Read 'today' on the Daily Stoic
- Write a very short gratitude journal
- Write an answer in my '5-year Q&A' book
- Only once the above has been done am I allowed to use or look at my phone
- Eat nothing or maybe a protein cookie then off to the gym
- Back home and eat breakfast (oats or eggs & my home-made rye bread)
- At my desk by 9 or 10am (depends on my mood and timekeeping)

The wake-up time also varies in seasons, when it's darker in winter I'm more likely to be up at 6:30AM. Spring and summer it's 6AM. In lockdown it was the same as above, except my workout was at home with dumbbells and resistance bands. I'm not a morning or a night person, or a day person… erm. I'm focused at any time, I suppose I prefer working at night but I also like mornings for self-work because it's quiet and the light is nice.

What do you do in your free time?
I love cooking, mainly Mexican, Italian, Jamaican and Punjabi (yes, my roti is round). I'm really picky too about the quality of ingredients, food is one thing I don't really have a budget for, because it is a vital part of

Tej Talks

our health but also, I can *taste the difference* between brands and 'types'. I cook every day; I bake bread weekly too. I love learning new recipes, styles, spice combinations and techniques. I feel at peace and very present when cooking, I've learnt from my family; my parents and grandparents all love cooking and would get me involved from a young age. I'm always learning from them and it connects me to them when we aren't together.

I love travelling, although that's been totally lock off for most of us in Lockdown *(apart from the #Dubai #Influencers)*. I've been to 11 different regions in Italy. I think it's one of the most beautiful places on earth, and so many places are not on 'the tourist map'. Of course, the food is out of this world and I love the language. The driving there is…fun.

I love learning languages, estoy aprendiendo español en mis tiempo libre y veo programas de televisión en español para practicar. Me encanta explorar nuevas culturas a través del lenguaje.

I dance, a lot. On my chair, in the office, in the kitchen, in the lounge… you get the picture. I used to dance Bhangra 'professionally' and I've performed at Wembley to 4,500 people. Afrobeats and dancehall are now my favourites to dance to.

I play Xbox on the weekends, yep, look at me, Mr. Property Guy and I'm not hustling 24/7!! What will people say. I'm a big fan of Star Wars games, anything by Rockstar, Assassins Creed, CoD and Battlefield. Obviously, FIFA too!

I really enjoy gardening and growing my own veg too, passed down to me from my Nani Ji, Dada Ji and Mum. House plants too.

What's been your biggest success in property?
Becoming financially free, buying 15 houses in 9 months using £648,000 of Investor finance and having a 100% payback record (then raising another £200,000 for my latest project in a few hours!). It was incredibly hard work, the stress was unreal… but the results are life changing, in a small way. It's left me with a £1.3m portfolio that cashflows enough to

cover everything and then some, and that's only going to increase as I grow.

Really though, my podcast and brand have been some of my biggest successes, the number of people who have taken my content and gone on to amazing things, read my book and done well, or who have been inspired by my podcasts is humbling. I love hearing from people, and what it's done for them, it really makes it worth it and shows that I am actually helping people. Which is nice! Especially since most of it is free.

I don't celebrate my successes that much, but it really makes me smile to know how much my content has helped people, that's meaningful.

What's an unusual or weird thing you love?
I don't think it's weird but I'm very fussy about the flour and pasta I eat. I like my Pasta to be di Gragnano I.G.P, with organic Italian semolina only through a bronze dye. I tend to only use Dove's farm organic bread and wholemeal flours. I really can't eat 'normal' pasta, it 100% does not taste the same!

What has property allowed you to do? What has it given you?
I'm standing in the Tesco car park *(other supermarkets are available),* it's 1pm on a Tuesday. The sky is blue, there is a light breeze and I'm wearing what can only be described as 'casual wear'. I've got 4 refurbishments on, I'm busy as ever. But,

I'm here.

At a time when most people are working, for someone else, maybe doing something they don't enjoy, in an office, with 101 things on their mind. They can't just leave and do this. At this moment I felt 'free', and I really appreciated what being self-employed can do for you. I wasn't making that much money; in fact, I was bleeding cash as I grew so quickly and had so much on. I had enough to be comfortable.

This might seem trivial, or mundane, but moments like this highlight what Property has allowed me to do. At the time of writing this, I haven't purchased a property for a year (lockdown + stupid crazy market) but my 12 BTLs are cash flowing £3,800+ a month with minimal work. So, if I want to do nothing today, I can. I have that freedom that's signified in the Tesco story. If I need to be somewhere quickly, look after family, or take a day off for a meaningful reason, I can. Without hesitation, regret or having to inform *the boss.*

I love property, seriously I walk around looking at houses and complimenting the brick, or the roof tiles, or thinking… what kind of re-pointing is that mate! I know I'm genuinely passionate and interested in it, so property has 'allowed me' to find something like this and thrive.

I'm usually listening to Burna Boy, eating Napoletana pizza with extra Bufala D.O.P and N'Duja, drinking tap water. I'm likely reading Ryan Holiday in my home office in the countryside whilst watching the Kites, Buzzards, Kestrels and Sparrowhawks soar above me, with my Fiancé.

WHAT'S NEXT?

Books, Podcasts, 'Free' info, Youtube etc. are all fantastic. That's what I used to learn, combined with networking and taking people for Nandos. However, I also lost £10,000s on lost profit, and business losses. If you follow me on IG, then you will have witnessed these. I can't encourage you to do the same as me, because I didn't do it in the most efficient or sensible way.

To the people who proclaim:

"Yeah, but me making mistakes myself makes me learn it deeply, innit"

So, you'd rather lose £1,000s just to 'learn' a lesson, when you could invest less than £1,000, one time, to learn from other's mistakes?

It's because deep down you think you won't make mistakes, isn't it?

I was exactly the same, hands up, I was. Plus, I was a tight arse with money so even worse.

When I saw the final figures on my last flip, which was supposed to make £20,000 profit, and it said £6,500 loss, I wasn't a happy bunny. I know the exact steps and decisions I made, which had I known better would have ensured I made profit. Luckily, I could cover it across the portfolio, but what if this was your first deal?

Can your starting cash pot cover this?

Protecting the downside is as important as maximizing profit!

Now, as I am moving into Development I am paying to up-skill myself and have the support I need as I move forward with deals. The costs here are even bigger, so I'm not playing when it comes to getting it right and investing in myself.

I created my eLearning platform to provide you with real education and insight into how to actually build your portfolio, avoid the mistakes I made, and how to ensure your cash isn't wasted. I'd say it's the most comprehensive and well-priced course on the market. Don't take my word for it though, just ask the many people who've used it to secure their first and many other deals from it. If you know me, you know I don't mess around, there is no upselling in it, this is IT, it's ALL here.

I'm going to breakdown my eLearning modules here, my Raising Finance module is up first, with the BRR ones to follow. tejtalks.learnworlds.com

RAISING FINANCE:
- 6 Guides, 3 contracts, 10 sections (Worth £100s)
- 550 minutes of learning
- 22 ways to find Investors
- Guest speakers' exclusive content (£5m+ raised)
- Bridging v JV v Investors
- How to pitch deals and build your Investor pack
- Where to find Investors and how to attract them
- Using Social Media
- Negotiation, % rates and security
- How to structure your Investors
- FCA Compliance & Due Diligence
- A Step-by-Step guide and everything you need to know to fund your deals

BRR PACKAGE:
- All 5 individual modules in one combination
- 15 eBooks, 5 Guest Speakers, 5 Graded Assessments
- 31+ hours of learning and education
- The entire process covered in detail – Buy, Refurbish, Refinance, Rent
- Special section on Property Flipping (Buy to Sell)
- All my tips, tricks, processes I used to buy 15 houses in 9 months
- Spreadsheets, documents, contracts & templates – everything included
- Pricing up refurbishments with actual prices on
- Visit the website to see every topic broken down further

FEEDBACK:

"...I asked the questions Tej taught me and knew that I could offer low. Every single thing you need to know is in the BRR package. Tej even helps you set your goals and foundations which is essential. I've calculated the numbers off this deal, and I should make £30,000 profit worst case scenario."
– Josh Alford

"The course is insightful and comprehensive, delivered with an honesty and frankness that can be lacking in the property industry. The money that I'll save far outweighs the investment in the eLearning!"
– Jodie Watts

"I like how Tej explains even the most basic aspects and talks through the entire process, of every aspect. Including insights from his own experience, the checklists and guides are so easy to use and put into practise. This platform bridges a very large knowledge gap and paints a very clear picture and filled me with confidence. I'd recommend to anyone, any day, this is fantastic."
– James Oliver

"I learnt so much more than I thought I would, from how to find my exact investment area, building my mindset and sourcing deals that nobody else has access to. Plus, so much more from Tej's experience, especially managing Builders which can be a very painful time. I'd recommend this to anyone who is serious about Property and wants to take their learning to the next level."
– Tashan McGregor

Tejtalks.learnworlds.com

Tej Talks

If you leave an Amazon review for this book, send me proof, I'll give you 25% EXTRA OFF the BRR and Raising Finance Package.

You might even get a Tej Talks T-Shirt. *Maybe.*

SAY HELLO

I post regularly on Social Media, especially Instagram. I respond to all of my DMs and emails, unless you're an askhole. Don't be afraid to chase me if I forget though!

You've probably read my first book, if you're reading this one, but it's a guide to BRR, it's very practical and talks a lot about mindset and the steps you should follow in BRR. It's on Amazon, go get it!

Make sure you follow and subscribe below:

IG - tej.talks

YouTube - Tej Talks Property

LinkedIn - Tej Singh

Facebook - The Tej Talks Podcast

Clubhouse - Tej Talks

The Tej Talks Podcast - ALL Podcast players

eLearning – tejsingh.me or tejtalks.learnworlds.com

Websites – tej-talks.com // tejinvests.com

Thank you, for the Amazon review you're about to leave. ;)

I'll leave you with this story taken from Steven Pressfields Virtues of War...

Big man like 'Alexander the Great' was crossing a path with his entourage, a Philosopher was blocking his direction and wasn't moving out of the way quick enough.

One of his crew was angered by the Philosophers apparent lack of respect, and/or recognition of his boss Alexander, and posed the question:

"This man *(Alexander the Great)* has conquered the world! What have you done!?"

The philosopher replied without an instant's hesitation,

"I have conquered the need to conquer the world."

Printed in Great Britain
by Amazon